FALLEN ANGELS
AND THE ORIGINS *of* EVIL

Once again Elizabeth Clare Prophet, author of *The Lost Years of Jesus,* challenges timeworn doctrine by shedding light on forgotten manuscripts. This time she examines the Book of Enoch, a text attributed to the great-grandfather of Noah—a man who Genesis says "walked with God" and "was not, for God took him."

The Book of Enoch reveals that God allowed Enoch to return to earth to give his children certain secrets. But the book was left out of the Bible. Why?

Was it to conceal Enoch's warning about the Watchers, fallen angels who took on human bodies and, because of their crimes against mankind, were doomed to remain on earth "as long as the world endures"?

If the fallen angels incarnated once, why not again—and again? Elizabeth Clare Prophet sets forth her bold thesis that the fallen angels Enoch warned about *have reincarnated today.* And that they are still wreaking havoc—starting wars, polluting the environment, manipulating economies, and spoiling the dreams of God and man.

ARCHANGEL GABRIEL, MESSENGER OF GOD

FALLEN ANGELS

AND THE | ORIGINS *of* EVIL

WHY CHURCH FATHERS SUPPRESSED
THE BOOK OF ENOCH AND
ITS STARTLING REVELATIONS

ELIZABETH
CLARE PROPHET

SUMMIT UNIVERSITY 🐚 PRESS®

Corwin Springs, Montana

FALLEN ANGELS AND THE ORIGINS OF EVIL
*Why Church Fathers Suppressed the Book of Enoch
and Its Startling Revelations* by Elizabeth Clare Prophet
Copyright © 2000 Summit University Press
All rights reserved

Previously published as *The Forbidden Mysteries of Enoch:
Fallen Angels and the Origins of Evil,* Summit University
Press, © 1983, 1992. All rights reserved.

Library of Congress Catalog Card Number: 99-67263
ISBN: 0-922729-43-3

SUMMIT UNIVERSITY ❧ PRESS®

Summit University Press and ❧ are registered trademarks.

Cover design: Roger Gefvert
Book design: Lynn M. Wilbert

Printed in the United States of America
05 04 03 02 01   6 5 4 3 2

CONTENTS

Illustrations

TO THE CHILDREN OF ENOCH

And now, my children, lay thought on your hearts, mark well the words of your father, which are all come to you from the Lord's lips.

Take these books of your father's handwriting and read them.

For the books are many, and in them you will learn all the Lord's works, all that has been from the beginning of creation, and will be till the end of time....

...Distribute the books to your children, into all your generations, and amongst the nations who shall have the sense to fear God, let them receive them, and may they come to love them more than any food or earthly sweets, and read them and apply themselves to them.

And those who understand not the Lord, who fear not God, who accept not, but reject, who do not receive them, a terrible judgement awaits these.

Enoch to his children
The Book of the Secrets of Enoch

FORBIDDEN MYSTERIES OF ENOCH

THE UNTOLD STORY OF MEN AND ANGELS

THE FALLEN ANGELS ON THE WING

FORBIDDEN MYSTERIES OF ENOCH
THE UNTOLD STORY OF MEN AND ANGELS

With the incredibly fast pace of modern life, most of us don't take a lot of time to think about angels. But it was not always so. Back in the fourth century, for instance, when the warring Visigoths stormed the Roman Empire, when civil disorder and social corruption reached an all-time high, when a regulated economy triggered double-digit inflation—people were thinking about angels.

And it was more than quaint musings about how many angels could fit on the head of a pin. No, they were asking questions that had serious and far-reaching ramifications.

The hottest debate revolved around a single crucial issue: Were angels ever transformed into flesh-and-blood beings in order to perform earthly deeds? Though most of the debate seems to have escaped history's chronicling pen, we can, and should, reconstruct a few of its questions—for reasons that will soon become clear.

If angels ever did become fleshly beings that looked

like ordinary men, what would they be like? How would you pick one out from among your neighbors? Would he be extra good, a sweet cherub of a person? Or extra evil, one of those fiendish fallen angels?

Regarding the latter, what began as a casual curiosity of the cloth has taken on the cloak of a Sherlock Holmes detective story, a probe into ancient cosmological history through fragmentary documents that piece together the missing links of much more than a mere theological dissertation on the nature and origin of evil.

I believe that my investigations, though by no means complete, uncover in the Book of Enoch, the texts of Origen, and related Scripture and apocrypha (not excluding mythological texts and ancient artifacts) the key to certain historical facts concerning the evolution of men and angels on this and other systems of worlds. I believe that these facts have been concealed from the children of the Light for thousands of years by deliberate design and that, once exposed and acted upon by dedicated hearts, they will be the essential ingredient in the turning of worlds toward a new age of peace and enlightenment.

Although the scope of this introduction does not permit the full presentation of the facts at hand, it does afford me the opportunity to begin to unravel the forbidden mysteries of Enoch concerning the true nature of the fallen angels known as the *Watchers*. Enoch passed on these mysteries to his sons and their households to preserve for a far-distant generation.

Based on convincing evidence from a number of sources, our thesis confirms the Book of Enoch—that there are indeed fallen angels, that they have embodied on earth and corrupted the souls of her people, and that they will be judged by the Elect One in the day of the coming of his elect servants. Our thesis must also by force of logic put forth the corollary that these fallen ones (together with the progeny of the *Nephilim* who were cast out of heaven by Michael the Archangel) have continued to embody on earth without interruption for at least half a million years.

Therefore, I am prepared to prove and document that they are with us today in positions of power in church and state as prime movers in matters of war and finance, sitting in the banking houses and on policy-making councils that determine the actual fate of mankind by population control and genetic engineering, the control of energy and commodities, education and the media, and by ideological and psychopolitical strategies of divide and conquer on all fronts.

The untold story of men and angels is a crack in the door of the full and final exposé of the Manipulators and the manipulated, the Oppressors and the oppressed. When I shall have penned the last word of the last volume of my ongoing essay, it will be clear, by the grace of God and his Holy Spirit—my Comforter and Teacher—that the embodied fallen angels, who are the main subject of Enoch's prophecy, have been from the beginning the spoilers of the dreams of God and man.

At every hand, they are turning the best efforts of the noblest hearts to a mockery of the Word incarnate and setting in motion the relentless spirals of degeneration and death in both Western and Eastern civilization. All of their ungodly deeds can and shall be reversed by the judgments of the Son of God—true and righteous— and by his Light within his own.

To this end and for the quickening of those who elect to be instruments of God's will, I am including my investigation into the history of fallen angels as an introduction to this paperback edition of the Book of Enoch and the Book of the Secrets of Enoch. I believe that these accounts of Enoch's experiences with our beloved Father are crucial to the understanding of an ancient conspiracy that is still with the mankind of earth and will be with us until children of the Light receive the true knowledge concerning the *seed of the Wicked One and the seed of the Son of God.*

In this and other works, I have and shall continue to make plain, for those who have ears to hear, the modus operandi of the fallen ones and the way of the anointed of the Lord. By their fruits shall all know them—those who are from 'above' and those who are from 'beneath'. And then by free will shall all choose whom they will serve: the Light or the darkness—and be judged according to their works.

The question that has become the subject of my research is this: If evil angels used to be around on earth and, as Scripture seems to indicate, wore the guise of common men, why couldn't they *still* be around? Given the state of affairs on planet earth, where would we find them today? Do they manipulate our government? Mismanage the economy?

Who are they anyway?

Fourth-century men had some of the answers, preserved in little-known, hard-to-procure books, some of which have never been translated into English. A little digging into the archives of Christianity's early Church Fathers turns up the intriguing fact that they indeed knew something about the incarnation of angels— knowledge so dangerous it was banned as heresy.

Back in the first few centuries after Christ, the Church Fathers were philosophizing on the origin of evil in God's universe—especially on earth. All agreed that evil was rooted in the angels who fell from heaven— the familiar scriptural account about an archangel's rebellion against the Almighty and the angels who were cast out with him.[1]

Usually these angels were depicted as immaterial, winged creatures, dark and shadowy demons tempting man to err, whispering wicked thoughts into his ear. But certain key passages in the holy books indicated that there might be more substance—literally and physically—to the fallen angels.

The materiality of angels seems to have been an age-old belief. There was the angel with whom Jacob wrestled—physical enough to cripple him at least temporarily, if not for life. So tangible was this angel that the author of the Book of Genesis calls him a man, although elsewhere Scripture reveals that he was an angel.[2] The 'angel' said to Jacob, "*Let me go,* for the day breaketh." How could Jacob have had hold upon an *incorporeal* angel?

The angels who came to visit Sodom had to be bolted indoors in Lot's house in order to protect them from an intended sexual assault by local townspeople— Sodomites who wanted to get to 'know' the angels.[3] And Manoah offered to cook dinner for his guest—presumed to be an ordinary man until he ascended to heaven in the fire Manoah had lit. Only then did Manoah know that the "man of God" was "an angel of the Lord."[4]

The bad angels, the fallen ones, were no less physical, according to certain religious scriptures of the world.

Zarathustra, the great Persian prophet, reportedly dashed the angels' *bodies* to pieces because they had used them to wreak evil. The angels (according to the story) had instigated illicit love affairs with earthly women—hard to accomplish without physical bodies, especially since the tale attributed offspring to them.[5] The story of corporeal angels, despite its questionability, at least made sense of scripture and legend.

THE STORY OF THE WATCHERS: THE GREAT LOSS AND THE GREAT FIND

And then there was the Book of Enoch. Once cherished by Jews and Christians alike, this book later fell into disfavor with powerful theologians—precisely because of its controversial statements on the nature and deeds of the fallen angels.

Its theme so infuriated the later Church Fathers that one, Filastrius, actually condemned it as heresy.[6] Nor did the rabbis deign to give credence to the book's teaching about angels. Rabbi Simeon ben Jochai in the second century A.D. pronounced a curse upon those who believed it.[7]

So the book was denounced, banned, cursed, no doubt burned and shredded—and last but not least, lost (and conveniently forgotten) for a thousand years. But with an uncanny persistence, the Book of Enoch found its way back into circulation two centuries ago.

In 1773, rumors of a surviving copy of the book drew Scottish explorer James Bruce to distant Ethiopia. True to hearsay, the Book of Enoch had been preserved by the Ethiopic church, which put it right alongside the other books of the Bible.

Bruce secured not one, but three Ethiopic copies of the precious book and brought them back to Europe and Britain. When in 1821 Dr. Richard Laurence, a Hebrew professor at Oxford, produced the first English translation of the work, the modern world gained its first glimpse of the forbidden mysteries of Enoch.[8]

The Book of Enoch speaks from that obscure realm where history and mythology overlap. Privy to those unfathomable founts of ancient lore, its author draws for the reader a brimming cup of secret wisdom.

A primordial drama of good and evil, light and dark, unfolds. The book tracks Enoch's footsteps back to antiquity's timelessness—back to the first hint of corruption upon a pristine world: earth.

The trouble began, according to the Book of Enoch, when the heavenly angels and their leader named Samyaza developed an insatiable lust for the 'daughters of men' upon earth and an irrepressible desire to beget children by these women. Samyaza feared to descend alone to the daughters of men, and so he convinced two hundred angels called Watchers to accompany him on his mission of pleasure.

Then the angels took oaths and bound themselves to the undertaking by "mutual execrations"—curses. Once such a pact was sealed, betrayal was punishable by unnamed horrors.

In their gang-inspired bravado, the angels descended and took wives from among the daughters of men. They taught the women sorcery, incantations, and divination—twisted versions of the secrets of heaven.

The plot thickens like a science-fiction thriller—easier to take as fantasy than as fact. The women conceive children from these angels—evil giants. The giants devour all the food that the men of earth can produce. Nothing satiates their hunger. They kill and eat birds, beasts, reptiles, and fish. To their gargantuan appetites, nothing is sacrosanct. Soon even Homo sapiens becomes a delicacy. (7:1–15)

As the story goes, one spiteful angel named Azazyel

creates accouterments for their consorts—like eye makeup and fancy bracelets—to enhance their sex appeal. As for the men, Azazyel teaches them "every species of iniquity," including the means for making swords, knives, shields, breastplates—all the instruments of war. (8:1–9)

There, millennia ago, someone explained war not as a man-invented or God-sent plague, but as a vengeful act of a fallen angel barred from the planes of God's power. The implication is that man, through one form of manipulation or another, latched on to the war games of the fallen angels and allowed himself to commit genocide in defense of their archrivalries.

But there is more to Enoch's account of the Watchers. When the men of earth cry out against the atrocities heaped upon them, heaven hears their plea. The mighty archangels—Michael, Gabriel, Raphael, Suryal, and Uriel—appeal on behalf of earth's people before the Most High, the King of kings. (9:1–14)

The Lord orders Raphael to bind Azazyel hand and foot. Gabriel is sent to destroy the "children of fornication," the offspring of the Watchers—by inciting them to their own self-destruction in mutual slaughter. Michael is then authorized to bind Samyaza and his wicked offspring "for seventy generations underneath the earth, even to the day of judgment."[9] And God sends the Great Flood to wipe out the evil giants, the children of the Watchers.

But in succeeding generations (after the sinking of

the continent of Atlantis) the giants return once again to haunt mankind. Likewise it seems that the Watchers will hold power over man (in some curiously undefined way) until the final judgment of these angels comes, which, the author implies, is long overdue.

There is also a most significant passage near the end of the book that speaks of the latter days upon earth:

> In those days will the angels return and hurl themselves upon the East, ... to stir up the kings and provoke in them a spirit of unrest....
>
> And they will march up to and tread under foot the land of His elect ones....
>
> They will begin to fight amongst themselves ... till the number of corpses through their slaughter is beyond count, and their punishment be no idle one.[10]

This seems a chilling prophecy of our own time— with wars and rumors of wars in "the East" and the countless corpses in a holy land. There is no date stamped on the prediction, but a few word changes in the right places would make it duplicate today's headlines.

The main theme of the Book of Enoch is the final judgment of these fallen angels, the Watchers, and their progeny, the evil spirits.[11] But several other scenarios are also noteworthy.

In chapter 12 of the book, the Lord says to Enoch, scribe of righteousness,

> Go tell the Watchers of heaven, who have deserted the lofty sky, and their holy everlasting station,

who have been polluted with women,*

　　And have done as the sons of men do, by taking to themselves wives, and who have been greatly corrupted on the earth;

　　That on the earth they shall never obtain peace and remission of sin. For they shall not rejoice in their offspring; they shall behold the slaughter of their beloved; shall lament for the destruction of their sons; and shall petition for ever; but shall not obtain mercy and peace. (12:5–7)

In chapter 13 Enoch declares the Lord's judgment to Azazyel:

Thou shalt not obtain peace. A great sentence is gone forth against thee. He shall bind thee;

　　Neither shall relief, mercy, and supplication be thine, on account of the oppression which thou hast taught;

　　And on account of every act of blasphemy, tyranny, and sin, which thou hast discovered to the children of men. (13:1–3)

Chapter 13 also describes how the Watchers became terrified and trembled and besought Enoch to write for them a prayer for forgiveness, that he might cause their prayer to ascend to God, since they themselves could not address him on account of their offense, their sins being so grievous. Enoch then reports to the Watchers:

---

*Refers to the fact that as heavenly beings the Watchers were not sexual.

I have written your petition; and in my vision it has been shown me, that what you request will not be granted you as long as the world endures.

Judgment has been passed upon you: your request will not be granted you.

From this time forward, never shall you ascend into heaven; He has said, that on the earth He will bind you, as long as the world endures.

But before these things you shall behold the destruction of your beloved sons; you shall not possess them, but they shall fall before you by the sword.

Neither shall you entreat for them, nor for yourselves;

But you shall weep and supplicate in silence. (14:2–7)

In chapter 15, the Glorious and the Effulgent, the Lord God, speaks again to righteous Enoch.

Go, say to the Watchers of heaven, who have sent thee to pray for them, You ought to pray for men, and not men for you....

You being spiritual, holy, and possessing a life which is eternal, have polluted yourselves with women; have begotten in carnal blood; have lusted in the blood of men; and have done as those who are flesh and blood do.

These however die and perish.

Therefore have I given to them wives, that they might cohabit with them; that sons might be born of them; and that this might be transacted upon earth.

But you from the beginning were made spiritual, possessing a life which is eternal, and not subject to death for ever.

Therefore I made not wives for you, because, being spiritual, your dwelling is in heaven.* (15:1, 3–7)

The Lord further explains to Enoch the nature of the offspring of the Watchers and the evil that they wreak upon the earth:

Now the giants, who have been born of spirit and of flesh, shall be called upon earth evil spirits, and on earth shall be their habitation. Evil spirits shall proceed from their flesh, because they were created from above; from the holy Watchers was their beginning and primary foundation. Evil spirits shall they be upon earth, and the spirits of the wicked shall they be called. The habitation of the spirits of heaven shall be in heaven; but upon earth shall be the habitation of terrestrial spirits, who are born on earth.

The spirits of the giants shall be like clouds, which shall oppress, corrupt, fall, contend, and bruise upon earth.

They shall cause lamentation. No food shall they eat; and they shall be thirsty; they shall be

---

*A reference to the fact that the Watchers had once shared with the holy Kumaras the heavenly offices of the Great Silent Watchers and the World Teachers as guardians of the soul purity and the evolution of the I AM Race.[12]

concealed, and shall not rise up against the sons of men, and against women; for they come forth during the days of slaughter and destruction.

And as to the death of the giants, wheresoever their spirits depart from their bodies, let their flesh, that which is perishable, be without judgment. Thus shall they perish, until the day of the great consummation of the great world. A destruction shall take place of the Watchers and the impious. (15:8–10; 16:1)

Because of so great a sin, the Lord tells the Watchers, "Never therefore shall you obtain peace." According to the text of the Book of Enoch, the Lord's judgment against the Watchers prevails—then and now.

The author of the book also describes in powerful majesty and moving praise certain visions of heaven given to him. He writes of his instruction from the archangels regarding the awesome judgment of the fallen ones before God's throne. He delivers three heavenly parables (or similitudes) describing the glories of the Kingdom and the ineffable Ancient of Days and the Son of man who, it is said, shall bring the final judgment upon the wicked of the earth. There is also a major section of the work devoted to astronomical description, as well as a lengthy prophecy concerning the future of the elect.

So runs the text of the Book of Enoch as we have the manuscripts today. The studious reader will note that the manuscript translated here feels somewhat disjointed and therefore might be compiled of old fragments loosely stitched together in ancient times—perhaps even a crudely edited version of a larger corpus of Enoch books that no longer exists.

CHRIST APPROVES OF
THE BOOK OF ENOCH

Most scholars say that the present form of the story in the Book of Enoch was penned sometime during the second century B.C. and was popular for at least five hundred years. The earliest Ethiopic text was apparently made from a Greek manuscript of the Book of Enoch, which itself was a copy of an earlier text. The original was apparently written in a Semitic language, now thought to be Aramaic.

Though it was once believed to be post-Christian (the similarities to Christian terminology and teachings are striking), discoveries of copies of the book among the Dead Sea Scrolls found at Qumran prove that the book was in existence before the time of Jesus Christ. But the date of the original writing upon which the Qumran copies of the second century B.C. were based is shrouded in obscurity. It is, in a word, old.

It has largely been the opinion of historians that the book does not really contain the authentic words of the ancient biblical patriarch Enoch, since he would have lived (according to the chronologies in the Book of Genesis) several thousand years earlier than the first known appearance of the book attributed to him.

But, of course, the contemporary historians' knowledge of Judaic scriptural history is by no means complete. As time progresses, new discoveries may help clarify the picture painted by the rabbinical tradition in the Zohar, which implies that Enoch's writings were passed faithfully from generation to generation.[13]

Despite its unknown origins, Christians once accepted the words of this Book of Enoch as authentic scripture, especially the part about the fallen angels and their prophesied judgment. In fact, many of the key concepts used by Jesus Christ himself seem directly connected to terms and ideas in the Book of Enoch.

Thus, it is hard to avoid the conclusion that Jesus had not only studied the book, but also respected it highly enough to adopt and elaborate on its specific descriptions of the coming kingdom and its theme of inevitable judgment descending upon "the wicked"— the term most often used in the Old Testament to describe the Watchers.[14]

There is abundant proof that Christ approved of the Book of Enoch. Over a hundred phrases in the New Testament find precedents in the Book of Enoch. Our Lord's beatitude "Blessed are the meek: for they shall inherit the earth"[15] perhaps renders Enoch 6:9, "The elect shall possess light, joy, and peace; and they shall inherit the earth."

Likewise, Jesus' scolding

> Woe unto that man by whom the Son of man is betrayed! it had been good for that man if he had not been born[16]

is reminiscent of Enoch's

> Where [will be] the place of rest for those who have rejected the Lord of spirits? It would have been better for them, had they never been born.[17]

The Book of Enoch also contains precedents for Jesus' assertion of "many mansions" in the Father's house.[18] Enoch 39:4 reads:

> I saw the habitations and couches of the saints. There my eyes beheld their habitations with the angels, and their couches with the holy ones. They were entreating, supplicating, and praying for the sons of men; while righteousness like water flowed before them.

Another Enochian parallel is found in Luke 18:7:

> And shall not God avenge his own elect, which cry day and night unto him, though he bear long with them?

In Enoch 47, verse 2, we read:

> In that day shall the holy ones assemble, who dwell above the heavens, and with united voice petition, supplicate, praise, laud, and bless the name of the Lord of spirits, on account of the blood of the righteous which has been shed; that the prayer of the righteous may not be intermitted before the

Lord of spirits; that for them he would execute judgment; and that his patience may not endure for ever.

Jesus' "well of water springing up into everlasting life"[19] perhaps parallels Enoch 48:1, the "fountain of righteousness, which never failed." The biblical term "children of light"[20] is a term that possibly stems from Enoch's "generation of light." Enoch 105:25 reads:

And now will I call the spirits of the good from the generation of light, and will change those who have been born in darkness.

Jesus' explanation of the afterlife of the righteous is nearly identical to Enoch 50:4: "All the righteous shall become angels in heaven." Matthew records Jesus as saying, "For in the resurrection they...are as the angels of God in heaven."[21]

And the "woe unto you that are rich"[22] of Jesus Christ is found almost verbatim in Enoch:

Woe to you who are rich, for in your riches have you trusted; but from your riches you shall be removed; because you have not remembered the Most High in the days of your prosperity.[23]

The list of parallels runs longer than can be summarized here (therefore we have listed them beginning on page 263), but two further themes central both to Christ's teaching and to the Book of Enoch ought to be noted.

First, the term "Son of man," often used by Jesus, finds great elaboration in the Book of Enoch. It has long been thought that Jesus' use of the term "Son of man" in referring to himself originated with Daniel 7:13. But prominent scholars believe that it was the Book of Enoch which provided this key term to Jesus.[24]

Although Laurence's translation does not reflect it, it seems that Enoch himself was called by God "Son of man." Biblical scholar H. H. Rowley points out that various translators have hedged on this passage, mistranslating it or even attempting to change the original text that applies the words "Thou art the Son of man" to Enoch.[25]

Laurence's translation of the key passage, perhaps for doctrinal reasons, substitutes the words "offspring of man" for the literal translation "Son of man." By contrast, when the term "Son of man" clearly refers to Jesus Christ, Laurence uses it without hesitation. Laurence's translation reads:

> Then that angel came to me, and with his voice saluted me, saying, Thou art the **offspring of man,** who art born for righteousness, and righteousness has rested on thee.[26]

Laurence's choice of words is duly noted in this volume in the Book of Enoch. See page 180.

The second theme important to both the Book of Enoch and the teachings of Jesus Christ concerns the judgment and the great tribulation. Jesus depicts the

Gentile judgment executed by the Son of man, his angels with him, as recorded in Matthew 25:31–32, 41, 46.

> When the Son of man shall come in his glory, and all the holy angels with him, then shall he sit upon the throne of his glory:
>
> And before him shall be gathered all Gentiles: and he shall separate them one from another, as a shepherd divideth his sheep from the goats....
>
> Next he will say to those on his left hand, "Go away from me, with your curse upon you [the judgment of God upon the Watchers], to the eternal fire prepared for the devil and his [fallen] angels." *(Jerusalem Bible)*[27]
>
> And these shall go away into everlasting punishment: but the righteous into life eternal.

The same scene is described in Enoch 45:3 and 66:5–7.

> In that day shall the Elect One sit upon a throne of glory; and shall choose their conditions and countless habitations (while their spirits within them shall be strengthened, when they behold my Elect One), shall choose them for those who have fled for protection to my holy and glorious name....
>
> I beheld that valley in which there was great perturbation, and where the waters were troubled.
>
> And when all this was effected, from the fluid

mass of fire, and the perturbation which prevailed in that place, there arose a strong smell of sulphur, which became mixed with the waters; and the valley of the angels, who had been guilty of seduction, burned underneath its soil.

Through that valley also rivers of fire were flowing, to which those angels shall be condemned, who seduced the inhabitants of the earth.

In Matthew 24:7, 21–22, 29-30 Jesus' prophecy on the great tribulation is recorded:

> For nation shall rise against nation, and kingdom against kingdom: and there shall be famines, and pestilences, and earthquakes, in divers places....
>
> For then shall be great tribulation, such as was not since the beginning of the world to this time, no, nor ever shall be.
>
> And except those days should be shortened, there should no flesh be saved: but for the elect's sake those days shall be shortened....
>
> Immediately after the tribulation of those days shall the sun be darkened, and the moon shall not give her light, and the stars shall fall from heaven, and the powers of the heavens shall be shaken:
>
> And then shall appear the sign of the Son of man in heaven: and then shall all the tribes of the earth mourn, and they shall see the Son of man coming in the clouds of heaven with power and great glory.

These passages are entirely consistent with the great drama of the judgment as it unfolds in the Book of Enoch. In Enoch 79, Archangel Uriel gives Enoch the vision of those things that the Son of man would also tell us must be fulfilled.

> In those days Uriel answered and said to me, Behold, I have showed thee all things, O Enoch;
>
> And all things have I revealed to thee. Thou seest the sun, the moon, and those which conduct the stars of heaven, which cause all their operations, seasons, and arrivals to return.
>
> In the days of sinners the years shall be shortened.
>
> Their seed shall be backward in their prolific soil; and everything done on earth shall be subverted, and disappear in its season. The rain shall be restrained, and heaven shall stand still.
>
> In those days the fruits of the earth shall be late, and not flourish in their season; and in their season the fruits of the trees shall be withholden.
>
> The moon shall change its laws, and not be seen at its proper period. But in those days shall heaven be seen; and barrenness shall take place in the borders of the great chariots in the west. Heaven shall shine more than when illuminated by the orders of light; while many chiefs among the stars of authority shall err, perverting their ways and works.
>
> Those shall not appear in their season, who command them, and all the classes of the stars shall be shut up against sinners. (79:1–7)

Note that in Enoch the stars are revealed to be a hierarchy of angels, some of whom pervert their ways and works, while Jesus says they shall fall from heaven and their powers be shaken, and Mother Mary declares in the Magnificat that her Son shall put down the mighty Watchers from their seats of authority on earth which they have usurped from the children of the Light—"them of low degree."[28]

The idea that Jesus' teachings may have been "dependent," in a broad sense, upon a former theological work, rather than an all-new and never-before-revealed teaching straight from heaven, has troubled some. In 1891, Reverend William J. Deane protested against connecting Jesus' teaching to the newly published Book of Enoch, noting indignantly, "We are asked to believe that our Lord and His apostles, consciously or unconsciously, introduced into their speech and writings ideas and expressions most decidedly derived from Enoch."[29]

But one can only conclude that it was a conscious decision on the part of the beloved Rabbi (Teacher) to include Enoch among the Old Testament prophets he so frequently cited.[30] Even as a boy of twelve, Jesus revealed his understanding of the Scriptures to the doctors of the temple at Jerusalem, who were astonished at his questions *and* his answers. In his Sermon on the Mount, Jesus declared himself to be the fulfillment of both the law and the prophets: "Think not that I am come to destroy the law, or the prophets: I am not come to destroy, but to fulfil."[31]

When Jesus returned from the temptation in the wilderness to Galilee in the power of the Spirit, he went into the synagogue at Nazareth and announced his ministry as the fulfillment of the prophecy of Isaiah 61:1–2.[32] Since the Master was obviously familiar with the Book of Enoch in some form, might not his reference to the law and the prophets have included the great work of the prophet who was the father of Methuselah and the great-grandfather of Noah?

I believe that Jesus came to pick up the mantle of Enoch as the messenger of the Ancient of Days and his ongoing prophecy to the Watchers. I believe that the son of David came with the authority of our Father Enoch, who said, "So has He created and given to me the power of reproving the Watchers, the offspring of heaven."[33] Indeed, Jesus came to fulfill the law and the prophecy of the judgment by the incarnate Word!

Both in his fierce rebuke of those scribes and Pharisees who prated the letter but had not the spirit of Moses and in his concise statement of his mission: "For judgment I am come,"[34] Jesus made clear that he knew of the prophesied judgment and saw it occurring both in his time and at the end of the age. He studiously understood the mechanism of the judgment of the fallen angels as an authority given by the Father to the Son.

For the Father judgeth no man, but hath committed all judgment unto the Son:

That all men should honour the Son, even as

they honour the Father. He that honoureth not the Son honoureth not the Father which hath sent him. . . .

For as the Father hath life in himself; so hath he given to the Son to have life in himself;

And hath given him authority to execute judgment also, because he is the Son of man.[35]

This power to execute judgment Jesus transferred to his apostles (Enoch's *elect*)[36] because he was the Son of man.

Verily I say unto you, that ye which have followed me, in the regeneration when the Son of man shall sit in the throne of his glory, ye also shall sit upon twelve thrones, judging the twelve tribes of Israel.[37]

And I appoint unto you a kingdom, as my Father hath appointed unto me; that ye may eat and drink at my table in my kingdom, and sit on thrones judging the twelve tribes of Israel.[38]

In addition to the familiar references to the Old Testament, Jesus may have even alluded to prophecies in apocryphal texts not included by the Church Fathers or the rabbis who selected the books that comprise our current Christian Bible and Judaic Scriptures. A number of previously unknown texts discovered at Qumran and Nag Hammadi indicate that Jesus taught from other writings in the manner of an ancient wisdom teacher.

Yale professor Charles Cutler Torrey cites evidence that Jesus quoted from a now-lost apocryphal work.[39] He points to Luke 11:49–51, which reads:

> Therefore also said the wisdom of God, I will send them prophets and apostles, and some of them they shall slay and persecute:
>
> That the blood of all the prophets, which was shed from the foundation of the world, may be required of this generation;
>
> From the blood of Abel unto the blood of Zacharias, which perished between the altar and the temple: verily I say unto you, It shall be required of this generation.

Although partial phrases and some of the above subject matter may be found in the Old Testament,[40] this statement of Jesus is not to be found intact anywhere in the Hebrew Scriptures. It is Torrey's contention that Luke's introductory phrase "said the wisdom of God" indicates that Jesus is quoting directly from a source that is now apparently lost.

It is my opinion that not only did Jesus quote material from sources not included in the Old Testament but that he did so in order to further elaborate on the judgment as the coming due of the accountability of the Watchers for their murder of the light-bearers, which these fallen ones had carried on continuously "from the foundation of the world."

Furthermore, Torrey notes there are other references in the New Testament to scriptural works that have now vanished but which were known to the apostles. One such reference can be found in Matthew 27:9–10:

> Then was fulfilled that which was spoken by Jeremy the prophet, saying, And they took the thirty pieces of silver, the price of him that was valued, whom they of the children of Israel did value;
> And gave them for the potter's field, as the Lord appointed me.

The text Matthew says he is quoting from Jeremiah is not in the prophet's book found in the Old Testament today. But the fourth-century Church Father Jerome wrote that a member of the Nazarene sect showed him an "apocryphal" text of Jeremiah in which Matthew's quotation could be seen in its exact form.[41] Thus, it appears that Matthew's version of the Book of Jeremiah had teachings that had been deleted by the time of the fourth century.

The idea that Jesus might have quoted from a book he felt was inspired with the spirit of the patriarch Enoch just as readily as he might quote from the Torah of Moses is not as preposterous as Deane chose to believe. Why else would the apostle Jude (who is believed to be the brother of Jesus) base an entire epistle on the story of fallen angels as told in Enoch?

I believe he was quoting his Lord's emphatic exegesis on the patriarch's work and that Jesus saw himself as one who came to expose the generation of the seed of the wicked (the Watchers), whom he and John the Baptist called vipers,[42] among other epithets, and to save from the intrigue of the incarnate angels the descendants of Adam through Seth, the sons of Jared—the children of the seed of Light. Jesus came to pick up the thread of Enoch—to build upon the very teaching, the crux in theological history, where Enoch left off.

ENOCH'S INFLUENCE ON THE APOSTLES

Enochian scholar Dr. R. H. Charles noted at the turn of the twentieth century that "the influence of Enoch on the New Testament has been greater than that of all the other apocryphal and pseudepigraphal books taken together."[43] Although scarce few had even heard of the influential book until the modern era, Dr. Charles points out that "all the writers of the New Testament were familiar with it, and were more or less influenced by it in thought and diction."[44]

For example, Dr. Charles Francis Potter notes that "with Paul, it [the Book of Enoch] is said to have been his *vade mecum,* literally, his 'go with me,' his pocketbook, his manual for frequent reference."[45] Perhaps Paul quotes the Book of Enoch indirectly in I Timothy 6:16 in his description of the Lord Jesus Christ, the Immortal One. He speaks of him as the one who only hath immortality, dwelling in the light which no man can approach unto; whom no man hath seen, nor can see: to whom be honour and power everlasting.

This description is much like that of the Book of Enoch, which reads:

No angel was capable of penetrating to view the face of Him, the Glorious and the Effulgent; nor could any mortal behold Him. A fire was flaming around Him.... Not one of those who surrounded Him was capable of approaching Him.[46]

The same book also seems to be the source of Paul's chastisement of the Gentiles "They sacrifice to devils, and not to God,"[47] as did the profane men in Enoch's book, which reads:

And being numerous in appearance [the fallen angels] made men profane, and caused them to err; so that they sacrificed to devils as to gods.[48]

Paul's story of a "man in Christ" who was "caught up to the third heaven," either in the body or out of the body (Paul could not tell), may reference Enoch's description of several heavens, implied in the main book of Enoch and directly stated in the Book of the Secrets of Enoch.[49]

Furthermore, one apocryphal New Testament work called the Revelation of Paul describes Paul's journey through those several heavens, including Paul's meeting with a hoary-headed man of joyful countenance—who turns out to be none other than the patriarch Enoch.

This is how the author tells his story:

> And the angel says to me: Hast thou seen all these things? And I answered: Yes, my lord. And again he said to me: Come, follow me, and I shall show thee the place of the righteous. And I followed him, and he set me before the doors of the city. And I saw a golden gate, and two golden pillars before it, and two golden plates upon it full of inscriptions. And the angel said to me: Blessed is he who shall enter into these doors; because not every one goeth in, but only those who have single-mindedness, and guiltlessness, and a pure heart.... And straightway the gate was opened, and there came forth a hoary-headed man to meet us; and he said to me: Welcome, Paul, beloved of God! and, with a joyful countenance, he kissed me with tears. And I said to him: Father, why weepest thou? And he said to me: Because God hath prepared many good things for men, and they do not His will in order that they may enjoy them. And I asked the angel: My lord, who is this? And he said to me: This is Enoch, the witness of the last day.[50]

The apostle John, author and amanuensis for the biblical Revelation of Jesus Christ, came even closer to Enochian symbolism, tone, and description. Many of his visions familiar to lovers of the Bible can also be found in the Book of Enoch: the "Lord of lords, and King of kings," the casting down of the devil into the lake of fire, the vision of the seven Spirits of God, the tree whose fruit is for the elect, the four beasts round the throne, the horse wading up to his breast in blood, and the book of life.[51]

Some believe it was Revelation's close similarity to the apocryphal Book of Enoch that nearly prevented it from becoming canonical scripture—which status it gained by a very close call. (In the third century, Dionysius of Alexandria, along with many others from the churches in Syria and Asia Minor, rejected the Revelation on literary grounds as being inauthentic.)[52]

Acts 10:34 quotes Peter as saying that "God is no respecter of persons"—a phrase also used by Paul which is found in the Book of Enoch as well as in Deuteronomy, Chronicles, and intermittently throughout the Old Testament. The Book of Enoch may have been the source of all of these biblical usages.

Both of Peter's letters in the New Testament seem to be predicated upon the Book of Enoch.[53] Peter's second letter, discussing the binding and casting down to hell of the angels who sinned, denounces the wicked in terms Enoch himself might have used. Peter writes:

> Spots they are and blemishes, sporting themselves with their own deceivings while they feast with you;
> Having eyes full of adultery, and that cannot cease from sin; beguiling unstable souls: an heart

they have exercised with covetous practices; cursed children.... [54]

Greek specialists Rendel Harris and M. R. James, among others, have speculated that Peter's first epistle may have originally contained an explicit reference to Enoch by name which was deleted—whether by error or direct intent—in later copies of Scripture.[55]

Yet there is even more dramatic evidence of the early Christian acceptance of the Book of Enoch. The Epistle of Jude clearly discusses the content of the Book of Enoch, noting that

> there are certain men crept in unawares, who were before of old ordained to this condemnation, ungodly men, turning the grace of our God into lasciviousness....
>
> These are spots in your feasts of charity, when they feast with you, feeding themselves without fear: clouds they are without water, carried about of winds; trees whose fruit withereth, without fruit, twice dead, plucked up by the roots;
>
> Raging waves of the sea, foaming out their own shame; wandering stars, to whom is reserved the blackness of darkness for ever.[56]

Jude actually *quotes* Enoch directly and refers to him by name, saying:

> And Enoch also, the seventh from Adam, prophesied of these, saying, Behold, the Lord

cometh with ten thousands of his saints,

To execute judgment upon all, and to convince all that are ungodly among them of all their ungodly deeds which they have ungodly committed, and of all their hard speeches which ungodly sinners have spoken against him.[57]

Note that the entire premise and conclusion of the Book of Enoch—i.e., the judgment of the Watchers as the key to the liberation of the souls of Light and as a necessary planetary purge prior to the Lord's kingdom come—is predicated to occur "in a generation which is to succeed at a distant period, *on account of the elect.*" (En. 1:2)

Who are the elect? We define the elect as those who elect to be instruments of God's will, according to their calling from the Father and the Son to be bearers of the Light of the Elect One—keepers of the flame of the prophecy of the Holy and Mighty One, the God of the World.

We take Enoch 1:2 to mean that the judgment is a direct and inevitable consequence of the coming of the Elect One—the incarnate Word—and his chosen in this and succeeding centuries.

The judgment prophesied by Enoch will come through the Christ Light that the Son has ignited in the hearts of his own. The Light is of the "inner man," known to Paul as "*Christ in you*, the hope of glory."[58] Our hope is in Christ the eternal Judge; for if he come, and he will surely come 'quickly' with "ten thousands of his saints,"[59] then the glory of the Lord will shine on earth through the anointed hearts who confirm the Word of the Lord—on earth as it is in heaven.

Enoch's prophecy on the judgment is quoted by Jude as acceptable scriptural evidence of "the ungodly." Jude based his entire epistle upon this Enochian theme. But when Enoch's book was later questioned, Jude himself also became suspect, his letter barely remaining among the canonical books of the Bible.

Another remarkable bit of evidence for the early Christians' acceptance of the Book of Enoch was for many years buried under the King James Bible's mistranslation of Luke 9:35, describing the transfiguration of Christ: "And there came a voice out of the cloud, saying, This is my beloved Son: hear him." Apparently the translator here wished to make this verse agree with a similar verse in Matthew and Mark. But Luke's verse in the original Greek reads: "This is my Son, the *Elect One*.[60] Hear him."

The "Elect One" is a most significant term in the Book of Enoch. If the book was indeed known to the apostles, with its abundant descriptions of the Elect One who should "sit upon a throne of glory" and the Elect One who should "dwell in the midst of them,"[61] then great scriptural authenticity is accorded to the Book of Enoch when the "voice out of the cloud" tells the apostles, "This is my Son, the Elect One"—the one promised in the Book of Enoch.

The Book of Enoch was also much loved by the Essenes, the new-age community that had a large monastery at Qumran on the Dead Sea at the time of Jesus Christ. "The motif of the fallen angels," Dr. Potter notes, "was a favorite legend among the Essenes."[62]

Fragments of ten Enoch manuscripts were found among the Dead Sea Scrolls. The famous scrolls actually comprise only one part of the total findings at Qumran. Much of the rest was Enochian literature, copies of the Book of Enoch, and other apocryphal works in the Enochian tradition, like the Book of Jubilees. With so many copies around, the Essenes could well have used Enoch as a community prayer book or teacher's manual and study text.

The Essenes were waiting for the coming Messiah to deliver them from the persecution they suffered, which they attributed to the "sons of Belial"—undoubtedly the fallen angels. They awaited the coming of the Elect One; for as the Book of Enoch had prophesied, "You shall behold my Elect One, sitting upon the throne of my glory. And he shall judge Azazeel [Azazyel], all his associates, and all his hosts."[63]

In this same tradition, Jesus himself said, "Now is the judgment of this world-system [of the Watchers]: now shall the prince of this world be cast out."[64] Certainly his listeners, well-versed as they were in the teachings of the Book of Enoch, would have caught Jesus' clear inference: that he came to implement the judgment of the fallen angels prophesied in the Book of Enoch.

In essence, Jesus revealed himself as the Messiah, the Elect One of the Book of Enoch, who came not only to fulfill the prophecies of the Old Testament but also to fulfill one very special prophecy in the Book of Enoch—namely, the judgment of the Watchers and their offspring.

The Book of Enoch was also used by writers of the noncanonical (i.e., apocryphal or "hidden") texts. The author of the apocryphal Epistle of Barnabas quotes the Book of Enoch three times, twice calling it "the Scripture," a term specifically denoting the inspired Word of God.[65] Other apocryphal works reflect knowledge of the Enoch story of the Watchers, notably the Testaments of the Twelve Patriarchs and the Book of Jubilees. (See "Enoch in the Forgotten Books" in this volume.)

CHURCH FATHERS AGREE WITH ENOCH ON THE PHYSICALITY OF FALLEN ANGELS

Everybody loved and respected the Book of Enoch. *At least for a time.* The turning point of opinions came in the fourth century, during the era of the Church Fathers. These highly respected interpreters of Christ's theology were the prominent leaders and teachers of the Christian Church who thrived from the first to the eighth centuries A.D.

At first the Fathers devoted much attention to the subject of the fall of the angel whom they knew as the biblical Satan. They also addressed the subject of the personalities of other fallen angels, the modus operandi of wicked spirits, and the nature of evil itself.

Convinced that these ancient wicked ones were still quite active in the world, the early Fathers often quoted the Book of Enoch to make their case for good against evil. Indeed, Dr. Charles points out that "with the earlier Fathers and Apologists it [the Book of Enoch] had all the weight of a canonical book."[66]

In the second century A.D., for example, Justin Martyr ascribed all evil to demons whom he alleged to be the offspring of the angels who fell through lust for the daughters of men—precisely the Enochian story.

The fallen angels seem to have occupied far more of Justin's thought than the good angels, and the consciousness of the demonic element in the universe was central to Justin's cosmology. Justin, in his *Second Apology*, agrees with Enoch that the angels fell through lust.[67] Moreover, explains Justin,

> they subsequently subjected the human race to themselves, partly by magic writings, partly by the fear they instilled into them and the punishments they inflicted upon them, and partly by instructing them in the use of sacrifices, incense, and libations, which they really needed after becoming slaves of their lustful passions; and among men they engendered murders, wars, adulteries, all sorts of dissipation, and every species of sin.[68]

Here Justin makes a strong statement reinforcing the argument that these angels actually dwelt among men as physical beings.

Athenagoras, writing in his work called *Legatio* in about A.D. 170, regards Enoch as a true prophet. He describes the angels which "violated both their own nature and their office":

These include the prince over matter and material things and others who are of those stationed at the first firmament (do realize that we say nothing unsupported by evidence but that we are exponents of what the prophets uttered); the latter are the angels who fell to lusting after maidens and let themselves be conquered by the flesh, the former failed his responsibility and operated wickedly in the administration of what had been entrusted to him.

Now from those who went after maidens were born the so-called giants. Do not be surprised that a partial account of the giants has been set forth also by poets. Worldly wisdom and prophetic wisdom differ from one another as truth differs from probability—the one is heavenly, the other earthly and in harmony with the prince of matter [who says]: We know how to tell many falsehoods which have the form of truth.

These angels, then, who fell from heaven busy themselves about the air and the earth and are no longer able to rise to the realms above the heavens. The souls of the giants are the demons who wander about the world. Both angels and demons produce movements [i.e., agitations, vibrations][69]—demons, movements which are akin to the natures they received, and angels, movements which are akin to the lusts with which they were possessed.[70]

The teaching that "the souls of the giants are the demons who wander about the world" is directly from Enoch. Athenagoras also discusses the fact that the angels "let themselves be conquered by flesh." Herein he may be implying that these angels were (or at least at one time had been) physical beings. The physicality of the fallen angels is nowhere more graphic than in Enoch's description of the wicked deeds of their giant offspring who devoured man and beast in their voracious appetites and even drank their blood.[71]

Most of the other early Church Fathers, as well as the early Jews, apparently held this same belief in the physicality of the fallen angels. Two Christian apologists, Lactantius and Tatian, speculated in detail on that idea of the incarnation of the fallen angels in matter.

Lactantius (260–330) believed that the fall resulted in a degradation of the angelic nature itself—that the once-heavenly angels had in fact become quite earthly. The earlier apologist Tatian (110–172) went into greater detail regarding this degradation. He described how the angels became engrossed in material things, and he believed that their very nature became coarse, gross, and material.[72]

A contemporary Catholic scholar, Emil Schneweis, summarizing Tatian's view, says the Father believed that "the fallen angels sank deeper and deeper into matter, becoming the slaves of concupiscence and lust."[73] Tatian actually says their bodies were "of fire and air"—not material flesh as are the bodies of men but in the broad sense "from matter."

Might Tatian have conjectured that the demons were physical, yet of a different sort of substance than other forms of life known to the five senses? Or might his thesis have gone so far as to speculate that the demons dwelt only in the astral realms "beneath"?

We may never know precisely how Tatian defined his terms. But even though Tatian and Lactantius both qualified their statements regarding the physicality of angels, saying that the substance composing their bodies was a fiery, airy material, later theologians totally dismissed the entire idea of material-clad angels.

Seventeenth-century editors of Tatian's work warned the reader to beware of the passage where Tatian "seems rashly to imagine the demons to be material creatures." Tatian says that the demons,

> having received their structure **from matter** and obtained the spirit which inheres in it, became intemperate and greedy; some few, indeed, turning to what was purer but others choosing what was inferior **in matter** and conforming their manner of life to it.[74]

Just in case Tatian's reader thinks Tatian is saying

these demons were physical beings (drawing the obvious conclusion from the above text), the respected collection of Church writings *The Ante-Nicene, Nicene, and Post-Nicene Fathers* to this day reprints the warning in a footnote to prevent such an 'error'.[75]

"In the course of time," says the 1967 *New Catholic Encyclopedia*, "theology has purified the obscurity and error contained in traditional views about angels. In this way, theology... [now] specifies that the nature of angels is completely spiritual and no longer merely a very fine material, firelike and vaporous."[76]

Irenaeus, Bishop of Lyons in the third century, makes several direct references to the Enoch story, including Enoch's announcement of the condemnation of the fallen Watchers. Irenaeus accuses a magically inclined Gnostic of his day of obtaining

> wonders of power that is utterly severed from God and apostate, which Satan, thy true father, enables thee still to accomplish by means of Azazel, that fallen and yet mighty angel.[77]

Azazel (or Azazyel) in the Book of Enoch is the fallen Watcher to whom the Lord "ascribes the whole crime" of the corruption of earth by his wicked inventions, including the instruments of war. Irenaeus, for one, believed Azazyel was still around.

Tertullian, who lived between A.D. 160 and 230, is most enthusiastic about the Book of Enoch. He calls the Book of Enoch "Scripture." He says:

As for the details of how some of the angels, of their own accord, were perverted and then constituted the source of the even more corrupt race of devils, a race damned by God together with the originators of the race and him whom we have mentioned as their leader, the account is found in Sacred Scripture.[78]

Tertullian wrote an entire work discussing the apparel of women in which he adjures women to dress modestly, without adornment, or what he calls "the tricks of beautifying themselves." He uses the Book of Enoch as the sturdiest evidence in his case against such "trappings":

For those, too, who invented these things are condemned to the penalty of death, namely, those angels who rushed from heaven upon the daughters of men.... For when these fallen angels had revealed certain well-hidden material substances, and numerous other arts that were only faintly revealed, to an age much more ignorant than ours...they granted to women as their special and, as it were, personal property these means of feminine vanity: the radiance of precious stones with which necklaces are decorated in different colors, the bracelets of gold which they wrap around their arms, the colored preparations which are used to dye wool, and that black powder which they use to enhance the beauty of their eyes. If you want to know what kind of things these are, you can easily learn from the character of those who taught these arts. Have sinners ever been able to show and provide anything conducive to holiness, unlawful lovers anything contributing to chastity, rebel angels anything promoting the fear of God? If, indeed, we must call what they have passed on 'teachings', then evil teachers must of necessity have taught evil lessons; if these are the wages of sin, then there can be nothing beautiful about the reward for something evil. But why should they have taught and granted such things?

Are we to think that women without the material of adornment or without the tricks of beautifying themselves would not have been able to please men when these same women, unadorned and uncouth and, as I might say, crude and rude, were able to impress angels? Or would the latter have appeared beggarly lovers who insolently demanded favors for nothing, unless they had brought some gift to the women they had attracted into marriage? But this is hardly conceivable. The women who possessed angels as husbands could not desire anything further, for surely they had already made a fine match.

The angels, on the other hand, who certainly thought sometimes of the place whence they had fallen and longed for heaven after the heated impulses of lust had quickly passed, rewarded in this way the very gift of woman's natural beauty as the cause of evil, that is, that woman should not profit from her happiness, but, rather, drawn away from the ways of innocence and sincerity, should be united with them in sin against God. They must have been certain that all ostentation, ambition, and love achieved by carnal pleasure would be displeasing God. You see, these are the angels whom we are destined to judge,[79] these are the angels whom we renounce in baptism, these are the very things on account of which they deserved to be judged by men.[80]

Tertullian, in this context, seems to hold women's beauty responsible for the fall of the angels, but he notes further on that angels are the guilty ones who "deserved to be judged by men."

Paul, too, seems to have been concerned about the connection between women's beauty and the fallen angels. In his first letter to the Corinthians, chapter 11, Paul at length admonishes women to cover their heads in church when men need not do so. Then comes the curious verse 10, translated in the King James Version as

> For this cause ought the woman to have power on her head because of the angels.

But the verse literally reads:

> For this ought the woman to have a covering on her head—because of the angels.

Most Bible commentaries explain that Paul meant a woman's uncovered head is an offense to the angels who observe church gatherings, but Tertullian believes Paul was referring specifically to the fallen angels spoken of in Enoch, who, Tertullian says, would be incited to wantonness by unveiled women with beautiful hair.[81] Having seen Paul's respect for the Book of Enoch, this interpretation does not seem unlikely.

Clement of Alexandria (150–220) speaks of the angels "who renounced the beauty of God for a beauty which fades, and so fell from heaven to earth"[82]— undeniably a reference to the Enoch story, which Clement did not question.

The *Clementine Homilies*—a Christian work written between the second and fourth centuries A.D. but not recognized as authoritative by the churches—also affirms the account of the mating of lustful angels with daughters of men, saying that angels *changed themselves into the nature of men* and partook of human lust.[83] This is a direct statement on the physicality of the fallen angels, who would have required flesh bodies in order to partake of that human lust.

Several other Church Fathers—Methodius of Philippi, Minucius Felix, Commodianus, and Ambrose of Milan—also approved the story in Enoch. Origen (186–255), a student of Clement and a highly original as well as intuitive thinker, more than once calls Enoch a prophet and freely quotes the Book of Enoch to support his own theories.[84] But Origen notes that the Book of Enoch was not accepted by the churches of his day as divine and that it was not held in respect by the Jews.

Since so many of Origen's works were later banned by the Church, perhaps his complete statement on the Book of Enoch has not survived. On the basis of Origen's half-dozen or so references to it, Enoch scholars conclude that Origen approved of the Book of Enoch, while Catholic scholars claim that Origen rejected it, maintaining that Origen "had no inclination to accept the legend of angelic fornication," as they call it.[85]

But the fragments of his writings that remain preserve one important key to the thought of this prolific Church Father: Origen surely would not have denied the Enoch account of the fall of the angels through lust on the ground that it implied a physical incarnation of the angels, because Origen himself believed that angels could embody as men. (See *The Origen Conspiracy*, page 367ff.)

Whether or not the early Church Fathers realized it, the ramifications of their statements were far-reaching. They suggest, for example, that the evil ones in our midst—the Hitlers past and present and nameless killers without conscience—might be of an entirely different psychological and spiritual makeup than other souls on planet Earth.

Such killers have an extraordinary power. When angered, they respond with a bloodthirstiness that is inhuman, a depravity that derives from their godlessness devoid of the divine spark. For these "evil spirits," murder is sheer joy—some even refer to it as "the most intimate act."

Is it because through it they get as close as they

ever will to the life-essence (i.e., the 'God-essence') of a son of God? Few realize that in the piercing of the heart of the son of God and in the spilling of the blood, an extraordinary light is released. This excites and enlivens the 'living dead' as they 'taste' and 'drink in' this vital energy that comes only from God, only through his embodied lightbearers.

The author of Hebrews calls the Watchers not sons of God but "bastards," who are without chastening because their final judgment is sealed, for the Lord chastens only the beloved sons whom he would receive to his heart. It should be understandable that these evildoers whose souls are condemned to the 'second death'[86] would be lovers of death rather than life. And their death cult—their pleasure in sensual stimulation expending the life-force* in riotous and rancorous living—has become a shroud upon a planet and her people.

Renowned psychologist Erich Fromm comments that these "necrophiles" have "precisely the reverse of the values we connect with normal life: not life, but death excites and satisfies them"[87]—death in all of the sensational downward spirals of a selfish, purposeless existence.

Few have ever understood the "why" of this alternate generation, who seem the antithesis of the life-loving sons of God—the angry, the blasphemous, raging, restless, dying race whose core is rotten, rebellious and irresponsible toward the Light and the Honor of

---

*The 'God-force', also called the sacred fire, or the Kundalini.

God. But then, few have explored the teaching of Enoch and the early Church Fathers on the incarnation of demons and fallen angels.

Perhaps the Book of Enoch also explains where these devils get the energy to do their despicable deeds. Since they have already lost the divine spark and their place in heaven—God told them, "Never shall you ascend into heaven," and "Never shall you obtain peace"—they have nothing else to lose and everything to gain from the shedding of the blood (the life-essence) of the sons of God.

They have no remorse for their misconduct, for the way of penance and forgiveness is not open to them. Without a heart flame, they have no pity for their victims, no ability to 'feel' for them. They do not identify with them in murder, or in the mass murders the Watchers legitimize with the term "war," as in "wars of liberation."

As a substitute for the loving rapport between our Father and his beloved sons that they have rejected, the Watchers and their seed have entered into a symbiotic relationship with the discarnate spirits of the "giants" who yet roam the astral plane oppressing, corrupting, and contending for the minds of their victims. Devoid of the mind of Christ, the evolutionary chain of the Watchers become demon-possessed tools of dark forces from whom they derive both the energy and the cunning for their crimes.

Jesus called them "whited sepulchres, which indeed appear beautiful outward, but are within full of dead men's bones, and of all uncleanness."[88] The truth is that these fallen ones are so dead that they cannot respond to the cries of the people to stop waging arms races, nor do they give adequate answer to appeals to stop misappropriating the people's money in the inner sanctums of their 'bank-tums'. Instead, the Watchers take the people's gold and give them inflated, worthless currency in exchange for their sacred labor.

The Watchers, by their words and their deeds, have been eroding our planet for a long, long time—our civilization, our religion, and, if they could, our very souls.

Why do we stand by and let the Watchers feed their alcohol to our sons and daughters? Why do we let them pump our children full of their death drugs? Why do we let them destroy the nations and the international economy before our children can even grow up to enjoy this beautiful world God gave us?

Our state of nonawareness and noninvolvement has let them get away with cold-blooded murder—for centuries. By our inaction we have allowed the streets of America to be turned into combat zones where innocent people are murdered, raped, or robbed at gunpoint. We have allowed violent crime to go unchecked by tolerating a legal system that turns killers, rapists, and child molesters back on the streets to strike again.

International terrorists, the Mafia, and deranged kidnappers make life uncertain for every public servant.

Today the risks of representative government are so high that the defenders of the people must carefully consider that they may be stopped by torturous blackmail or a hideous death if they raise their hand in defense of the Light. But has it not been so for as long as the servants of justice and truth can remember?

See how the Watchers manipulate the food of the world in order to gain their military objectives. See how they rob the nations' granaries to feed the enemies of the Light in order to achieve political ends. Whose side are they on anyway?—surely not the people's!

See their disdain for the human race whom they regard as nothing more than "an experiment" to do their bidding, whom they have so far managed to contain by regulation of the basic necessities of life and population control (by making war and abortion an easy out for the people's unresolved emotional conflicts). No one but the Watchers and their embodied offspring could have masterminded such a complex and cunning scheme to subjugate the people of earth to their total domination—body, mind, and soul, by any and every means and madness.

I write this detailed exposé of a spiritual fraud perpetrated against all the God-fearing of the planet so that you may realize somewhat the enormity of the conspiracy against our very hearts to be the vessels on earth of our Lord's sacred heart.

Now let us examine how the later Church Fathers turned away from the concept of embodied angels and the Book of Enoch, thus unwittingly playing into their hands.

LATER CHURCH FATHERS DENOUNCE ENOCH AS HERESY— BELIEF IN EMBODIED ANGELS BANNED AS BLASPHEMY

The later Church Fathers did indeed have difficulty with the Enoch viewpoint and sought another explanation for the fall of the angels. Perhaps they were uncomfortable with the implications of the story of some among us who are not of us—men who are not men but fallen angels. So they looked to the record of Lucifer's fall in Isaiah 14:12–15, which reads:

> How art thou fallen from heaven, O Lucifer, son of the morning! how art thou cut down to the ground, which didst weaken the nations!
>
> For thou hast said in thine heart, I will ascend into heaven, I will exalt my throne above the stars of God: I will sit also upon the mount of the congregation, in the sides of the north:
>
> I will ascend above the heights of the clouds; I will be like the most High.
>
> Yet thou shalt be brought down to hell, to the sides of the pit.

Some Church Fathers saw in these verses of Isaiah the story of the fall of an archangel and subsequently that of his underlings, drawing by "his tail" (pride), according to Revelation 12:4, "the third part of the stars [angels] of heaven." Thus, they saw the fall as being through pride rather than through lust, as in the Enoch account.

The Fathers, it seems, came up with an idea—an easy way to avoid the troublesome tale of embodied evil angels. They unanimously chose the version of the fall of the angels through pride *instead of* the Enochian version of the fall through lust, making it an either/or equation.

The question is: Was their motivation in challenging the Book of Enoch to avoid the controversial doctrine of the corporeality of the wicked angels and their bodily presence upon earth? And if so... why?

Perhaps we can reconstruct the logic of their argument. If the angels fell through lust, they must have had (or gotten) physical bodies to outplay their physical desires. But if the angels merely fell through pride, a corruption of mind and heart, they need not have had bodies to consummate their sin. They could simply be those bat-winged demons that whisper into men's ears, inciting *them* to vanity of vanities.

The latter explanation was, in theological terms, less problematical. And to this very day—though the Genghis Khans, et al., have made their grandiose entrances and exits, parading their superhuman or subhuman vileness, as the case may be—that belief prevails.

I for one do not believe that the sin of pride does not require a physical body to outplay itself. The preening of these devils—their body fixations and perversions ad nauseam and a physical culture based entirely on the pride of the eye, from body-building to fashion to the decadence of the Cain civilization—is rooted in both pride *and* lust and is the proving ground for fallen egos vying for attention and acclaim through the success cult.

The love of money is also rooted in both pride and lust. These vices feed on each other as acts of lust become an assertion of pride in sexual prowess. Yes, pride is a physical boasting—"See me, see how beautiful I am, see how I can do all things better than the sons of God. See how I can defy the Almighty, commit any crime, abuse every law, spurn his love—and get away with it!"

In fact, the sin of lust itself technically does not require a physical body to stain the soul and life record of men or angels. For did not Jesus teach that the sin of lust could be carried out mentally and spiritually through an impure heart? "Whosoever looketh on a woman to lust after her hath committed adultery with her already in his heart." (Matt. 5:28)

It would seem that to dwell upon the flesh-and-blood aspects of sin should cause a digression from the fact that the state of sinfulness or virtue is a condition of the soul which may be carried to its logical conclusion in contempt of the Almighty on any plane of habitation by either men or angels, whether clothed with bodies earthly, astral, or ethereal.

Notwithstanding, the Church Fathers who grasped

at a few verses of Isaiah as salvation from their Enochian dilemma overlooked the most astounding story of all. The narrative, after detailing the fall of the archangel Lucifer, outlines the contemptuous deeds, the *earthly* deeds, of this ambitious "son of the morning," calling him outright "the man that made the earth to tremble."

> They that see thee shall narrowly look upon thee, and consider thee, saying, Is this **the man** that made the earth to tremble, that did shake kingdoms;
>
> That made the world as a wilderness, and destroyed the cities thereof; that opened not the house of his prisoners?
>
> All the kings of the nations, even all of them, lie in glory, every one in his own house.
>
> But thou art cast out of thy grave like an abominable branch, and as the raiment of those that are slain, thrust through with a sword, that go down to the stones of the pit; as a carcase trodden under feet.[89]

Isaiah called Lucifer a *man*—giving strong indication that he believed that the "cast down one" had walked the earth in the flesh, had moved among mortals as one of them.[90]

Cyprian (200–258), a pupil of Tertullian, noted the specific use of the word *man* and used it as proof that the Antichrist—Lucifer—would someday come as a man. Aphrahat, a fourth-century Christian theologian from Persia, believed that Lucifer had already incarnated—as Nebuchadnezzar, king of ancient Babylon.[91]

But this phenomenal piece of evidence for the incarnation of fallen angels was brushed aside by the other Church Fathers—if they ever recognized it for what it was—who instead used the Isaiah passage to launch another debate: the pride-versus-lust controversy.

Christian writer Julius Africanus (200–245) first opposed the traditional story of the fall of the angels through lust. He even tackled Genesis 6, verses 1–4, about the "sons of God" and the "daughters of men" —a parallel to the Book of Enoch in approved Scripture. The pivotal verses read:

> And it came to pass, when men began to multiply on the face of the earth, and daughters were born unto them,
>
> That the sons of God saw the daughters of men that they were fair; and they took them wives of all which they chose.
>
> And the Lord said, My spirit shall not always strive with man, for that he also is flesh: yet his days shall be an hundred and twenty years.
>
> There were giants in the earth in those days; and also after that, when the sons of God came in unto the daughters of men, and they bare children to them, the same became mighty men which were of old, men of renown.

Julius Africanus preferred to believe that the "sons of God" in Genesis 6:2 who "saw the daughters of men" and "took them wives" didn't refer at all to angels, despite the fact that certain translations of the Bible in his day explicitly read "angels of God" rather than "sons of God."[92]

Julius Africanus thought that the verse referred instead to the righteous sons of Seth who "fell" (in the moral sense) by taking wives of the inferior daughters of Cain.[93] He formed his opinion in spite of the fact that both the Book of Enoch and the Book of Jude refer to angels who left their first (heavenly) estate,[94] which Julius should have known, and also in spite of the fact that the term "sons of God" is elsewhere used in the Old Testament to indicate angels,[95] which Julius also should have known.

The opinions of the Church Fathers soon flocked to this interpretation. In the early fourth century, the Syrian authority Ephraem also declared that Genesis 6 referred to the Sethites and Cainites—and therefore not to the fall of angels through lust.[96]

Hilary of Tours casually mentions the tale of the lustful fall of angels as if it were folly—"about which," he says, "some book or other exists," but notes, "We need not know those things which are not contained in the book of the Law."[97] Syrian theologian Theodoret simply called believers of the story in Enoch "stupid and very silly."[98]

Then Jerome (348–420), Doctor of the Church and scholarly Hebraist, got into the argument. Jerome branded Enoch as apocryphal and declared its teaching similar to the Manichaean teachings—which Jerome emphatically denounced as heretical. These are Jerome's words:

> We have read in a certain apocryphal book* that when the sons of God were coming down to the daughters of men, they descended upon Mount Hermon and there entered into an agreement to come to the daughters of men and make them their wives. This book is quite explicit and is classified as apocryphal. The ancient exegetes have at various times referred to it, but we are citing it, not as authoritative, but merely to bring it to your attention....I have read about this apocryphal book in the work of a particular author who used it to confirm his own heresy. What does he say? He says: The sons of God who came down from heaven upon Mount Hermon and coveted the daughters of men are angels descending from the heavens and souls that desired bodies since bodies are the daughters of men. Do you detect the source of the teachings of Manichaeus, the ignorant? Just as the Manichaeans say that souls desired human bodies to be united in pleasure, do not they who say that angels desired bodies—or the daughters of men—seem to you to be saying the same thing as the Manichaeans? It would take too long to refute them now, but I merely wanted to indicate the coinci-

---

*Jerome elsewhere mentions the Book of Enoch by name and is clearly referring to it here.

dence, as it were, of the book that opportunely confirmed their dogma.[99]

Note the sarcasm of Jerome in his statement that the Book of Enoch "opportunely" confirmed the dogma of "Manichaeus, the ignorant"—as if to say that the author of Enoch was responsible for the supposed heresies of the Manichaeans. By implying that the teachings of the Book of Enoch were in cahoots with Manichaean doctrines, Jerome castigated the book severely.

Manichaeanism, a powerful competitor of the Church, was founded in about 240 A.D. by a Persian visionary named Mani who claimed apostleship under Jesus Christ. Mani believed himself an embodiment of the promised Paraclete and preached a synthesis of several major religions including Buddhism, Zoroastrianism, and Christianity. He also taught reincarnation and wrote a book (now destroyed) about the wicked giants.[100] Needless to say, Mani was blacklisted by the Church—and he was martyred in southwest Persia by fanatical Zoroastrians.

Jerome's statement that the Book of Enoch's doctrines supported Manichaeanism certainly would have cast aspersions upon the book's spiritual integrity. And not surprisingly, the core of Jerome's argument is against the Manichaean doctrine that "souls desired human bodies to be united in pleasure"—which Jerome compares to the Enochian fall of the angels through lust, a teaching he rejected.

Church Father Chrysostom (346–407) took the case against Enoch one step further. Who were those "sons of God" in Genesis 6? Certainly not angels, says Chrysostom. He thought that opinion was totally absurd and refuted it with vigor. To quote him in his own outraged words:

> Here is, first, the most audacious idea, of which we are going to show you the absurdity, by presenting to your meditation the true meaning of the Scripture, so that you do not listen to those who utter such blasphemy.... They say that it is not men that are referred to here, but angels, and that it is the angels that are called "sons of God."... It would be folly to accept such insane blasphemy, saying that an incorporeal and spiritual nature could have united itself to human bodies![101]

With Chrysostom, the problem presented by the Book of Enoch finally gets fully defined. It was not *really* just a question of whether angels fell through pride or through lust—it was the bigger question of whether angels ever took on human bodies at all in their fall.

This very issue—the descent of the angels into the physical world through lust—infuriated Chrysostom and caused him to issue his judgment of the "insane blasphemy" of the account in the Book of Enoch. Chrysostom's edict that angels were spiritual and men were physical (and never the twain should meet) was ratified by Caesarius of Arles, who also insisted that angels were incorporeal and therefore could not have mated with women.[102]

But the final axe was yet to fall upon the Book of Enoch. Filastrius, in the late fourth century, condemned the teaching in Enoch as actual heresy. In his long list of heresies, of which Enoch's account of the Watchers is heresy number 108, Filastrius declared:

> There is no doubt that the angels, who were cast down from heaven, are not similar to human nature, if only because to suggest such a thing would be blasphemy and contrary to the law.... Moreover, if he who thought it to be correct that the angels, having been transformed into the flesh, sinned in such a way that they remained in this very flesh or thus did such carnal deeds—this one discerns history with a convoluted logic.[103]

Doubtless the threat of having one's logic "convoluted" by such a "blasphemy" turned many away from the Book of Enoch.

The issue was settled once and for all with the logical and technical arguments of Augustine (354–430), who rejected the tale of the fall of angels through a physical lust and mating with women as implying an impossibility for angelic natures. In his *City of God*, Augustine declared:

> We made a passing reference to this question, but did not decide whether angels, inasmuch as they are

spirits, could have bodily intercourse with women. For it is written, "Who maketh His angels spirits," that is, He makes those who are by nature spirits His angels by appointing them to the duty of bearing His messages.... However, the same trustworthy Scripture testifies that angels have appeared to men in such bodies as could not only be seen, but also touched. There is, too, a very general rumour, which many have verified by their own experience, or which trustworthy persons who have heard the experience of others corroborate, that sylvans and fauns, who are commonly called "incubi," had often made wicked assaults upon women, and satisfied their lust upon them; and that certain devils...are constantly attempting and effecting this impurity is so generally affirmed, that it were impudent to deny it. From these assertions, indeed, I dare not determine whether there be some spirits embodied in an aerial substance...and who are capable of lust and of mingling sensibly with women; but certainly I could by no means believe that God's holy angels could at that time have so fallen.[104]

Augustine continues with a long proof that the phrase "sons of God" in Genesis 6 refers to the righteous sons of Seth who married the daughters of Cain, reaching the same conclusion as Julius Africanus—an escape route used by most Fathers to avoid the admission of the incarnation of angels. He concludes:

Let us omit, then, the fables of those scriptures which are called apocryphal, because their obscure origin was unknown to the fathers from whom the authority of the true Scriptures has been transmitted to us by a most certain and well-ascertained succession. For though there is some truth in these apocryphal writings, yet they contain so many false statements, that they have no canonical authority. We cannot deny that Enoch, the seventh from Adam, left some divine writings, for this is asserted by the Apostle Jude in his canonical epistle. But it is not without reason that these writings have no place in that canon of Scripture which was preserved in the temple of the Hebrew people by the diligence of successive priests; for their antiquity brought them under suspicion, and it was impossible to ascertain whether these were his genuine writings, and they were not brought forward as genuine by the persons who were found to have carefully preserved the canonical books by a successive transmission. So that the writings which are produced under his name, and which contain these fables about the giants, saying that their fathers were not men [but angels], are properly judged by prudent men to be not genuine; just as many writings are produced by heretics under the names both of other prophets, and, more recently, under the names of the apostles, all of which, after careful examination, have been set apart from canonical authority under the title of Apocrypha.[105]

Augustine had decided the issue. After his time, the "sons of God" in Genesis 6 are no longer angels but simply the sons of Seth, the "daughters of men" being Cainites. This has since become the standard interpretation of Catholic and Protestant exegetes down to the present day.[106] And the controversy over the likelihood of fallen angels incarnating as men was laid to rest for centuries.

What do Church theologians think of Enoch's tale today? *A Catholic Dictionary of Theology* calls the story in Enoch that angels could assume bodies a "wild improbability."[107] The *New Catholic Encyclopedia* points out several times that the Book of Enoch is based on a "misinterpretation of Genesis 6:1–4."[108] The nature of angels, it declares, is completely spiritual.

The logical conclusion of this premise of the incorporeality of angels was also noted by Thomas Aquinas, who with Augustine would not allow that angels could have any other sin than pride or envy—sins not dependent upon body or sense.[109] In this view, therefore, angels simply cannot commit gross sins through bodily passion because their nature is not "bodily."

The question that the Church could never answer was, How on earth could incorporeal angels mate with corporeal daughters of men? Rather than admit that the angels must have incarnated in flesh bodies to perform the task, the Church Fathers, as we have seen, preferred to say that the angels weren't angels at all, but the descendants of Seth, thereby ousting Enoch's story in its entirety. Besides, the fall of the angels could be completely (and easily) explained by the rebellion of a proud archangel.

The Church's fourth-century Synod of Laodicea struck another sharp blow against the Book of Enoch's angelology—this time, against the *good* angels in the book. This council, two centuries earlier than the one which banned Origen's views on angels becoming men, decreed that the only angels which could be named were Michael, Gabriel, and Raphael, who are the only angels mentioned in the Church's Scriptures.[110]

The council also "prohibited by a canon that prayer should be offered to angels" on the grounds that "it was a species of idolatry and detracted from the worship due to Christ." A commentary notes that the synod held its meeting at Laodicea in Phrygia because the people there believed angels to be defenders of the Law and were therefore supposedly "worshiping" them.[111]

The commentary also notes that Pope Zachary in 745 A.D. held a Roman council against one Aldebert, "who was found to invoke by name eight angels in his prayers."[112] No wonder the intricate angelology in the Book of Enoch—which names far more than three angels—was condemned!

When Rabbi Simeon ben Jochai pronounced an actual curse on those who held the "sons of God" in Genesis 6:2 to be angels, although that had been the age-old Jewish interpretation of the verse,[113] he turned the world of Judaism against the Book of Enoch. The rabbi's second-century curse was apparently effective, because from that point onwards, sparse mention is made in Jewish literature of the book.

It could have been his knowledge of the rabbi's curse which prompted Origen's remark a century later that the Book of Enoch was not accepted among the Jews. And it may have been the work of even earlier rabbis that first began to hide the book away in the shadows of Judaic tradition so that, as Augustine noted, it was not found among the approved Scriptures of the Jews.

What eventually happened to the book? In a recent study of the apocrypha, writer Nicholas de Lange cites a revealing passage found in some texts of the Talmud in the context of the statement of Rabbi Akiba (c. 40–135) that "whoever reads the 'excluded books' has no share in the world to come." Following this, the Babylonian teacher Rab Joseph is then quoted as saying, "It is also forbidden to read the book of Ben Sira [another apocryphal work]. But we may teach the good things it contains." Other texts, however, in place of this last sentence, read, "If the rabbis had not hidden this book away, we should be able to teach the good things it contains."[114]

De Lange points out that the expression "hiding away" denotes the process applied to sacred texts and other sacred objects which were no longer considered fit for use. According to the Talmud, he continues, the sages had even considered hiding away the Book of

Ezekiel on account of the supposedly "misleading" teachings it contained.[115]

Undoubtedly there were some apocryphal writings that would have been judged even by laymen as devoid of the Lord's spirit. These counterfeits have survived perhaps in much greater number than apocrypha of authentic spiritual value, which have come down to us either in severely edited copies or not at all.

Also central to the question of the disappearance of the Book of Enoch from religious scriptures is the fact that books were generally produced in small quantities in this era before the invention of the printing press. In order for a book to survive, it would need to be continually recopied by scribes. The easiest way to suppress a text was simply not to have it copied. Once a book fell into disapproval with the authorities, the scribes were hardly likely to copy it. The book then was allowed to fade into obscurity.

And so the words of Enoch 'faded' from the source books of civilization. It might not be irrelevant or irreverent to ask, Who made the deletions—men or angels? Who so wanted to keep the presence of fallen ones upon earth a guarded secret?

In the guise and garb of Christian and Jew, 'they'— the fallen angels and those who they influenced— denounced and suppressed the Book of Enoch's record of the fall of angels through the lusts of the flesh. Their verdicts of heresy and blasphemy rested against Enoch for over fifteen hundred years.

MILESTONES IN
ENOCHIAN SCHOLARSHIP

Then the twentieth-century discovery of several Aramaic Enoch texts among the Dead Sea Scrolls prompted Catholic scholar J. T. Milik to compile a complete history of the Enoch legends, including translations of the Aramaic manuscripts.

Milik's 400-page book, published in 1976 by Oxford,[116] is a milestone in Enochian scholarship, and Milik himself is no doubt one of the world's finest experts on the subject. His opinions, based as they are on years of in-depth research, are highly respected.

Milik notes the obviously close interdependence of the story of the fallen angels in Enoch and the story of the "sons of God" in the Book of Genesis. But he does not draw the same conclusion as the Church Fathers, namely that the Book of Enoch misinterpreted the earlier Genesis account and was therefore irrelevant.

Milik, rather, arrives at a surprising yet well-justified conclusion: that not only is the history of the fallen angels in Enoch *older* than Genesis 6—but Genesis 6 is in fact a direct *summary* of the earlier Enoch account.[117]

This is what Milik calls the "ineluctable solution": it is Genesis 6 that is based on Enoch and not the other way around. Milik thinks that the text of Genesis 6, by its abridged and allusive formulation and direct quoting of two or three phrases of Enoch, must be the later of the two, making the Enoch legend earlier than the definitive chapters in Genesis.[118]

Milik has thus deftly turned the tables on the late Church Fathers who banned the records of fallen angels mating with daughters of men and who labeled Enoch's teaching a heretical misinterpretation of Genesis 6. For if Genesis 6 was really based on the Book of Enoch, then obviously Genesis 6 is retelling the same event as Enoch: the lusting of the fallen angels after the daughters of men. Enoch's account *was* in the Bible, right in the approved text of Genesis, all along.

If Milik is right—and the evidence leans in his favor—then the criteria upon which the Fathers based their judgments against the Book of Enoch are fully invalidated and their testimony against Enoch is refuted. Their arguments have no ground. Enoch's case must be reopened and retried.

But the astute reader will ask, If Genesis 6 tells of the fall of the angels through lust, what about the *other* biblical fall of the archangel through pride, as told in Isaiah and as noted (or rather, used) by the later Church Fathers long ago? Here again, twentieth-century scholarship provides an answer that was unavailable in the patristic era.

In an unparalleled and detailed probing into the specific meaning of the passage, Hebrew scholar Julian Morgenstern discovered that tied up in the Genesis verses are traces of "two distinct and originally entirely unrelated myths dealing with gods or angels."[119]

In his remarkable exegesis (Hebrew Union College, 1939), Morgenstern proves that originally two accounts of separate falls of the angels were known: one, that of the archangel's rebellion against the authority of God and his subsequent fall through pride, in which he was followed by a multitude of lesser angels, biblically called the *Nephilim* (the "fallen ones"); and two, the other account, recorded faithfully in the Book of Enoch—the later fall of the angels, called *Watchers*, through inordinate lust for the daughters of men.[120] And so, Morgenstern concludes, the angels fell not once but *twice*.

Morgenstern explains that the very construction of Genesis 6:4, one of the most intricate and obscure Old Testament verses, implies that it is a synthesis of two different stories. The verse reads in literal English:

> The Nephilim were on the earth at that time (and even afterward) when the sons of God resorted to the daughters of man, and had children by them.[121]

The text specifically sets side by side two facts: one, there used to be beings called Nephilim on earth; and two, they were still around when the sons of God came down and mated with the daughters of men. Clearly, says Morgenstern, the Nephilim are fallen angels who were *already* on the earth when the sons of God—the other angels which Enoch depicted—also fell through their own lust.

But how did the Nephilim fallen angels get here to earth in the first place? That, states Morgenstern, is where the rebellious archangel and the fall through pride fits in. That is the earlier of two entirely separate celestial events.[122]

What seems to have caused scriptural confusion in later times is the many-faceted meaning of the word *Nephilim*. The synopsis in Genesis 6 is so terse and abbreviated that it apparently became all but unreadable to later Jews.

Some seem to have thought the Nephilim were the same as the "sons of God" in that verse, while others thought the Nephilim were the evil children of the sons of God and the daughters of men. The latter misunderstanding cropped up in the Book of Jubilees and in some editions of the Enoch material.[123]

On top of this confusion, the Greek Septuagint, a late translation of the Hebrew Scriptures, rendered the word *Nephilim* as "giants," eliminating all connotations of "fallen angels." The evil giant children born to the Watchers and daughters of men were known to the Hebrews specifically as *Gibborim* (literally "heroes" or "mighty men"), but later editors, in the confusion, mixed up the Nephilim with these Gibborim and also with the giants of Numbers 13:33, the Anakim.[124]

Morgenstern further notes that the term *Nephilim* is in the passive voice, i.e., "those who were made to fall" or "those who were cast down."[125] The New Testament Greek term *eblēthēsan* conveys precisely the same meaning. ("And the great dragon was *cast out*, that old serpent, called the Devil, and Satan, which deceiveth the whole world: he was *cast out* into the earth, and his angels were *cast out* with him.")[126]

This form of the word *Nephilim* is entirely different from the active voice of the verbal form, i.e., *Nophelim,* those who fell of their own accord or in a natural manner. Elsewhere the Bible confirms that these fallen ones were "cast down" and "delivered into chains of darkness"[127]—they did not descend by their own free will but were forcibly removed from heaven.

In time, it appears, the original meaning of the term *Nephilim* (the "cast down ones") became more generalized and applied to whoever or whatever was wicked. Thus, the giant Gibborim born to the lustful Watchers and the daughters of men might have been labeled Nephilim simply because they were of fallen character like the original Nephilim who already walked the earth and seemed like "giants" in their own right.

With so many definitions and misunderstandings piled on top of the word, it is not surprising that the history of the original Nephilim who fell with the archangel through pride got lost in the translation.

But the account in Revelation 12 is well worth examining. The angels who had fallen in rank with the fall of the proud archangel were forced to surrender their position in the hierarchy of heaven by none other than Archangel Michael. This "great prince"[128] of the celestial orders had to wage a cosmic war and engage in direct combat with the rebels in order to force them to surrender their position.

The Gospel of Bartholomew elaborates upon the reason for the archangel's fall. This apocryphal work explains that the archangel revealed his pride when he refused to bend the knee (to confess the Christ) before the man made by the Lord.

The account in Revelation 12 gives force to this apocryphal theme. The great dragon in Revelation, "called the Devil, and Satan," is threatened by the birth of the Manchild to the Woman "clothed with the sun" and therefore seeks "to devour her child as soon as it is born." The dragon's disrespect for the Manchild, son of the Woman and Son of God, cost him his high rung on the ladder of the heavenly hierarchy.

The same proud refusal to bend the knee before God's newly created man is evident in the Gospel of Bartholomew. "I am fire of fire," boasts the archangel. "I was the first angel formed, and shall I worship clay and matter?"[129] His refusal to worship the man—as the Son of God (or the Son of God *within* the Son of man)—was the original act of rebellion.

The apocryphal Book of John the Evangelist contains a description of the consequences of the archangel's pride: physical incarnation. The apostle John asks the Lord, "When Satan fell, in what place dwelt he?" The Lord replies, "My Father changed his appearance because of his pride, and the light was taken from him, and his face became like unto heated iron, and his face became wholly *like that of a man*."[130]

Revelation 12:9 ("he was cast out *into the earth*") confirms the incarnation of the Nephilim in the earth plane in earth bodies. Genesis 6:4 confirms not only the physical incarnation of the Nephilim (the "giants" *in the earth*) but also that of the Watchers, as we have seen. So not only were there two falls—there were two (or at *least* two) separate incarnations of fallen angels upon earth. The Nephilim were "made to fall" or "cast down"; the Watchers "fell" of their own accord— we might therefore call the latter *Nophelim*.

Strike two for the Church Fathers and rabbis who banned the Book of Enoch. The seeming contradiction between two falls of angels, eventually used by the Fathers against Enoch, disappears if there are separate stories of two falls.

Enoch's book, then, is a trustworthy preservation of the one fall, the one through lust, that would other- wise have been lost to posterity but for a few other brief apocryphal references.

The later Church Fathers' denial of the Book of Enoch thus clouded man's understanding of the fallen angels for centuries. Furthermore, the statements of the later Church Fathers against the idea of physical incarnation of angels are far from authoritative. Lin- guistic proof supports the theory that the Jews of ancient times believed the fallen angels physically incarnated in flesh bodies.

THE "ACTUAL ANGELIC INCARNATION" OF THE FALLEN ONES

In a respected scriptural study in the late nineteenth century, Franz Delitzsch shows that the wife-choosing of the fallen angels was a contract of actual and lasting marriages, as shown by the Hebrew verb phrase *(lakach ishsha)* used to describe them. "To make this to a certain degree conceivable," says Delitzsch, "we must admit an assumption of human bodies by angels; and hence not merely transitory appearances of angels in human form, but actual angelic incarnation."[131]

J. H. Kurtz, a nineteenth-century professor of theology, agreed with Delitzsch that the angels of Genesis 6 were not mere incorporeal spirits but possessed bodies.

"We may perhaps not regard it as quite impossible," he wrote, "that the angels should have not only desired to look into this mystery of human nature, but also to share in it." More explicitly, Kurtz declares, "We can only conceive a sexual connection between angels and daughters of men if the idea of corporeity attaches to the former."[132]

Morgenstern also hints that for the early Jews, the fallen angels were quite physical, noting that the crime of the "sons of God" was one which was characteristic of the *human* level of existence. He shows that God's punishment of these angels was that they take on the nature and quality of the human women with whom they had associated themselves carnally and that they become *mortal*. Morgenstern says, "No other conclusion is possible."[133] Sentenced to an earthly life, the angels thereafter became as mortal men.

One by one the arguments against the Book of Enoch fade away. The day may soon arrive when the final complaints about the Book of Enoch's lack of historicity and "late date" are also silenced by new evidence of the book's real antiquity.

There is also a more metaphysical explanation of how the Book of Enoch may be of late date yet still carry the words of the ancient father Enoch. Tertullian proposed that the book could have been reproduced after the Flood through the inspiration of the Holy Spirit.[134] Likewise did Ezra, according to Jewish legend, reproduce (through God's dictation) the text of all the scriptures destroyed when the Torah was burned.[135] An unknown prophet inspired by the Holy Spirit might also have restored this ancient book of Enoch to a later era that had lost the original.

Not only could the book be authentically the ancient story of the real Enoch, it could also be the answer to the philosophers' conundrum of the origin of evil in God's universe. According to Harvard's Dr. Paul D. Hanson, the myth of the fallen angels "offers an etiology of evil in the world: all of the evil in the world stems from a heavenly event, the rebellion of certain divine beings, and more immediately, from the resulting generation of their pernicious offspring in the world."[136]

The Book of Enoch may also explain the apparent differential of stature and power among men—like the control by certain 'elite' men over others more 'common'. We may turn from the ancient history of the Nophelim (Watchers) and the Nephilim to consider those on earth today who have that magnetic personality and greater sense of self-importance to which the 'little people' always defer. Imposing and ingratiating men and women are these whose birthright (they believe) it is to rule the lesser endowed. The latter, being thoroughly intimidated and stupefied by the former, easily become the idolaters of these masterminds.

Voilà! Now you've got their number (their genetic code): for thousands of years the fallen angels have been propagating themselves and propping themselves up—up, up on the social and success-cult ladder. From the original prototype, they have cloned and carbon-copied an oppressive—and godless—power elite. The Pilates and the Herods, with emperors and high priests, senators and warlords, moneychangers and lawyers—secure in their private clubs and retreats, in firm control, with money and sex as their gods—they will rule the world until the heirs of Enoch take the torch of illumination to challenge and consume their infamy.

That Jesus spoke of two distinct evolutions, one that came from God, the I AM Presence, and one that came from the lower order of fallen ones, is specifically concealed in the Lord's conversation with Nicodemus: "Except a man be born again, he cannot see the kingdom of God"[137]—so the translation usually reads. But the original Greek reads: "Except a man be born *from above,* he cannot see the kingdom of God." ("And no man hath ascended up to heaven, but he that came down from heaven, even the Son of man which is in heaven," John 3:13.) The phrase "born from above" is reminiscent of Jesus' later statement to the Pharisees, "Ye are from beneath; I am from above."[138]

But in chapter 8 of the Gospel of John, Jesus is quoted as making an even stronger statement to distinguish these two evolutions. Here he declares that the Pharisees are the seed of the 'devil'.*

Now, just who was Jesus talking about when he used the term "devil" and "seed of the devil"? The root of the word is "slanderer," one who defames the name of God and elevates his own, or one who 'deifies' evil *(de-evil)* in place of the Light and Person of Christ. In the sense that the original Devil, and devils in general, invert the creation and pervert the name of the Godhead, both Nephilim and Watchers, as the angels who were either cast down or fell of their own volition, would be termed devils.

I believe our Lord was identifying the Pharisees as an evolution entirely apart from the children of God,

---

*The seed of the Wicked One, the conspiring enemies of Israel against whom David cries out to God repeatedly in his psalms. David refers to the Watchers as "the wicked." Other biblical designations of the Watchers include "evildoers," "evil men," "wicked men," "mighty men," "pagans," and "heathen." See "Concealed References to the Watchers (and Nephilim) in Scripture," p. 295.

but one which through intermarriage had eventually embodied in any or all races, retaining the characteristics of the proud and lustful, murderous and slanderous fallen angels from which they descended—or whose souls they in fact were.

Jesus may have even been identifying the Pharisees as the same Nephilim who originally fell or as the reincarnated Watchers—rather than as their descendants. If so, his condemnation might have been spoken to the very ones to whom Enoch had delivered the message of the Lord "Never shall you ascend into heaven! Never shall you obtain peace!" aeons ago in the mists of a forgotten antiquity.

I find no other legitimate means of interpreting the following passage from the Gospel of John than through this grand and forbidden thesis of the Book of Enoch.

> I speak that which I have seen with my Father: and ye do that which ye have seen with your father.
>
> They answered and said unto him, Abraham is our father. Jesus saith unto them, If ye were Abraham's children, ye would do the works of Abraham.
>
> But now ye seek to kill me, a man that hath told you the truth, which I have heard of God: this did not Abraham.
>
> Ye do the deeds of your father. Then said they to him, We be not born of [angelic] fornication; we have one Father, even God.

> Jesus said unto them, If God were your Father, ye would love me: for I proceeded forth and came from God; neither came I of myself, but he sent me.
>
> Why do ye not understand my speech? even because ye cannot hear my word.
>
> Ye are of your father the devil, and the lusts of your father ye will do. He was a murderer from the beginning, and abode not in the truth, because there is no truth in him. When he speaketh a lie, he speaketh of his own: for he is a liar, and the father of it....
>
> He that is of God heareth God's words: ye therefore hear them not, because ye are not of God.[139]

So much for the words of the Son of God who ofttimes has been worshiped as a god instead of followed as the great exemplar of the Christ of our hearts and the revolutionary of Truth who gave his life that the princes of this world might be exposed and the living Word triumph over the death and hell they have created to torment the children of the Elect One.

We cannot follow in his footsteps if we do not understand the prophecy of Daniel concerning the time of trouble and the resurrection of souls—the Great Awakening to true identity to take place in the last days:

> And at that time shall Michael stand up, the great prince which standeth for the children of thy people: and there shall be a time of trouble, such as never was since there was a nation even to that same time: and at that time thy people shall be delivered,

every one that shall be found written in the book.

And many of them that sleep in the dust of the earth shall awake, some to everlasting life, and some to shame and everlasting contempt.

And they that be wise shall shine as the brightness of the firmament; and they that turn many to righteousness as the stars for ever and ever.[140]

Now it is crystal clear: we know who Jesus Christ was talking about when he gave to his disciples a private interpretation of his parable of the tares of the field:

He that soweth the good seed is the Son of man;

The field is the world; the good seed are the sons of the kingdom; but the tares are the sons of the Wicked One;

The enemy that sowed them is the devil; the harvest is the end of the world; and the reapers are the angels.

As therefore the tares are gathered and burned in the fire; so shall it be in the end of this world.

The Son of man shall send forth his angels, and they shall gather out of his kingdom all things that offend, and them which do iniquity;

And shall cast them into a furnace of fire: there shall be wailing and gnashing of teeth.

Then shall the righteous shine forth as the sun in the kingdom of their Father. Who hath ears to hear, let him hear.[141]

We recall that Enoch foresaw the final judgment of the Watchers "in a generation which is to succeed at a distant period, on account of the elect."[142] If the "distant generation" he envisioned was in fact the twentieth century and beyond, heralded by many as a time of judgment, the legacy of the Book of Enoch may at last find its intended audience—one receptive to the true history of men and angels.

John the Baptist and Jesus Christ embodied to show us the distinction between the children of the Light and the power elite—a statement already made, loud and clear, by the prophets before them. And this, their most important message, has been lost because subsequent theologians covered over the basic elements of the hypothesis. In their attempt to destroy the works of Enoch and Origen, the Church Fathers (consciously or unconsciously, it does not matter) effectively destroyed the work of both Christ and his fiery forerunner.

The World Teacher and his supreme teaching no longer belonged to the people. The Beloved One, their spokesman and advocate before God, and the godless, was now silenced in church as well as in state. And this exposé, fundamental to all others, unmasking the gods and their creation, was lost to the children of Enoch.

Why has the Church refused to acknowledge what Jesus Christ taught outright: that the tares, the sons of the Wicked One, have been genetically sown among the good seed of the sons of God and walk among us as fallen angels incarnate—who maintain the meticulous outer appearance of the sons of God but who are wanting in the inner splendor?

No racism or religious separatism is permitted when dealing with the tares and the wheat. Souls who are the seed of God are embodied in every race and nation—descendants of every tribe and culture, adherents of every religion. Their oppressors, the seed of the father of lies, have followed them within and amongst all peoples as Christian and Jew, Moslem, Buddhist, or Hindu, atheist, agnostic, or pagan.

The Watchers would like us to think they are one of us, for in their anonymity lies their "equal protection" under the mercy of God's laws. And their children would like us to think that they are also the children of Enoch. But they are not! They are the archdeceivers who murdered, for one, Saint Thomas Becket at the altar of God in Canterbury Cathedral and, for another, Saint Thomas More!

Thus the Lord condemned these 'children' of the murderous Watchers: "Woe unto you! for ye build the sepulchres of the prophets, and your fathers killed them. Truly ye bear witness that ye allow the deeds of your fathers: for they indeed killed them, and ye build their sepulchres." Therefore the blood of all the prophets which was shed from the foundation of the world shall be required of this generation of the Watchers![143]

The Christed ones of all ages—from the unborn to innocent children to the responsible citizens of the world who dare to challenge the ignoble Watchers— have been slaughtered by the Satans,[144] whose progeny yet carry on the tradition of their bloodletting and blood-drinking rite in the civilized as well as primitive cultures of the world. Yes!

They are the murderers of the Messiah who even now is aborning in the hearts of Christians and Jews alike and all who love God in the pure and undefiled religion of the heart. They are the tormentors of children, the purveyors of every temptation, physical and moral, to steal the souls of the lightbearers from the breast of the Divine Mother.

And last but not least, to the present hour the Watchers allied with the Nephilim heap the guilt for their crimes against humanity upon specific races or karmic groups by appearing to be Italian or German, Jew or Japanese, black or white, Russian...or American, thereby escaping the divine and human justice that is long overdue. First their divide-and-conquer strategy setting brother against brother, then their holocaust: This has been their deadly game played against all children of God from then until now.

How long, O Lord, shall the Watchers triumph?[145] How long, O Lord, holy and true, dost thou not judge and avenge our blood on the Watchers that dwell on the earth?[146] How long, O people of God, wilt thou neglect the holy cause of the Faithful and True!

That the honest seeker for Truth may evaluate the evidence, I am republishing this long-suppressed

Book of Enoch. Because I believe it is the key to the life and mission of the prophets of Israel, and of John the Baptist and Jesus Christ two thousand years ago—and today.

Elizabeth Clare Prophet

NOTES

Note: All Bible passages are quoted from the King James Version unless otherwise indicated.

1. Isa. 14:12–15; Rev. 12:9.
2. Gen. 32:24–26; Hos. 12:4.
3. Gen. 19:1–11.
4. Judg. 13:3–21.
5. Franz Delitzsch, *A New Commentary on Genesis,* trans. Sophia Taylor, 2 vols. (Edinburgh: T. & T. Clark, 1888), 1:225.
6. Filastrius, *Liber de Haeresibus,* no. 108.
7. Delitzsch, p. 223.
8. Dr. Laurence's translation (1883 edition) is reprinted in this book, updated with new explanatory footnotes.
9. En. 10:15. I believe that the seventy generations have long passed and that this is the era of judgment. The offspring of the Watchers are unbound and have been loosed on the earth for the final testing of the souls of Light.
10. R. H. Charles, ed. and trans., *The Book of Enoch* (Oxford: Clarendon Press, 1893), pp. 148–50.
11. En. 15:8.
12. The Great Silent Watchers guard the purity of the Christ consciousness and Christ image out of which souls of Light are created. Some of the Watchers were sent by God to instruct the children of men, according to the Book of Jubilees 4:15. These Watchers subsequently fell when they began to cohabit with the "daughters of men." G. B. Caird *(Principalities and Powers)* cites the Apocalypse of Baruch, which says that it was "the physical nature of man which not only became a danger to his own soul, but resulted in the fall of the angels" (*A Dictionary of Angels,* s.v. "fallen angels").

   The I AM Race is defined as the seed of the Son of God who are "from above" (see pp. 78–79), having the divine spark from their source, the I AM Presence, the Tree of Life, the crystal cord, and the true Self, the anointed of the Lord. (See "Chart of Your Divine Self," pp. 359–62.)
13. Zohar 1:55a–55b.

14. See "Concealed References to the Watchers...," p. 297.

15. Matt. 5:5.

16. Matt. 26:24.

17. En. 38:2.

18. John 14:2.

19. John 4:14.

20. Luke 16:8; John 12:36; Eph. 5:8; I Thess. 5:5.

21. Matt. 22:30.

22. Luke 6:24.

23. En. 93:7.

24. Charles, pp. 312–17; R. Otto, "The Kingdom of God and the Son of Man," cited by H. H. Rowley, *The Relevance of Apocalyptic,* rev. ed. (New York: Harper & Brothers, 1946), p. 58, n. 1.

25. Rowley, pp. 57–58.

26. En. 70:17, 23. See p. 180, n. 74.

27. *The Jerusalem Bible,* ed. Alexander Jones (Garden City, N.Y.: Doubleday & Co., 1966).

28. Luke 1:52.

29. Charles Francis Potter, *The Lost Years of Jesus Revealed,* rev. ed. (Greenwich, Conn.: Fawcett, 1962), p. 109.

30. See Appendix I, "The Law and the Prophets Quoted by Jesus Christ," pp. 503–5.

31. Matt. 5:17.

32. Luke 4:14–21.

33. En. 14:2.

34. John 9:39.

35. John 5:22–23, 26–27.

36. En. 1:1, 2, 7, et passim.

37. Matt. 19:28.

38. Luke 22:29–30.

39. Charles Cutler Torrey, *The Apocryphal Literature: A Brief Introduction* (New Haven: Yale University Press, 1945), p. 18.

40. See II Chron. 24:19–22; 36:15–16; Gen. 4:8; Ezek. 3:18, 20; 33:6, 8.

41. Torrey, p. 18.

42. Matt. 3:7; 12:34; 23:33; Luke 3:7. See Appendix II, "Con-

frontations: the Watchers vs. John the Baptist and Jesus Christ,"
pp. 509–11.

43. Charles, p. 41.
44. Ibid., p. 1.
45. Potter, p. 93.
46. En. 14:23–24.
47. I Cor. 10:20.
48. En. 19:2.
49. II Cor. 12:2. See also the Book of the Secrets of Enoch in this volume, p. 413 ff.
50. "Revelation of Paul," trans. Alexander Walker, in *Fathers of the Third and Fourth Centuries,* ed. A. Cleveland Coxe, *The Ante-Nicene Fathers,* ed. Alexander Roberts and James Donaldson, 10 vols. to date (1867–1895; reprint ed., Grand Rapids, Mich.: Wm. B. Eerdmans, 1978–), 8(1871): 577.
51. For further similarities, see "Biblical Parallels to the Book of Enoch," pp. 263–93.
52. *New Catholic Encyclopedia,* s.v. "Bible, III," p. 394. To this day there are some who hold that Revelation was not written by the apostle John because its literary style is entirely different from John's Gospel. As if the Revelation of our Lord Jesus Christ "sent and signified by his angel" to the near ninety-year-old John on the isle of Patmos (whom they had already boiled in oil but could not destroy or deter from being the Lord's messenger until his work was throughly finished) ought to conform to any author's style—or that if the Lord himself inspired upon John his Gospel, he could not have chosen from any number of literary styles to dictate, in symbolism and cypher, a message which would be understood only by those for whom it was intended—those who had "ears to hear"—to whom the Lord would also give the key by his Holy Spirit (Rev. 10:7). This argument points up a recurring problem in the history of the Church: the idea that God and his Son and the saints in heaven must speak and act according to man's set standards. Severe doctrinal limitation is thereby placed upon all followers of God because of the demand for clerical conformism to an orthodox

tradition, which may appear to be in keeping with the interpretation of apostles and Gospel writers, but may in fact differ sharply with Christ's own words and works as perceived through his own eyes and those of the Holy Spirit.

53. I Pet. 3:18–20; II Pet. 2:4.

54. II Pet. 2:13–14.

55. Potter, p. 98.

56. Jude 4, 12–13.

57. Jude 14–15.

58. Eph. 3:16; Col. 1:27.

59. Rev. 22:20; Deut. 33:2; Jude 14.

60. From the Greek *ho eklelegmenos,* lit., "the elect one."

61. En. 45:3–4.

62. Potter, p. 97.

63. En. 54:5.

64. John 12:31. See *The Scofield Reference Bible* (New York: Oxford University Press, 1945), p. 1133, marginal notation d.

65. Epis. Barn. 4:3; 16:5–6.

66. Charles, p. 1.

67. Justin Martyr, "The Second Apology," *Writings of Saint Justin Martyr,* trans. Thomas B. Falls (New York: New York Christian Heritage, 1948), p. 124.

68. Ibid.

69. As in the 'troubling' of the waters by the angel who charged the pool of Bethesda with a healing energy (John 5:4)—so good and bad angels, whether embodied or not, retain the ability to affect the environment with positive or negative vibrations. Originally in their holy offices they were charged by God with the responsibility for bringing man the vibrations of joy, hope, peace, faith, freedom, etc. Their nature predisposes them to be able to transform a temple, a house, or a soul by the qualification of matter as well as Spirit with the consciousness of God. At the molecular level and within the neurons of the brain and nervous system, angels can cause 'movements' that alter both mind and matter.

70. Athenagoras, "Legatio," ed. and trans. William R. Schoedel,

Oxford Early Christian Texts: Legatio and De Resurrectione (Oxford: Clarendon Press, 1972), p. 61.

71. En. 7:12–14.

72. Emil Schneweis, *Angels and Demons according to Lactantius* (Washington, D.C.: Catholic University of America Press, 1944), p. 103.

73. Ibid., p. 127.

74. Tatian, "Address to the Greeks," Ante-Nicene Fathers, 2:70.

75. Ibid.

76. *New Catholic Encyclopedia,* s.v. "angels."

77. Irenaeus, "Adv. Haereses" [Against Heresies], Ante-Nicene Fathers, 1:340. See also 1:481, 516.

78. Tertullian, "Apology," *Apologetical Works,* Fathers of the Church, 69 vols. to date (Washington, D.C.: Catholic University of America Press, 1947–), 10(1950): 69.

79. I Cor. 6:3.

80. Tertullian, "The Apparel of Women," *Disciplinary, Moral, and Ascetical Works,* Fathers of the Church, 40:118–20.

81. Tertullian, "On the Veiling of Virgins," Ante-Nicene Fathers, 4:31–32. See also Charles, p. 46.

82. Clement, "The Instructor," Ante-Nicene Fathers, 2:274.

83. *The Clementine Homilies,* Ante-Nicene Fathers, 8:272–73.

84. *De Principiis* 1:3:3; 4:1:35; *Commentary on John* 6:25.

85. *A Catholic Dictionary of Theology,* s.v. "devil."

86. Rev. 20:14; 21:8.

87. Erich Fromm, "Necrophilia and Biophilia," in *War within Man,* Beyond Deterrence Series (Philadelphia: American Friends Service Committee, 1963), p. 9.

88. Matt. 23:27. I believe that this description "dead men's bones" refers to the fact that the Watchers' temples, devoid of the Holy Spirit, were infested with discarnates, the cast-off sheaths of the disembodied spirits.

89. Isa. 14:16–19.

90. Unless it is uncovered that etymologically the term "man" was applied in certain instances to other than earthlings—i.e., to extraterrestrials or the Nephilim gods—the application of

"man" to Lucifer gives strong indication that Isaiah believed that the "cast down one" was embodied as a mortal man.

91. Cyprian, "The Treatises of Cyprian," Ante-Nicene Fathers, 5:556; Aphrahat, "Select Demonstrations," in _Gregory the Great, Ephraim Syrus, Aphrahat,_ ed. James Barmby and John Gwynn, A Select Library of Nicene and Post-Nicene Fathers of the Christian Church, ed. Philip Schaff and Henry Wace, 2d ser., 14 vols. to date (1890–1899; reprint ed., Grand Rapids, Mich.: Wm. B. Eerdmans, 1979–), 13(1898): 353.

92. Some copies of the Greek Septuagint translated the Hebrew words "sons of God" (Gen. 6:2) as "angels of God." See Charles, p. 62.

93. Bernard Jacob Bamberger, _Fallen Angels_ (Philadelphia: Jewish Publication Society of America, 1962), pp. 78–79; Julius Africanus, "The Extant Fragments...of the Chronography of Julius Africanus," Ante-Nicene Fathers, 6:131.

94. Jude 6.

95. J. H. Kurtz, _History of the Old Covenant_ (Edinburgh: T. & T. Clark, 1859), 1:98. See also Job 1:6; 2:1; and the commentaries on 1:6 in the _Jerusalem Bible_ and the _Ryrie Study Bible._ Cp. Pss. 29:1; 82:1; 89:6. The "sons of God" in Deut. 32:8 _(Jerusalem Bible)_ are in most cases understood by scholars to be angels—specifically, the guardian angels assigned to the nations. One theory has it that the Massoretic scribes of the sixth to tenth centuries thought that this idea might lead to the worship of these guardian angels, and therefore they changed the original Hebrew words "sons of God" (which they knew to mean "angels") to "children of Israel"—which then found its way into the King James Version of the Bible. Pre-Massoretic manuscripts recently discovered prove that "sons of God" was the original term in the Hebrew Scripture.

It ought to be considered that the term "sons of God" might have originally referred to sons of God in heaven, Christed ones of whom Jesus was one. Some of these sons of God might have fallen, out of the misplaced ambition to create on earth by their Christic seed a superrace who could lead mere earthlings or the creation of the Nephilim on the paths of right-eousness and to ultimate reunion with God. Though well-intended in their desire to upgrade the evolutions of the planet, these sons of God might not have had the divine approba-tion. Therefore the Watchers, once fallen and judged as un-worthy of the ascent to God, having lost the sacred fire of their original anointing, would have determined in any case to dom-inate the scene of earth life with their superior intellect and overwhelming presence yet residual from their lost estate. If in fact the Watchers were the fallen sons of God and the Nephilim the fallen angels, we can understand both the difference of their modus operandi and reason for being and the dissimilarity of their natures which remains observable to the present.

The doctrine of the only begotten Son of God having been misconstrued to designate one son only, namely Jesus, the Anointed, would of course make this theory preposterous to today's Christian. However, when correctly understood, the Christ, "the only begotten Son of God," is revealed to the soul by the Holy Spirit to be the true Self of every son of God, "the Light which lighteth [ignites the divine spark in] *every man* that cometh into the world." Christ, the Light, the Word, is therefore an office and a mantle which the son of God by the Father's grace may 'put on' and 'become', fully integrating with and assimilat-ing the only begotten of God until he does embody or incarnate that Christ—i.e., that Christ-flame or Christ-consciousness which Jesus as the embodiment of the Son of God had the power to ignite, as John writes: "As many as received him, to them gave he power to become the sons* of God, even to them that believe on his name: which were born, not of blood, nor of the will of the flesh, nor of the will of man, but of God" (John 1:12–13).

I believe that John and Paul both received this teaching from Jesus. For John also says, "Beloved, now are we the sons* of God, and it doth not yet appear what we shall be: but we know that, when he shall appear, we shall be like him; for we shall see him as he is. And every man that hath this hope in him

---

*Gk. *tekna*, "children" or "offspring."

purifieth himself, even as he is pure" (I John 3:2–3).

Paul, who was taught directly by the ascended master Jesus Christ, mentions the oneness of Christ as well as the "inner man" in several key passages: "To be strengthened with might by his Spirit in the inner man; that Christ may dwell in your hearts" (Eph. 3:16–17). "Because ye are sons, God hath sent forth the Spirit of his Son into your hearts, crying, Abba, Father. Wherefore thou art no more a servant, but a son; and if a son, then an heir of God through Christ" (Gal. 4:6–7). "I live; yet not I, but Christ liveth in me" (Gal. 2:20). "God would make known what is the riches of the glory of this mystery among the Gentiles; which is Christ in you, the hope of glory" (Col. 1:27). "For as many as are led by the Spirit of God, they are the sons of God. For ye have not received the spirit of bondage again to fear; but ye have received the Spirit of adoption, whereby we cry, Abba, Father. The Spirit itself beareth witness with our spirit, that we are the children of God: and if children, then heirs; heirs of God, and joint-heirs with Christ; if so be that we suffer with him, that we may be also glorified together. . . . For the earnest expectation of the creature waiteth for the manifestation of the sons of God" (Rom. 8:14–17, 19). "That ye may be blameless and harmless, the sons* of God, without rebuke, in the midst of a crooked and perverse nation, among whom ye shine as lights in the world" (Phil. 2:15).

Although the Bible speaks distinctly of sons of God in heaven and angels in heaven, it seems that the distinction between these two types of spiritual beings holding two distinct types of heavenly offices has been lost to the understanding of the children of God on earth. It seems that the term "son of God" designates one of greater light and attainment, who had been crowned with more glory and honor than that bestowed upon the angels, but who must yet grow into the fullness of the stature of the one Jesus Christ chosen by the Father to be the incarnate Word, nourisher of our souls.

96. Bamberger, p. 79.

---

*Gk. *tekna*, "children" or "offspring."

97. Ibid.

98. Theodoret, *Quaestiones in Gen. Interrogatio XLVII.*

99. Saint Jerome, *Homily 45 on Psalm 132 (133),* trans. Marie Liguori Ewald, Fathers of the Church, 48(1964): 338–39.

100. Mani was well acquainted with the Book of Enoch and even refers to "Enoch, the apostle" in his *Book of Giants.* Mani's book, though it has survived in very fragmentary form, can be found in the *Bulletin of the School of Oriental and African Studies, University of London,* 11, pt. 1 (1943): 52–74.

101. Jean Chrysostom, "Homelies sur la Genèse," *Saint Jean Chrysostome Oeuvres Complètes,* trans. M. Jeannin and ed. L. Guerin (Paris, 1865), 5:136–37.

102. Bamberger, p. 80.

103. Filastrius, *Liber de Haeresibus,* no. 108.

104. Augustine, *The City of God,* ed. and trans. Marcus Dods, 2 vols. (New York: Hafner, 1948), 2:92–93.

105. Ibid., 2:95–96.

106. Bamberger, p. 80.

107. *A Catholic Dictionary of Theology,* s.v. "devil."

108. *New Catholic Encyclopedia,* s.v. "demon (theology of)."

109. Bamberger, pp. 204–5.

110. Synod of Laodicea, "Cannon XXXV," Nicene and Post-Nicene Fathers, 14:150. Josephus notes that one of the sacred rites of the Essenes was their swearing to preserve the names of the angels (*War of the Jews,* 2:8).

111. Synod of Laodicea, "Cannon XXXV," Nicene and Post-Nicene Fathers, 14:150.

112. Ibid.

113. Philip S. Alexander, "The Targumim and Early Exegesis of 'Sons of God' in Genesis 6," *Journal of Jewish Studies* 23 (1972): 60–61.

114. Nicholas de Lange, *Apocrypha: Jewish Literature of the Hellenistic Age* (New York: Viking Press, 1978), pp. 9–10.

115. Ibid., p. 10.

116. J. T. Milik, ed. and trans., *The Books of Enoch: Aramaic Fragments of Qumran Cave 4* (Oxford: Clarendon Press, 1976).

117. Ibid., p. 31.

118. Ibid.

119. Julian Morgenstern, "The Mythological Background of Psalm 82," *Hebrew Union College Annual* 14 (1939): 106.

120. Ibid., pp. 106–7.

121. *Jerusalem Bible.*

122. Morgenstern, p. 107.

123. Bk. Jub. 7:22; Milik, p. 178.

124. Morgenstern, pp. 84–85; 106, n. 135; Kurtz, p. 99.

125. Morgenstern, pp. 106–7, n. 135a.

126. Rev. 12:9.

127. II Pet. 2:4.

128. Dan. 12:1.

129. Montague Rhodes James, trans. "The Gospel of Bartholomew," in *The Apocryphal New Testament* (Oxford: Clarendon Press, 1924), p. 178.

130. James, trans. "The Book of John the Evangelist," in *The Apocryphal New Testament,* p. 189.

131. Delitzsch, 1:225.

132. Kurtz, pp. 100–101.

133. Morgenstern, p. 82.

134. Tertullian, "The Apparel of Women," p. 15.

135. Apoc. Ezra (4 Ezra) 14.

136. Paul D. Hanson, "Rebellion in Heaven, Azazel, and Euhemeristic Heroes in 1 Enoch 6–11," *Journal of Biblical Literature* 96, no. 2 (1977): 218.

137. John 3:3.

138. John 8:23.

139. John 8:38–44, 47.

140. Dan. 12:1–3.

141. Matt. 13:37–43.

142. En. 1:2.

143. Luke 11:47–51.

144. En. 40:7.

145. Ps. 94:3.

146. Rev. 6:10.

SELECT BIBLIOGRAPHY

Alexander, Philip S. "The Targumim and Early Exegesis of 'Sons of God' in Genesis 6." *Journal of Jewish Studies* 23 (1972): 60–71.

Bamberger, Bernard Jacob. *Fallen Angels*. Philadelphia: Jewish Publication Society of America, 1962.

Charles, R. H., ed. and trans. *The Book of Enoch*. Oxford: Clarendon Press, 1893.

DeLange, Nicholas. *Apocrypha: Jewish Literature of the Hellenistic Age*. New York: Viking Press, 1978.

James, Montague Rhodes, trans. *The Apocryphal New Testament*. Oxford: Clarendon Press, 1924.

Knibb, Michael A., ed. and trans. *The Ethiopic Book of Enoch*. Oxford: Clarendon Press, 1978.

Kurtz, J. H. *History of the Old Covenant*. Edinburgh: T. & T. Clark, 1859.

Laurence, Richard. *The Book of Enoch the Prophet*. London: Kegan Paul, Trench & Co., 1883.

Milik, J. T. *The Books of Enoch: Aramaic Fragments of Qumran Cave 4*. Oxford: Clarendon Press, 1976.

Moore, Thomas, "The Loves of the Angels." (poem)

Morgenstern, Julian. "The Mythological Background of Psalm 82." *Hebrew Union College Annual* 14:29–126.

Potter, Charles Francis. *The Lost Years of Jesus Revealed*. Greenwich, Conn.: Fawcett, 1962.

Roberts, Alexander and Donaldson, James, eds. *The Ante-Nicene Fathers*. 1885–96. Reprint, 10 vols. Grand Rapids, Mich.: Wm. B. Eerdmans, 1978–.

Schaff, Philip. *A Select Library of Nicene and Post-Nicene Fathers*. First series. 1886–90. Reprint, 14 vols. Grand Rapids, Mich.: Wm. B. Eerdmans, 1978–.

Schaff, Philip and Wace, Henry. *A Select Library of Nicene and Post-Nicene Fathers*. Second series. 1890–1899. Reprint, 14 vols. Grand Rapids, Mich.: Wm. B. Eerdmans, 1978–.

Schneweis, Emil. *Angels and Demons According to Lactantius*. Washington, D.C.: Catholic University of America Press, 1944.

Torrey, Charles Cutler. *The Apocryphal Literature: A Brief Introduction*. New Haven: Yale University Press, 1945.

*When men had begun to be plentiful
on the earth, and daughters had been born
to them.*

*The sons of God [the Watchers], looking
at the daughters of men, saw they were pleasing, so they married as many as they chose.*

*Yahweh said, "My spirit must not for ever
be disgraced in man, for he is but flesh; his life
shall last no more than a hundred and twenty
years."*

*The Nephilim were on the earth at that
time (and even afterward) when the sons of
God [the Watchers] resorted to the daughters
of man, and had children by them. These are
the heroes of days gone by, the famous men.*

Genesis 6:1–4
Jerusalm Bible

THE BOOK OF ENOCH

TRANSLATED BY
RICHARD LAURENCE, LL.D.

ANGELS IN PURSUIT OF SATAN

THE BOOK OF ENOCH

CHAPTER 1

1 The word of the blessing of Enoch, how he blessed the elect and the righteous, who were to exist in the time of trouble; rejecting all the wicked and ungodly. Enoch, a righteous man, who *was*[1] with God, answered and spoke, while his eyes were open, and *while* he saw a holy vision in the heavens. This the angels showed me.

2 From them I heard all things, and understood what I saw; that which will not take place in this generation, but in a generation which is to succeed at a distant period, on account of the elect.

3 Upon their account I spoke and conversed with him, who will go forth from his habitation, the Holy and Mighty One, the God of the world:

4 Who will hereafter tread upon Mount Sinai; appear with his hosts; and be manifested in the strength of his power from heaven.

1. N.B. The italicized words supply a gap in the text.

5 All shall be afraid, and the Watchers be terrified.

6 Great fear and trembling shall seize them, even to the ends of the earth. The lofty mountains shall be troubled, and the exalted hills depressed, melting like a honeycomb in the flame. The earth shall be immerged, and all things which are in it perish; while judgment shall come upon all, even upon all the righteous:

7 But to them shall he give peace: he shall preserve the elect, and towards them exercise clemency.

8 Then shall all belong to God; be happy and blessed; and the splendour of the Godhead shall illuminate them.

CHAPTER 2

Behold, he comes with ten thousands of his saints, to execute judgment upon them, and destroy the wicked, and reprove all the carnal for everything which the sinful and ungodly have done, and committed against him.[2]

CHAPTER 3

1 All who are in the heavens know what is transacted *there*.

2 *They know* that the heavenly luminaries change not their paths; that each rises and sets regularly, every one at its proper period, without transgressing the commands *which they have received*. They behold the earth, and understand what is there transacted, from the beginning to the end of it.

3 *They see* that every work of God is invariable in

---

2. Quoted by Jude, vss. 14, 15.

the period of its appearance. They behold summer and winter: *perceiving* that the whole earth is full of water; and that the cloud, the dew, and the rain refresh it.

CHAPTER 4

They consider and behold every tree, how it appears to wither, and every leaf to fall off, except of fourteen trees, which are not deciduous; which wait from the old, to the appearance of the new *leaf*, for two or three winters.

CHAPTER 5

Again they consider the days of summer, that the sun is upon it at its very beginning; while you seek for a covered and shady spot on account of the burning sun; while the earth is scorched up with fervid heat, and you become incapable of walking either upon the ground or upon the rocks in consequence of that heat.

CHAPTER 6

1 They consider how the trees, when they put forth their green leaves, become covered, and produce fruit; understanding everything, and knowing that He who lives for ever does all these things for you:

2 *That* the works at the beginning of every existing year, that all his works, are subservient to him, and invariable; yet as God has appointed, so are all things brought to pass.

3 They see, too, how the seas and the rivers together complete their respective operations:

4 *But* you endure not patiently, nor fulfil the commandments of the Lord; but you transgress and calumniate *his* greatness; and malignant are the words in your polluted mouths against his Majesty.

5 Ye withered in heart, no peace shall be to you!

6 Therefore your days shall you curse, and the years of your lives shall perish; perpetual execration shall be multiplied, and you shall not obtain mercy.

7 In those days shall you resign your peace with the eternal maledictions of all the righteous, and sinners shall perpetually execrate you;

8 *Shall execrate you* with the ungodly.

9 The elect shall possess light, joy, and peace; and they shall inherit the earth.

10 But you, ye unholy, shall be accursed.

11 Then shall wisdom be given to the elect, all of whom shall live, and not again transgress by impiety or pride; but shall humble themselves, possessing prudence, and shall not repeat transgression.

12 They shall not be condemned the whole period of their lives, nor die in torment and indignation; but the sum of their days shall be completed, and they shall grow old in peace; while the years of their happiness shall be multiplied with joy, and with peace, for ever, the whole duration of their existence.

CHAPTER 7

1 It happened after the sons of men had multiplied in those days, that daughters were born to

them, elegant and beautiful.

2 And when the angels,[3] the sons of heaven, beheld them, they became enamoured of them, saying to each other, Come, let us select for ourselves wives from the progeny of men, and let us beget children.

3 Then their leader Samyaza said to them; I fear that you may perhaps be indisposed to the performance of this enterprise;

4 And that I alone shall suffer for so grievous a crime.

5 But they answered him and said; We all swear;

6 And bind ourselves by mutual execrations, that we will not change our intention, but execute our projected undertaking.

7 Then they swore all together, and all bound themselves by mutual execrations. Their whole number was two hundred, who descended upon Ardis,[4] which is the top of mount Armon.

8 That mountain therefore was called Armon, because they had sworn upon it,[5] and bound themselves by mutual execrations.

9 These are the names of their chiefs: Samyaza, who was their leader, Urakabarameel, Akibeel, Tamiel, Ramuel, Danel, Azkeel, Saraknyal, Asael, Armers, Batraal,

---

3. An Aramaic text reads "Watchers" here (J. T. Milik, *Aramaic Fragments of Qumran Cave 4* [Oxford: Clarendon Press, 1976], p. 167).
4. **Upon Ardis.** Or, "in the days of Jared" (R. H. Charles, ed. and trans., *The Book of Enoch* [Oxford: Clarendon Press, 1893], p. 63).
5. Mt. Armon, or Mt. Hermon, seems to derive its name from the Hebrew word *hērem,* a curse (Charles, p. 63).

Anane, Zavebe, Samsaveel, Ertael, Turel, Yomyael, Arazyal. These were the prefects of the two hundred angels, and the remainder were all with them.[6]

10 Then they took wives, each choosing for himself; whom they began to approach, and with whom they cohabited; teaching them sorcery, incantations, and the dividing of roots and trees.

11 And the women conceiving brought forth giants,[7]

12 Whose stature was each three hundred cubits. These devoured all *which* the labour of men *produced;* until it became impossible to feed them;

13 When they turned themselves against men, in order to devour them;

14 And began to injure birds, beasts, reptiles, and fishes, to eat their flesh one after another,[8] and to drink their blood.

15 Then the earth reproved the unrighteous.

---

6. The Aramaic texts preserve an earlier list of names of these Watchers: Šemîhazah; ʾArʿtqoph; Ramtʾel; Kôkabʾel; Raʿmʾel; Danîʾel; Zêqîʾel; Baraqʾel; ʿAsaʾel; Hermonî; Matarʾel; ʿAnanʾel; Śʿtawʾel; Šamšîʾel; Sahrîʾel; Tummîʾel; Tûrîʾel; Yomîʾel; Yʿhaddîʾel (Milik, p. 151).

7. The Greek texts vary considerably from the Ethiopic text here. One Greek manuscript adds to this section, "And they [the women] bore to them [the Watchers] three races—first, the great giants. The giants brought forth [some say "slew"] the Naphelim, and the Naphelim brought forth [or "slew"] the Elioud. And they existed, increasing in power according to their greatness." See the account in the Book of Jubilees in this volume.

8. **Their flesh one after another.** Or, "one another's flesh." R. H. Charles notes that this phrase may refer to the destruction of one class of giants by another (Charles, p. 65).

CHAPTER 8

1 Moreover Azazyel taught men to make swords, knives, shields, breastplates, the fabrication of mirrors, and the workmanship of bracelets and ornaments, the use of paint, the beautifying of the eyebrows, *the use of* stones of every valuable and select kind, and of all sorts of dyes, so that the world became altered.

2 Impiety increased; fornication multiplied; and they transgressed and corrupted all their ways.

3 Amazarak taught all the sorcerers, and dividers of roots:

4 Armers *taught* the solution of sorcery;

5 Barkayal *taught* the observers of the stars;[9]

6 Akibeel *taught* signs;

7 Tamiel taught astronomy;

8 And Asaradel taught the motion of the moon.

9 And men, being destroyed, cried out; and their voice reached to heaven.

CHAPTER 9

1 Then Michael and Gabriel, Raphael, Suryal, and Uriel, looked down from heaven, and saw the quantity of blood which was shed on earth, and all the iniquity which was done upon it, and said one to another, *It is* the voice of their cries;

2 The earth deprived *of her children* has cried even to the gate of heaven.

3 And now to you, O ye holy ones of heaven, the

___

9. Observers of the stars. Astrologers (Charles, p. 67).

souls of men complain, saying, Obtain Justice for us with[10] the Most High. Then they said to their Lord, the King, *Thou art* Lord of lords, God of gods, King of kings. The throne of thy glory is for ever and ever, and for ever and ever is thy name sanctified and glorified. Thou art blessed and glorified.

4 Thou hast made all things; thou possessest power over all things; and all things are open and manifest before thee. Thou beholdest all things, and nothing can be concealed from thee.

5 Thou hast seen what Azazyel has done, how he has taught every species of iniquity upon earth, and has disclosed to the world all the secret things which are done in the heavens.

6 Samyaza also has taught sorcery, to whom thou hast given authority over those who are associated with him. They have gone together to the daughters of men; have lain with them; have become polluted;

7 And have discovered crimes[11] to them.

8 The women likewise have brought forth giants.

9 Thus has the whole earth been filled with blood and with iniquity.

10 And now behold the souls of those who are dead, cry out.

11 And complain even to the gate of heaven.

---

10. **Obtain Justice for us with.** Literally, "Bring judgment to us from." (Richard Laurence, ed. and trans., *The Book of Enoch the Prophet* [London: Kegan Paul, Trench & Co., 1883], p. 9).
11. **Discovered crimes.** Or, "revealed these sins" (Charles, p. 70).

12 Their groaning ascends; nor can they escape from the unrighteousness which is committed on earth. Thou knowest all things, before they exist.

13 Thou knowest these things, and what has been done by them; yet thou dost not speak to us.

14 What on account of these things ought we to do to them?

CHAPTER 10

1 Then the Most High, the Great and Holy One spoke,

2 And sent Arsayalalyur[12] to the son of Lamech,

3 Saying, Say to him in my name, Conceal thyself.

4 Then explain to him the consummation which is about to take place; for all the earth shall perish; the waters of a deluge shall come over the whole earth, and all things which are in it shall be destroyed.

5 And now teach him how he may escape, and how his seed may remain in all the earth.

6 Again the Lord said to Raphael, Bind Azazyel hand and foot; cast him into darkness; and opening the desert which is in Dudael, cast him in there.

7 Throw upon him hurled and pointed stones, covering him with darkness;

8 There shall he remain for ever; cover his face, that he may not see the light.

9 And in the great day of judgment let him be cast into the fire.

---

12. Arsayalalyur. Here one Greek text reads "Uriel."

10 Restore the earth, which the angels have corrupted; and announce life to it, that I may revive it.

11 All the sons of men shall not perish in consequence of every secret, by which the Watchers have destroyed, and *which* they have taught, their offspring.

12 All the earth has been corrupted by the effects of the teaching of Azazyel. To him therefore ascribe the whole crime.

13 To Gabriel also the Lord said, Go to the biters,[13] to the reprobates, to the children of fornication; and destroy the children of fornication, the offspring of the Watchers, from among men; bring them forth, and excite them one against another. Let them perish by *mutual* slaughter; for length of days shall not be theirs.

14 They shall all entreat thee, but their fathers shall not obtain *their wishes* respecting them; for they shall hope for eternal life, and that they may live, each of them, five hundred years.

15 To Michael likewise the Lord said, Go and announce *his crime* to Samyaza, and to the others who are with him, who have been associated with women, that they might be polluted with all their impurity. And when all their sons shall be slain, when they shall see the perdition of their beloved, bind them for seventy generations underneath the earth, even to the day of judgment, and of consummation, until the judgment,

---

13. Biters. More accurately, "bastards" (Charles, p. 73; Michael A. Knibb, ed. and trans., *The Ethiopic Book of Enoch* [Oxford: Clarendon Press, 1978], p. 88).

the effect of which will last for ever, be completed.

16 Then shall they be taken away into the lowest depths of the fire in torments; and in confinement shall they be shut up for ever.

17 Immediately after this shall he,[14] together with them, burn and perish; they shall be bound until the consummation of many generations.

18 Destroy all the souls addicted to dalliance,[15] and the offspring of the Watchers, for they have tyrannized over mankind.

19 Let every oppressor perish from the face of the earth;

20 Let every evil work be destroyed;

21 The plant of righteousness and of rectitude appear, and its produce become a blessing.

22 Righteousness and rectitude shall be for ever planted with delight.

23 And then shall all the saints give thanks, and live until they have begotten a thousand *children,* while the whole period of their youth, and their sabbaths shall be completed in peace. In those days all the earth shall be cultivated in righteousness; it shall be wholly planted with trees, and filled with benediction; every tree of delight shall be planted in it.

24 In it shall vines be planted; and the vine which shall be planted in it shall yield fruit to satiety; every seed, which shall be sown in it, shall produce for one

14. He. I.e., Samyaza.
15. **Dalliance.** Or, "lust" (Knibb, p. 90; cp. Charles, p. 76).

measure a thousand; and one measure of olives shall produce ten presses of oil.

25 Purify the earth from all oppression, from all injustice, from all crime, from all impiety, and from all the pollution which is committed upon it. Exterminate them from the earth.

26 Then shall all the children of men be righteous, and all nations shall pay me divine honours, and bless me; and all shall adore me.

27 The earth shall be cleansed from all corruption, from every crime, from all punishment, and from all suffering; neither will I again send a deluge upon it from generation to generation for ever.

28 In those days I will open the treasures of blessing which are in heaven, that I may cause them to descend upon earth, and upon all the works and labour of man.

29 Peace and equity shall associate with the sons of men all the days of the world, in every generation of it.

(NO CHAPTER 11)

CHAPTER 12

1 Before all these things Enoch was concealed; nor did any one of the sons of men know where he was concealed, where he had been, and what had happened.

2 He was wholly engaged with the holy ones, and with the Watchers in his days.

3 I, Enoch, was blessing the great Lord and King of peace.

4 And behold the Watchers called me Enoch the scribe.

5 Then *the Lord* said to me: Enoch, scribe of righteousness, go tell the Watchers of heaven, who have deserted the lofty sky, and their holy everlasting station, *who* have been polluted with women.

6 And have done as the sons of men do, by taking to themselves wives, and *who* have been greatly corrupted on the earth;

7 That on the earth they shall never obtain peace and remission of sin. For they shall not rejoice in their offspring; they shall behold the slaughter of their beloved; shall lament for the destruction of their sons; and shall petition for ever; but shall not obtain mercy and peace.

CHAPTER 13

1 Then Enoch, passing on, said to Azazyel: Thou shalt not obtain peace. A great sentence is gone forth against thee. He shall bind thee;

2 Neither shall relief, mercy, and supplication be thine, on account of the oppression which thou hast taught;

3 And on account of every act of blasphemy, tyranny, and sin, which thou hast discovered to the children of men.

4 Then departing *from him* I spoke to them all together;

5 And they all became terrified, and trembled;

6 Beseeching me to write for them a memorial of supplication, that they might obtain forgiveness; and that I might make the memorial of their prayer ascend up before the God of heaven; because they could not themselves thenceforwards address him, nor raise up their eyes to heaven on account of the disgraceful offence for which they were judged.

7 Then I wrote a memorial of their prayer and supplication, for their spirits, for everything which they had done, and for the subject of their entreaty, that they might obtain remission and rest.

8 Proceeding on, I continued over the waters of Danbadan,[16] which is on the right to the west of Armon, reading the memorial of their prayer, until I fell asleep.

9 And behold a dream came to me, and visions appeared above me. I fell down and saw a vision of punishment, that I might relate it to the sons of heaven, and reprove them. When I awoke I went to them. All being collected together stood weeping in Oubelseyael, which is situated between Libanos and Seneser,[17] with their faces veiled.

10 I related in their presence all the visions which I had seen, and my dream;

11 And began to utter these words of righteouness, reproving the Watchers of heaven.

---

16. **Danbadan.** Dan in Dan (Knibb, p. 94).
17. **Libanos and Seneser.** Lebanon and Senir (near Damascus).

CHAPTER 14

1 This is the book of the words of righteousness, and of the reproof of the Watchers, who belong to the world,[18] according to that which He, who is holy and great, commanded in the vision. I perceived in my dream, that I was now speaking with a tongue of flesh, and with my breath, which the Mighty One has put into the mouth of men, that they might converse with it.

2 And understand with the heart. As he has created and given to men *the power of* comprehending the word of understanding, so has he created and given to me *the power of* reproving the Watchers, the off-spring of heaven. I have written your petition; and in my vision it has been shown me, that what you request will not be granted you as long as the world endures.

3 Judgment has been passed upon you: *your request* will not be granted you.

4 From this time forward, never shall you ascend into heaven; He has said, that on the earth He will bind you, as long as the world endures.

5 But before these things you shall behold the destruction of your beloved sons; you shall not possess them, but they shall fall before you by the sword.

6 Neither shall you entreat for them, nor for yourselves;

7 But you shall weep and supplicate in silence.

---

18. **Who belong to the world.** Or, "who (are) from eternity" (Knibb, p. 95).

The words of the book which I wrote.[19]

8 A vision thus appeared to me.

9 Behold, in *that* vision clouds and a mist invited me; agitated stars and flashes of lightning impelled and pressed me forwards, while winds in the vision assisted my flight, accelerating my progress.

10 They elevated me aloft to heaven. I proceeded, until I arrived at a wall built with stones of crystal. A vibrating flame[20] surrounded it, which began to strike me with terror.

11 Into this vibrating flame I entered;

12 And drew nigh to a spacious habitation built also with stones of crystal. Its walls too, as well as pavement, were *formed* with stones of crystal, and crystal likewise was the ground. Its roof had the appearance of agitated stars and flashes of lightning; and among them were cherubim of fire in a stormy sky.[21] A flame burned around its walls; and its portal blazed with fire. When I entered into this dwelling, it was hot as fire and cold as ice. No *trace* of delight or of life was there. Terror overwhelmed me, and a fearful shaking seized me.

13 Violently agitated and trembling, I fell upon my face. In the vision I looked,

---

19. **But you shall weep...I wrote.** Or, "Likewise despite your tears and prayers you will receive nothing whatever contained in the writing which I have written" (Charles, p. 80).

20. **Vibrating flame.** Literally, "a tongue of fire" (Laurence, p. 18).

21. **In a stormy sky.** Literally, "and their heaven was water" (Charles, p. 81).

14 And behold there was another habitation more spacious than *the former*, every entrance to which was open before me, erected in *the midst of* a vibrating flame.

15 So greatly did it excel in all points, in glory, in magnificence, and in magnitude, that it is impossible to describe to you either the splendour or the extent of it.

16 Its floor was on fire; above were lightnings and agitated stars, while its roof exhibited a blazing fire.

17 Attentively I surveyed it, and saw that it contained an exalted throne;

18 The appearance of which was like that of frost; while its circumference resembled the orb of the brilliant sun; and *there was* the voice of the cherubim.

19 From underneath this mighty throne rivers of flaming fire issued.

20 To look upon it was impossible.

21 One great in glory sat upon it:

22 Whose robe was brighter than the sun, and whiter than snow.

23 No angel was capable of penetrating to view the face of Him, the Glorious and the Effulgent; nor could any mortal behold Him. A fire was flaming around Him.

24 A fire also of great extent continued to rise up before Him; so that not one of those who surrounded Him was capable of approaching Him, among the myriads of myriads[22] who were before Him. To Him holy consultation was needless. Yet did not the sanc-

---

22. **Myriads of myriads.** Ten thousand times ten thousands (Knibb, p. 99).

tified, who were near Him, depart far from Him either by night or by day; nor were they removed from Him. I also was so far advanced, with a veil on my face, and trembling. Then the Lord with his *own* mouth called me, saying, Approach hither, Enoch, at my holy word.

25 And He raised me up, making me draw near even to the entrance. My eye was directed to the ground.

CHAPTER 15

1 Then addressing me, He spoke and said, Hear, neither be afraid, O righteous Enoch, thou scribe of righteousness: approach hither, and hear my voice. Go, say to the Watchers of heaven, who have sent thee to pray for them, You ought to pray for men, and not men for you.

2 Wherefore have you forsaken the lofty and holy heaven, which endures for ever, and have lain with women; have defiled yourselves with the daughters of men; have taken to yourselves wives; have acted like the sons of the earth, and have begotten an impious offspring?[23]

3 You being spiritual, holy, and possessing a life which is eternal, have polluted yourselves with women; have begotten in carnal blood; have lusted in the blood of men; and have done as those *who are* flesh and blood do.

4 These however die and perish.

5 Therefore have I given to them wives, that they might cohabit with them; that sons might be born of

---

23. An impious offspring. Literally, "giants" (Charles, p. 82; Knibb, p. 101).

them; and that this might be transacted upon earth.

6 But you from the beginning were made spiritual, possessing a life which is eternal, and not subject to death for ever.

7 Therefore I made not wives for you, because, being spiritual, your dwelling is in heaven.

8 Now the giants, who have been born of spirit and of flesh, shall be called upon earth evil spirits, and on earth shall be their habitation. Evil spirits shall proceed from their flesh, because they were created from above; from the holy Watchers was their beginning and primary foundation. Evil spirits shall they be upon earth, and the spirits of the wicked shall they be called. The habitation of the spirits of heaven shall be in heaven; but upon earth shall be the habitation of terrestrial spirits, who are born on earth.[24]

9 The spirits of the giants *shall be like clouds,*[25] which shall oppress, corrupt, fall, contend, and bruise upon earth.

10 They shall cause lamentation. No food shall they eat; and they shall be thirsty; they shall be concealed, and shall not[26] rise up against the sons of men,

24. Note the many implications of vss. 3–8 regarding the incarnation of the Watchers and the evil spirits in flesh bodies.

25. The Greek word for "clouds" here, *nephelas,* may disguise a more ancient reading, Naphēleim (Nephilim). Laurence's verb "shall be like" is only conjectural.

26. **Shall not.** Nearly all manuscripts contain this negative, but Charles, Knibb, and others believe the "not" should be deleted so the phrase reads "shall rise up."

and against women; for they come forth during the days of slaughter and destruction.

CHAPTER 16

1 And as to the death of the giants, wheresoever their spirits depart from their bodies, let their flesh, that which is perishable, be without judgment.[27] Thus shall they perish, until the day of the great consummation of the great world. A destruction shall take place of the Watchers and the impious.

2 And now to the Watchers, who have sent thee to pray for them, who in the beginning were in heaven,

3 *Say*, In heaven have you been; secret things, however, have not been manifested to you; yet have you known a reprobated mystery.

4 And this you have related to women in the hardness of your heart, and by that mystery have women and mankind multiplied evils upon the earth.

5 Say to them, Never therefore shall you obtain peace.

CHAPTER 17

1 They raised me up into a certain place, where there was[28] the appearance of a burning fire; and when they pleased they assumed the likeness of men.

2 They carried me to a lofty spot, to a mountain,

---

27. Let their flesh...be without judgment. Or, "their flesh shall be destroyed before the judgment" (Knibb, p. 102).

28. Where there was. Or, "where they [the angels] were like" (Knibb, p. 103).

the top of which reached to heaven.

3 And I beheld the receptacles of light and of thunder at the extremities of the place, where it was deepest. There was a bow of fire, and arrows in their quiver, a sword of fire, and every species of lightning.

4 Then they elevated me to a babbling stream,[29] and to a fire in the west, which received all the setting of the sun. I came to a river of fire, which flowed like water, and emptied itself into the great sea westwards.

5 I saw every large river, until I arrived at the great darkness. I went to where all of flesh migrate; and I beheld the mountains of the gloom which constitutes winter, and the place from which issues the water in every abyss.

6 I saw also the mouths of all the rivers in the world, and the mouths of the deep.

CHAPTER 18

1 I then surveyed the receptacles of all the winds, perceiving that they contributed to adorn the whole creation, and *to preserve* the foundation of the earth.

2 I surveyed the stone *which supports* the corners of the earth.

3 I also beheld the four winds, which bear up the earth, and the firmament of heaven.

4 And I beheld the winds occupying the exalted sky.

5 Arising in the midst of heaven and of earth, and

---

29. To a babbling stream. Literally, "to water of life, which spoke" (Laurence, p. 23).

constituting the pillars of heaven.

6 I saw the winds which turn the sky, which cause the orb of the sun and of all the stars to set; and over the earth I saw the winds which support the clouds.

7 I saw the path of the angels.

8 I perceived at the extremity of the earth the firmament of heaven above it. Then I passed on towards the south;

9 Where burnt, both by day and night, six mountains formed of glorious stones; three towards the east, and three towards the south.

10 Those which were towards the east were of a variegated stone; one of which was of margarite, and another of antimony. Those towards the south were of a red stone. The middle one reached to heaven like the throne of God; *a throne composed* of alabaster, the top of which was of sapphire. I saw, too, a blazing fire hanging over all the mountains.

11 And there I saw a place on the other side of an extended territory, where waters were collected.

12 I likewise beheld terrestrial fountains, deep in the fiery columns of heaven.

13 And in the columns of heaven I beheld fires, which descended without number, but neither on high, nor into the deep. Over these fountains also I perceived a place which had neither the firmament of heaven above it, nor the solid ground underneath it; neither was there water above it, nor anything on wing; but the spot was desolate.

14 And there I beheld seven stars, like great blazing mountains, and like spirits entreating me.

15 Then the angel said, This place, until the consummation of heaven and earth, will be the prison of the stars, and the host of heaven.

16 The stars which roll over fire are those which transgressed the commandment of God before their time arrived; for they came not in their proper season. Therefore was He offended with them, and bound them, until the period of the consummation of their crimes in the secret year.

CHAPTER 19

1 Then Uriel said, Here the angels, who cohabited with women, appointed their leaders,

2 And being numerous in appearance[30] made men profane, and caused them to err; so that they sacrificed to devils as to gods. For in the great day *there shall be* a judgment, with which they shall be judged, until they are consumed; and their wives also shall be *judged,* who led astray the angels of heaven that they might salute them.

3 And I, Enoch, I alone saw the likeness of the end of all things. Nor did any human being see it, as I saw it.

CHAPTER 20

1 These are the names of the angels who watch.

2 Uriel, one of the holy angels, who *presides*

---

30. **Being numerous in appearance.** Or, "assuming many forms" (Knibb, p. 106).

over clamour and terror.

3 Raphael, one of the holy angels, who *presides* over the spirits of men.

4 Raguel, one of the holy angels, who inflicts punishment on the world and the luminaries.

5 Michael, one of the holy angels, who, *presiding* over human virtue, commands the nations.

6 Sarakiel, one of the holy angels, who *presides* over the spirits of the children of men that transgress.

7 Gabriel, one of the holy angels, who *presides* over Ikisat,[31] over paradise, and over the cherubim.

CHAPTER 21

1 Then I made a circuit to a place in which nothing was completed.

2 And there I beheld neither the tremendous workmanship of an exalted heaven, nor of an established earth, but a desolate spot, prepared, and terrific.

3 There, too, I beheld seven stars of heaven bound in it together, like great mountains, and like a blazing fire. I exclaimed, For what species of crime have they been bound, and why have they been removed to this place? Then Uriel, one of the holy angels who was with me, and who conducted me, answered: Enoch, wherefore dost thou ask; wherefore reason with thyself, and anxiously inquire? These are those of the stars which have transgressed the commandment of the most high God; and are here bound, until the infinite number of

---

31. Ikisat. The serpents (Charles, p. 92; Knibb, p. 107).

the days of their crimes be completed.

4 From thence I afterwards passed on to another terrific place;

5 Where I beheld the operation of a great fire blazing and glittering, in the midst of which there was a division. Columns of fire struggled together to the end of the abyss, and deep was their descent. But neither its measurement nor magnitude was I able to discover; neither could I perceive its origin. Then I exclaimed, How terrible is this place, and how difficult to explore!

6 Uriel, one of the holy angels who was with me, answered and said: Enoch, why art thou alarmed and amazed at this terrific place, at the sight of this *place of* suffering? This, he said, is the prison of the angels; and here they are kept for ever.

CHAPTER 22

1 From thence I proceeded to another spot, where I saw on the west a great and lofty mountain, a strong rock, and four delightful places.

2 Internally it was deep, capacious, and very smooth; as smooth as if it had been rolled over: it was both deep and dark to behold.

3 Then Raphael, one of the holy angels who were with me, answered and said, These are the delightful places where the spirits, the souls of the dead, will be collected; for them were they formed; and here will be collected all the souls of the sons of men.

4 These places, in which they dwell, shall they occupy until the day of judgment, and until their appointed period.

5 Their appointed period will be long, even until the great judgment. And I saw the spirits of the sons of men who were dead; and their voices reached to heaven, while they were accusing.

6 Then I inquired of Raphael, an angel who was with me, and said, Whose spirit is that, the voice of which reaches *to heaven,* and accuses?

7 He answered, saying, This is the spirit of Abel, who was slain by Cain his brother; and who will accuse that brother, until his seed be destroyed from the face of the earth;

8 Until his seed perish from the seed of the human race.

9 At that time therefore I inquired respecting him, and respecting the general judgment, saying, Why is one separated from another? He answered, Three *separations* have been made between the spirits of the dead, and thus have the spirits of the righteous been separated.

10 Namely, *by* a chasm, *by* water, and *by* light above it.

11 And in the same way likewise are sinners separated when they die, and are buried in the earth; judgment not overtaking them in their lifetime.

12 Here their souls are separated. Moreover, abundant is their suffering until the time of the great

judgment, the castigation, and the torment of those who eternally execrate, whose souls are punished and bound there for ever.

13 And thus has it been from the beginning of the world. Thus has there existed a separation between the souls of those who utter complaints, and of those who watch for their destruction, to slaughter them in the day of sinners.

14 A receptacle of this sort has been formed for the souls of unrighteous men, and of sinners; of those who have completed crime, and associated with the impious, whom they resemble. Their souls shall not be annihilated in the day of judgment, neither shall they arise from this place. Then I blessed God,

15 And said, Blessed be my Lord, the Lord of glory and of righteousness, who reigns over all for ever and for ever.

CHAPTER 23

1 From thence I went to another place, towards the west, unto the extremities of the earth.

2 Where I beheld a fire blazing and running along without cessation, which intermitted its course neither by day nor by night; but continued always the same.

3 I inquired, saying, What is this, which never ceases?

4 Then Raguel, one of the holy angels who were with me, answered,

5 And said, This blazing fire, which thou beholdest

running towards the west, is *that of* all the luminaries of heaven.

CHAPTER 24

1 I went from thence to another place, and saw a mountain of fire flashing both by day and night. I proceeded towards it; and perceived seven splendid mountains, which were all different from each other.

2 Their stones were brilliant and beautiful; all were brilliant and splendid to behold; and beautiful was their surface. Three *mountains* were towards the east, and strengthened by being placed one upon another; and three were towards the south, strengthened in a similar manner. There were likewise deep valleys, which did not approach each other. And the seventh mountain was in the midst of them. In length they all resembled the seat of a throne, and odoriferous trees surrounded them.

3 Among these there was a tree of an unceasing smell; nor of those which were in Eden was there one of all the fragrant trees which smelt like this. Its leaf, its flower, and its bark never withered, and its fruit was beautiful.

4 Its fruit resembled the cluster of the palm. I exclaimed, Behold! this tree is goodly in aspect, pleasing in its leaf, and the sight of its fruit is delightful to the eye. Then Michael, one of the holy and glorious angels who were with me, and *one* who presided over them, answered,

5 And said: Enoch, why dost thou inquire respecting the odour of this tree?

6 *Why* art thou inquisitive to know it?

7 Then I, Enoch, replied to him, and said, Concerning everything I am desirous of instruction, but particularly concerning this tree.

8 He answered me, saying, That mountain which thou beholdest, the extent of whose head resembles the seat of the Lord, will be the seat on which shall sit the holy and great Lord of glory, the everlasting King, when he shall come and descend to visit the earth with goodness.

9 And that tree of an agreeable smell, not one of carnal *odour*, there shall be no power to touch, until the period of the great judgment. When all shall be punished and consumed for ever, this shall be bestowed on the righteous and humble. The fruit of this *tree* shall be given to the elect. For towards the north life shall be planted in the holy place, towards the habitation of the everlasting King.

10 Then shall they greatly rejoice and exult in the Holy One. The sweet odour shall enter into their bones; and they shall live a long life on the earth, as thy forefathers have lived; neither in their days shall sorrow, distress, trouble, and punishment afflict them.

11 And I blessed the Lord of glory, the everlasting King, because He has prepared *this tree* for the saints, formed it, and declared that He would give it to them.

CHAPTER 25

1 From thence I proceeded to the middle of the earth, and beheld a happy and fertile spot, which contained branches continually sprouting from the trees which were planted in it. There I saw a holy mountain, and underneath it water on the eastern side, which flowed towards the south. I saw also on the east another mountain as high as that; and between them there were deep, but not wide valleys.

2 Water ran towards the mountain to the west of this; and underneath there was likewise another mountain.

3 There was a valley, but not a wide one, below it; and in the midst of them were other deep and dry valleys towards the extremity of the three. All these valleys, which were deep, but not wide, consisted of a strong rock, with a tree which was planted in them. And I wondered at the rock and at the valleys, being extremely surprised.

CHAPTER 26

1 Then I said, What means this blessed land, all these lofty trees, and the accursed valley between them?

2 Then Uriel, one of the holy angels who were with me, replied, This valley is the accursed of the accursed for ever. Here shall be collected all who utter with their mouths unbecoming language against God,

and speak harsh things of His glory. Here shall they be collected. Here shall be their territory.

3 In the latter days an example of judgment shall be made of them in righteousness before the saints: while those who have received mercy shall for ever, all their days, bless God, the everlasting King.

4 And at the period of judgment shall they bless Him for his mercy, as He has distributed it to them. Then I blessed God, addressing myself to Him, and making mention, as was meet, of His greatness.

CHAPTER 27

1 From thence I proceeded towards the east, to the middle of the mountain in the desert, the level surface only of which I perceived.

2 It was full of trees of the seed alluded to; and water leaped down upon it.

3 There appeared a cataract composed as of many cataracts both towards the west and towards the east. Upon one side were trees; upon the other water and dew.

CHAPTER 28

1 Then I went to another place from the desert, towards the east of that mountain *which* I had approached.

2 There I beheld choice trees,[32] particularly *those which produce* the sweet-smelling drugs, frankincense

---

32. Choice trees. Literally, "trees of judgment" (Laurence, p. 35; Knibb, p. 117).

and myrrh; and trees unlike to each other.

3 And over it, above them, was the elevation of the eastern mountain at no great distance.

CHAPTER 29

1 I likewise saw another place with valleys of water which never wasted,

2 *Where* I perceived a goodly tree, which in smell resembled Zasakinon.[33]

3 And towards the sides of these valleys I perceived cinnamon of a sweet odour. Over them I advanced towards the east.

CHAPTER 30

1 Then I beheld another mountain containing trees, from which water flowed like Neketro.[34] Its name was Sarira, and Kalboneba.[35] And upon this mountain I beheld another mountain, upon which were trees of Alva.[36]

2 These trees were full, like almond trees, and strong; and when they produced fruit, it was superior to all perfume.

CHAPTER 31

1 After these things, surveying the entrances of the north, above the mountains, I perceived seven mountains replete with pure nard, odoriferous trees,

33. Zasakinon. The mastic tree (Knibb, p. 118).
34. Neketro. A nectar (Knibb, p. 119).
35. Sarira, and Kalboneba. Styrax and galbanum (Knibb, p. 119).
36. Alva. Aloe (Knibb, p. 119).

cinnamon and papyrus.

2 From thence I passed on above the summits of those mountains to some distance eastwards, and went over the Erythraean sea.[37] And when I was advanced far beyond it, I passed along above the angel Zateel, and arrived at the garden of righteousness. In this garden I beheld, among other trees, some which were numerous and large, and which flourished there.

3 Their fragrance was agreeable and powerful, and their appearance both varied and elegant. The tree of knowledge also was there, of which if any one eats, he becomes endowed with great wisdom.

4 It was like a species of the tamarind tree, bearing fruit which resembled grapes extremely fine; and its fragrance extended to a considerable distance. I exclaimed, How beautiful is this tree, and how delightful is its appearance!

5 Then holy Raphael, an angel who was with me, answered and said, This is the tree of knowledge, of which thy ancient father and thy aged mother ate, who were before thee; and who, obtaining knowledge, their eyes being opened, and knowing themselves to be naked, were expelled from the garden.

CHAPTER 32

1 From thence I went on towards the extremities of the earth; where I saw large beasts different from each other, and birds various in their countenances and

---

37. **Erythraean sea.** The Red Sea.

forms, as well as with notes of different sounds.

2 To the east of these beasts I perceived the extremities of the earth, where heaven ceased. The gates of heaven stood open, and I beheld the celestial stars come forth. I numbered them as they proceeded out of the gate, and wrote them all down, as they came out one by one according to their number. *I wrote down* their names altogether, their times and their seasons, as the angel Uriel, who was with me, pointed them out to me.

3 He showed them all to me, and wrote down *an account of* them.

4 He also wrote down for me their names, their regulations, and their operations.

CHAPTER 33

1 From thence I advanced on towards the north, to the extremities of the earth.

2 And there I saw a great and glorious wonder at the extremities of the whole earth.

3 I saw there heavenly gates opening into heaven; three of them distinctly separated. The northern winds proceeded from them, blowing cold, hail, frost, snow, dew, and rain.

4 From one of the gates they blew mildly; but when they blew from the two *other gates,* it was with violence and force. They blew over the earth strongly.

CHAPTER 34

1 From thence I went to the extremities of the world westwards;

2 Where I perceived three gates open, as I had seen in the north; the gates and passages through them being of equal magnitude.

CHAPTER 35

1 Then I proceeded to the extremities of the earth southwards; where I saw three gates open to the south, from which issued dew, rain, and wind.

2 From thence I went to the extremities of heaven eastwards; where I saw three heavenly gates open to the east, which had smaller gates within them. Through each of these small gates the stars of heaven passed on, and proceeded towards the west by a path which was seen by them, and that at every period *of their appearance.*

3 When I beheld *them,* I blessed; every time *in which they appeared,* I blessed the Lord of glory, who had made those great and splendid signs, that they might display the magnificence of his works to angels and to the souls of men; and that these might glorify all his works and operations; might see the effect of his power; might glorify the great labour of his hands; and bless him for ever.

(NO CHAPTER 36)

CHAPTER 37

1 The vision which he saw, the second vision of wisdom, which Enoch saw, the son of Jared, the son of Malaleel, the son of Canan, the son of Enos, the son of Seth, the son of Adam. This is the commencement

of the word of wisdom, which I received to declare and tell to those who dwell upon earth. Hear from the beginning, and understand to the end, the holy things which I utter in the presence of the Lord of spirits. Those who were before *us* thought it good to speak;

2 And let not us, who come after, obstruct the beginning of wisdom. Until the present period never has there been given before the Lord of spirits that which I have received, wisdom according to the capacity of my intellect, and according to the pleasure of the Lord of spirits; that which I have received from him, a portion of life eternal.

3 And I obtained three parables, which I declared to the inhabitants of the world.

CHAPTER 38

1 Parable the first. When the congregation of the righteous shall be manifested; and sinners be judged for their crimes, and be troubled in the sight of the world;

2 When righteousness shall be manifested[38] in the presence of the righteous themselves, who will be elected for their *good* works *duly* weighed by the Lord of spirits; and when the light of the righteous and the elect, who dwell on earth, shall be manifested; where will the habitation of sinners be? and where the place of rest for those who have rejected the Lord of spirits? It would have been better for them, had they never been born.

---

38. When righteousness shall be manifested. Or, "when the Righteous One appears" (Knibb, p. 125; cp. Charles, p. 112).

3 When, too, the secrets of the righteous shall be revealed, then shall sinners be judged; and impious men shall be afflicted in the presence of the righteous and the elect.

4 From that period those who possess the earth shall cease to be powerful and exalted. Neither shall they be capable of beholding the countenances of the holy; for the light of the countenances of the holy, the righteous, and the elect, has been seen by the Lord of spirits.[39]

5 Yet shall not the mighty kings of that period be destroyed; but be delivered into the hands of the righteous and the holy.

6 Nor thenceforwards shall any obtain commiseration from the Lord of spirits, because their lives *in this world* will have been completed.

CHAPTER 39

1 In those days shall the elect and holy race descend from the upper heavens, and their seed shall then be with the sons of men. Enoch received books of indignation and wrath, and books of hurry and agitation.

2 Never shall they obtain mercy, saith the Lord of spirits.

3 A cloud then snatched me up, and the wind raised me above the surface of the earth, placing me at the extremity of the heavens.

---

39. For the light...Lord of spirits. Or, "for the light of the Lord of Spirits will have appeared on the face of the holy, the righteous, and the chosen" (Knibb, p. 126).

4 There I saw another vision; I *saw* the habitations and couches of the saints. There my eyes beheld their habitations with the angels, and their couches with the holy ones. They were entreating, supplicating, and praying for the sons of men; while righteousness like water flowed before them, and mercy like dew *was scattered* over the earth. And thus *shall it be* with them for ever and for ever.

5 At that time my eyes beheld the dwelling of the elect, of truth, faith, and righteousness.

6 Countless shall be the number of the holy and the elect, in the presence of God for ever and for ever.

7 Their residence I beheld under the wings of the Lord of spirits. All the holy and the elect sung before him, in appearance like a blaze of fire; their mouths being full of blessings, and their lips glorifying the name of the Lord of spirits. And righteousness incessantly *dwelt* before him.

8 There was I desirous of remaining, and my soul longed for that habitation. There was my antecedent inheritance; for thus had I prevailed before the Lord of spirits.

9 At that time I glorified and extolled the name of the Lord of spirits with blessing and with praise; for he has established it with blessing and with praise, according to his own good pleasure.

10 That place long did my eyes contemplate. I blessed and said, Blessed be he, blessed from the beginning for ever. In the beginning, before the world

was created, and without end is his knowledge.

11 What is this world? Of every existing generation those shall bless thee who do not sleep *in the dust,* but stand before thy glory, blessing, glorifying, exalting thee, and saying, The holy, holy, Lord of spirits, fills the whole world of spirits.

12 There my eyes beheld all who, without sleeping, stand before him and bless him, saying, Blessed be thou, and blessed be the name of God for ever and for ever. Then my countenance became changed, until I was incapable of seeing.

CHAPTER 40

1 After this I beheld thousands of thousands, and myriads of myriads, and an infinite number of people, standing before the Lord of spirits.

2 On the four wings likewise of the Lord of spirits, on the four sides, I perceived others, besides those who were standing *before him.* Their names, too, I know; because the angel, who proceeded with me, declared them to me, discovering to me every secret thing.

3 Then I heard the voices of those upon the four sides magnifying the Lord of glory.

4 The first voice blessed the Lord of spirits for ever and for ever.

5 The second voice I heard blessing the elect One, and the elect who suffer on account of the Lords of spirits.

6 The third voice I heard petitioning and praying

for those who dwell upon earth, and supplicate the name of the Lord of spirits.

7 The fourth voice I heard expelling the impious angels,[40] and prohibiting them from entering into [the] presence of the Lord of spirits, to prefer accusations against[41] the inhabitants of the earth.

8 After this I besought the angel of peace, who proceeded with me, to explain all that was concealed. I said to him, Who are those *whom* I have seen on the four sides, and whose words I have heard and written down? He replied, The first is the merciful, the patient, the holy Michael.

9 The second is he who *presides* over every suffering and every affliction of the sons of men, the holy Raphael. The third, who *presides* over all that is powerful, is Gabriel. And the fourth, who *presides* over repentance, and the hope of those who will inherit eternal life, is Phanuel. These are the four angels of the most high God, and their four voices, which at that time I heard.

CHAPTER 41

1 After this I beheld the secrets of the heavens and of paradise, according to its divisions; and of human action, as they weigh it there in balances. I saw the habitations of the elect, and the habitations of the holy.

40. **Impious angels.** Literally, "the Satans" (Laurence, p. 45; Knibb, p. 128). *Ha-satan* in Hebrew ("the adversary") was originally the title of an office, not the name of an angel.

41. **Prefer accusations against.** Or, "to accuse" (Charles, p. 119).

And there my eyes beheld all the sinners, who denied the Lord of glory, and whom they were expelling from thence, and dragging away, as they stood *there;* no punishment proceeding against them from the Lord of spirits.

2 There, too, my eyes beheld the secrets of the lightning and the thunder; and the secrets of the winds, how they are distributed as they blow over the earth: the secrets of the winds, of the dew, and of the clouds. There I perceived the place from which they issued forth, and became saturated with the dust of the earth.

3 There I saw the wooden receptacles out of which the winds became separated, the receptacle of hail, the receptacle of snow, the receptacle of the clouds, and the cloud itself, *which* continued over the earth before *the creation of* the world.

4 I beheld also the receptacles of the moon, whence the moons came, whither they proceeded, their glorious return, and how one became more splendid than another. I *marked* their rich progress, their unchangeable progress, their disunited and undiminished progress; their observance of a mutual fidelity by a stable oath; their proceeding forth before the sun, and their adherence to the path *allotted* them,[42] in obedience to the command of the Lord of spirits. Potent is his name for ever and for ever.

---

42. Their proceeding forth...path allotted them. Or, "the sun goes out first and completes its journey" (Knibb, p. 129; cp. Charles, p. 122).

5 After this *I perceived, that* the path both concealed and manifest of the moon, as well as the progress of its path, was there completed by day and by night; while each, one with another, looked towards the Lord of spirits, magnifying and praising without cessation, since praise to them is rest; for in the splendid sun there is a frequent conversion to blessing and to malediction.

6 The course of the moon's path to the righteous is light, but to sinners it is darkness; in the name of the Lord of spirits, who created *a division* between light and darkness, and, separating the spirits of men, strengthened the spirits of the righteous in the name of his own righteousness.

7 Nor does the angel prevent *this,* neither is he endowed with the power of preventing it; for the Judge beholds them all, and judges them all in his own presence.

CHAPTER 42

1 Wisdom found not a place *on earth* where she could inhabit; her dwelling therefore is in heaven.

2 Wisdom went forth to dwell among the sons of men, but she obtained not *an habitation.* Wisdom returned to her place, and seated herself in the midst of the angels. But iniquity went forth after her return, who unwillingly found *an habitation,* and resided among them, as rain in the desert, and as a dew in a thirsty land.

CHAPTER 43

1 I beheld another splendour, and the stars of heaven. I observed that he called them all by their respective names, and that they heard. In a righteous balance I saw that he weighed out with their light the amplitude of their places, and the day of their appearance, and their conversion. Splendour produced splendour; and their conversion *was* into the number of the angels, and of the faithful.

2 Then I inquired of the angel, who proceeded with me, and explained to me secret things, What *their names* were. He answered, A similitude of those has the Lord of spirits shown thee. They are names of the righteous who dwell upon earth, and who believe in the name of the Lord of spirits for ever and for ever.

CHAPTER 44

Another thing also I saw respecting splendour; that it rises out of the stars, and becomes splendour; being incapable of forsaking them.

CHAPTER 45

1 Parable the second, respecting these who deny the name of the habitation of the holy ones, and of the Lord of spirits.

2 Heaven they shall not ascend, nor shall they come on the earth. This shall be the portion of sinners, who deny the name of the Lord of spirits, and who are thus reserved for the day of punishment and of affliction.

3 In that day shall the Elect One sit upon a throne of glory; and shall choose their conditions and countless habitations (while their spirits within them shall be strengthened, when they behold my Elect One), *shall choose them* for those who have fled for protection to my holy and glorious name.

4 In that day I will cause my Elect One to dwell in the midst of them; will change *the face of* heaven; will bless it, and illuminate it for ever.

5 I will also change *the face of* the earth; will bless it; and cause those whom I have elected to dwell upon it. But those who have committed sin and iniquity shall not inhabit it, for I have marked their proceedings. My righteous ones will I satisfy with peace, placing them before me; but the condemnation of sinners shall draw near, that I may destroy them from the face of the earth.

CHAPTER 46

1 There I beheld the Ancient of days, whose head was like white wool, and with him another, whose countenance resembled that of man. His countenance was full of grace, like *that of* one of the holy angels. Then I inquired of one of the angels, who went with me, and who showed me every secret thing, concerning this Son of man; who he was; whence he was; and why he accompanied the Ancient of days.

2 He answered and said to me, This is the Son of man, to whom righteousness belongs; with whom righteousness has dwelt; and who will reveal all the

treasures of that which is concealed: for the Lord of spirits has chosen him; and his portion has surpassed all before the Lord of spirits in everlasting uprightness.

3 This Son of man, whom thou beholdest, shall raise up kings and the mighty from their couches, and the powerful from their thrones; shall loosen the bridles of the powerful, and break in pieces the teeth of sinners.

4 He shall hurl kings from their thrones and their dominions; because they will not exalt and praise him, nor humble themselves *before him,* by whom their kingdoms were granted to them. The countenance likewise of the mighty shall He cast down, filling them with confusion. Darkness shall be their habitation, and worms shall be their bed; nor from *that* their bed shall they hope to be again raised, because they exalted not the name of the Lord of spirits.

5 They shall condemn the stars of heaven, shall lift up their hands against the Most High, shall tread upon and inhabit the earth, exhibiting all their works of iniquity, even their works of iniquity. Their strength shall be in their riches, and their faith in the gods whom they have formed with their own hands. They shall deny the name of the Lord of spirits, and shall expel him from the temples, in which they assemble;

6 And *with him* the faithful,[43] who suffer in the name of the Lord of spirits.

---

43. Shall expel him ... the faithful. Or, "will be driven from the houses of his congregation, and of the faithful" (Knibb, p. 132; cp. Charles, p. 131).

CHAPTER 47

1 In that day the prayer of the holy and the righteous, and the blood of the righteous, shall ascend from the earth into the presence of the Lord of spirits.

2 In that day shall the holy ones assemble, who dwell above the heavens, and with united voice petition, supplicate, praise, laud, and bless the name of the Lord of spirits, on account of the blood of the righteous which has been shed; that the prayer of the righteous may not be intermitted before the Lord of spirits; that for them he would execute judgment; and that his patience may not endure for ever.[44]

3 At that time I beheld the Ancient of days, while he sat upon the throne of his glory, *while* the book of the living was opened in his presence, and *while* all the powers which were above the heavens stood around and before him.

4 Then were the hearts of the saints full of joy, because the consummation of righteousness was arrived, the supplication of the saints heard, and the blood of the righteous appreciated by the Lord of spirits.

CHAPTER 48

1 In that place I beheld a fountain of righteousness, which never failed, encircled by many springs of wisdom. Of these all the thirsty drank, and were filled with wisdom, having their habitation with the

---

44. That his patience...endure for ever. Or, "(that) their patience may not have to last for ever" (Knibb, p. 133).

righteous, the elect, and the holy.

2 In that hour was this Son of man invoked before the Lord of spirits, and his name in the presence of the Ancient of days.

3 Before the sun and the signs were created, before the stars of heaven were formed, his name was invoked in the presence of the Lord of spirits. A support shall he be for the righteous and the holy to lean upon, without falling; and he shall be the light of nations.

4 He shall be the hope of those whose hearts are troubled. All, who dwell on earth, shall fall down and worship before him; shall bless and glorify him, and sing praises to the name of the Lord of spirits.

5 Therefore the Elect and the Concealed One existed in his presence, before the world was created, and for ever.

6 In his presence *he existed*, and has revealed to the saints and to the righteous the wisdom of the Lord of spirits; for he has preserved the lot of the righteous, because they have hated and rejected this world of iniquity, and have detested all its works and ways, in the name of the Lord of spirits.

7 For in his name shall they be preserved; and his will shall be their life. In those days shall the kings of the earth and the mighty men, who have gained the world by their achievements, become humble in countenance.

8 For in the day of their anxiety and trouble their souls shall not be saved; and *they shall be* in subjection

to those whom I have chosen.

9 I will cast them like hay into the fire, and like lead into the water. Thus shall they burn in the presence of the righteous, and sink in the presence of the holy; nor shall a tenth part of them be found.

10 But in the day of their trouble, the world shall obtain tranquillity.

11 In his presence shall they fall, and not be raised up again; nor shall there be any one to take them out of his hands, and to lift them up: for they have denied the Lord of spirits, and his Messiah. The name of the Lord of spirits shall be blessed.

CHAPTER 48A[45]

1 Wisdom is poured forth like water, and glory fails not before him for ever and ever; for potent is he in all the secrets of righteousness.

2 But iniquity passes away like a shadow, and possesses not a fixed station: for the Elect One stands before the Lord of spirits; and his glory is for ever and ever; and his power from generation to generation.

3 With him dwells the spirit of intellectual wisdom, the spirit of instruction and of power, and the spirit of those who sleep in righteousness; he shall judge secret things.

4 Nor shall any be able to utter a single word before him; for the Elect One is in the presence of the Lord of spirits, according to his own pleasure.

---

45. Two consecutive chapters are numbered "48."

CHAPTER 49

1 In those days the saints and the chosen shall undergo a change. The light of day shall rest upon

them; and the splendour and glory of the saints shall be changed.

2 In the day of trouble evil shall be heaped up upon sinners; but the righteous shall triumph in the name of the Lord of spirits.

3 Others shall be made to see, that they must repent, and forsake the works of their hands; and that glory awaits them not in the presence of the Lord of spirits; yet that by his name they may be saved. The Lord of spirits will have compassion on them: for great is his mercy; and righteousness is in his judgment, and in the presence of his glory; nor in his judgment shall iniquity stand. He who repents not before him shall perish.

4 Henceforward I will not have mercy on them, saith the Lord of spirits.

CHAPTER 50

1 In those days shall the earth deliver up from her womb, and hell deliver up from hers, that which it has received; and destruction shall restore that which it owes.

2 He shall select the righteous and holy from among them; for the day of their salvation has approached.

3 And in those days shall the Elect One sit upon his throne, while every secret of intellectual wisdom shall proceed from his mouth; for the Lord of spirits

has gifted and glorified him.

4 In those days the mountains shall skip like rams, and the hills shall leap like young sheep[46] satiated with milk; and all *the righteous* shall become angels in heaven.

5 Their countenance shall be bright with joy; for in those days shall the Elect One be exalted. The earth shall rejoice; the righteous shall inhabit it, and the elect possess it.

CHAPTER 51

1 After that period, in the place where I had seen every secret sight, I was snatched up in a whirlwind, and carried off westwards.

2 There my eyes beheld the secrets of heaven, and all which existed on earth; a mountain of iron, a mountain of copper, a mountain of silver, a mountain of gold, a mountain of fluid metal, and a mountain of lead.

3 And I inquired of the angel who went with me, saying, What are these things, which in secret I behold?

4 He said, All these things which thou beholdest shall be for the dominion of the Messiah, that he may command, and be powerful upon earth.

5 And that angel of peace answered me, saying, Wait but a short time, and thou shalt understand, and every secret thing shall be revealed to thee, which the Lord of spirits has decreed. Those mountains which thou hast seen, the mountain of iron, the mountain of copper, the mountain of silver, the mountain of gold, the mountain of fluid metal, and the mountain of lead,

46. Cp. Ps. 114:4.

all these in the presence of the Elect One shall be like a honeycomb before the fire, and like water descending from above upon these mountains; and shall become debilitated before his feet.

6 In those days men shall not be saved by gold and by silver.

7 Nor shall they have it in their power to secure themselves, and to fly.

8 There shall be neither iron for war, nor a coat of mail for the breast.

9 Copper shall be useless; useless also that which neither rusts nor consumes away; and lead shall not be coveted.

10 All these things shall be rejected, and perish from off the earth, when the Elect One shall appear in the presence of the Lord of spirits.

CHAPTER 52

1 There my eyes beheld a deep valley; and wide was its entrance.

2 All who dwell on land, on the sea, and in islands, shall bring to it gifts, presents, and offerings; yet that deep valley shall not be full. Their hands shall commit iniquity. Whatsoever they produce by labour, the sinners shall devour with crime. But they shall perish from the face of the Lord of spirits, and from the face of his earth. They shall stand up, and shall not fail for ever and ever.

3 I beheld the angels of punishment, who were dwelling *there,* and preparing every instrument of Satan.

4 Then I inquired of the angel of peace, who proceeded with me, for whom those instruments were preparing.

5 He said, These they are preparing for the kings and powerful ones of the earth, that thus they may perish.

6 After which the righteous and chosen house of his congregation shall appear, thenceforward unchangeable, in the name of the Lord of spirits.

7 Nor shall those mountains exist in his presence, as the earth and the hills, as the fountains of water *exist*. And the righteous shall be relieved from the vexation of sinners.

CHAPTER 53

1 Then I looked and turned myself to another part of the earth, where I beheld a deep valley burning with fire.

2 To this valley they brought monarchs and the mighty.

3 And there my eyes beheld the instruments which they were making, fetters of iron without weight.[47]

4 Then I inquired of the angel of peace, who proceeded with me, saying, For whom are these fetters and instruments prepared?

5 He replied, These are prepared for the host of Azazeel, that they may be delivered over and adjudged to the lowest condemnation; and that their angels may be overwhelmed with hurled stones, as the Lord

---

47. Without weight. Or, "of immeasurable weight" (Knibb, p. 138).

of spirits has commanded.

6 Michael and Gabriel, Raphael and Phanuel shall be strengthened in that day, and shall then cast them into a furnace of blazing fire, that the Lord of spirits may be avenged of them for their crimes; because they became ministers of Satan, and seduced those who dwell upon earth.

7 In those days shall punishment go forth from the Lord of spirits; and the receptacles of water which are above the heavens shall be opened, and the fountains likewise, which are under the heavens and under the earth.

8 All the waters, which are in the heavens and above them, shall be mixed together.

9 The water which is above heaven shall be the agent;[48]

10 And the water which is under the earth shall be the recipient:[49] and all shall be destroyed who dwell upon earth, and who dwell under the extremities of heaven.

11 By these means shall they understand the iniquity which they have committed on earth: and by these means shall they perish.

CHAPTER 54

1 Afterwards the Ancient of days repented, and said, In vain have I destroyed all the inhabitants of the earth.

48. **Agent.** Literally, "male" (Laurence, p. 61).
49. **Recipient.** Literally, "female" (Laurence, p. 61).

2 And he sware by his great name, *saying*, Henceforwards I will not act thus towards all those who dwell upon earth.

3 But I will place a sign in the heavens;[50] and it shall be a faithful witness between me and them for ever, as long as the days of heaven and earth last upon the earth.

4 Afterwards, according to this my decree, when I shall be disposed to seize them beforehand, by the instrumentality of angels, in the day of affliction and trouble, my wrath and my punishment shall remain upon them, my punishment and my wrath, saith God the Lord of spirits.

5 O ye kings, O ye mighty, who inhabit the world, you shall behold my Elect One, sitting upon the throne of my glory. And he shall judge Azazeel, all his associates, and all his hosts, in the name of the Lord of spirits.

6 There likewise I beheld hosts of angels who were moving in punishment, confined in a net-work of iron and brass. Then I inquired of the angel of peace, who proceeded with me, To whom those under confinement were going.

7 He said, To each of their elect and their beloved,[51] that they may be cast into the fountains and deep recesses of the valley.

---

50. Cp. Gen. 9:13, "I do set my bow in the cloud, and it shall be for a token of a covenant between me and the earth."

51. To each of...their beloved. Or, "Each to his own chosen ones and to his own beloved ones" (Knibb, p. 139).

8 And that valley shall be filled with their elect and beloved; the days of whose life shall be consumed, but the days of their error shall be innumerable.

9 Then shall princes[52] combine together, and conspire. The chiefs of the east, among the Parthians and Medes, shall remove kings, in whom a spirit of perturbation shall enter. They shall hurl them from their thrones, springing as lions from their dens, and like famished wolves into the midst of the flock.

10 They shall go up, and tread upon the land of their elect. The land of their elect shall be before them. The threshing-floor, the path, and the city of my righteous *people* shall impede *the progress of* their horses. They shall rise up to destroy each other; their right hand shall be strengthened; nor shall a man acknowledge his friend or his brother;

11 Nor the son his father and his mother; until the number of the dead bodies shall be *completed,* by their death and punishment. Neither shall this take place without cause.

12 In those days shall the mouth of hell be opened, into which they shall be immerged; hell shall destroy and swallow up sinners from the face of the elect.

CHAPTER 55

1 After this I beheld another army of chariots, with men riding in them.

2 And they came upon the wind from the east,

---

52. Princes. Or, "angels" (Charles, p. 149; Knibb, p. 140).

from the west, and from the south.[53]

3 The sound of the noise of their chariots was heard.

4 And when that agitation took place, the saints out of heaven perceived it; the pillar of the earth shook from its foundation; and the sound was heard from the extremities of the earth unto the extremities of heaven at the same time.

5 Then they all fell down, and worshipped the Lord of spirits.

6 This is the end of the second parable.

CHAPTER 56

1 I now began to utter the third parable, concerning the saints and the elect.

2 Blessed are ye, O saints and elect, for glorious is your lot.

3 The saints shall exist in the light of the sun, and the elect in the light of everlasting life, the days of whose life shall never terminate; nor shall the days of the saints be numbered, who seek for light, and obtain righteousness with the Lord of spirits.

4 Peace be to the saints with the Lord of the world.

5 Henceforward shall the saints be told to seek in heaven the secrets of righteousness, the portion of faith; for like the sun has it arisen upon the earth, while darkness has passed away. There shall be light inter-

---

53. **From the south.** Literally, "from the midst of the day" (Laurence, p. 63).

minable: nor shall they enter upon the enumeration of time; for darkness shall be previously destroyed, and light shall increase before the Lord of spirits; before the Lord of spirits shall the light of uprightness increase for ever.

CHAPTER 57

1 In those days my eyes beheld the secrets of the lightnings and the splendours, and the judgment belonging to them.

2 They lighten for a blessing and for a curse, according to the will of the Lord of spirits.

3 And there I saw the secrets of the thunder, when it rattles above in heaven, and its sound is heard.

4 The habitations also of the earth were shown to me. The sound of the thunder is for peace and for blessing, as well as for a curse, according to the word of the Lord of spirits.

5 Afterwards every secret of the splendours and of the lightnings was seen by me. For blessing and for fertility they lighten.

CHAPTER 58

1 In the five hundredth year, and in the seventh month, on the fourteenth *day* of the month, of the lifetime of Enoch, in that parable, I saw that the heaven of heavens shook; that it shook violently; and that the powers of the Most High, and the angels, thousands of thousands, and myriads of myriads, were agitated with great agitation. And when I looked, the Ancient of days

was sitting on the throne of his glory, while the angels and saints were standing around him. A great trembling came upon me, and terror seized me. My loins were bowed down and loosened; my reins were dissolved; and I fell upon my face. The holy Michael, another holy angel, one of the holy ones, was sent, who raised me up.

2 And when he raised me, my spirit returned; for I was incapable of enduring this vision of violence, its agitation, and the concussion of heaven.

3 Then holy Michael said to me, Wherefore art thou disturbed at this vision?

4 Hitherto has existed the day of mercy; and he has been merciful and longsuffering towards all who dwell upon the earth.

5 But when the time shall come, then *shall* the power, the punishment, and the judgment *take place,* which the Lord of spirits has prepared for those who prostrate themselves to the judgment of righteousness, for those who abjure that judgment, and for those who take *his* name in vain.

6 That day has been prepared for the elect *as a day of* covenant; and for sinners as a day of inquisition.

7 In that day shall be distributed *for food*[54] two monsters; a female monster, whose name is Leviathan, dwelling in the depths of the sea, above the springs of waters;

---

54. **Distributed for food.** Or, "separated from one another" (Knibb, p. 143).

8 And a male *monster*, whose name is Behemoth; which possesses, *moving* on his breast, the invisible wilderness.

9 His name was Dendayen in the east of the garden, where the elect and the righteous will dwell; where he received *it* from my ancestor, who was man, from Adam the first of men,[55] whom the Lord of spirits made.

10 Then I asked of another angel to show me the power of those monsters, how they became separated on the same day, one *being* in the depths of the sea, and one in the dry desert.

11 And he said, Thou, son of man, art here desirous of understanding secret things.

12 And the angel of peace, who was with me, said, These two monsters are by the power of God prepared to become food, that the punishment of God may not be in vain.

13 Then shall children be slain with their mothers, and sons with their fathers.

14 And when the punishment of the Lord of spirits shall continue, upon them shall it continue, that the punishment of the Lord of spirits may not take place in vain. After that, judgment shall exist with mercy and longsuffering.

---

55. He received it ... first of men. Or, "my [great-] grandfather was taken up, the seventh from Adam" (Charles, p. 155). This implies that this section of the book was written by Noah, Enoch's descendant, rather than Enoch. Scholars have speculated that this portion of the book may contain fragments of the lost Apocalypse of Noah.

CHAPTER 59

1 Then another angel, who proceeded with me, spoke to me;

2 And showed me the first and last secrets in heaven above, and in the depths of the earth:

3 In the extremities of heaven, and in the foundations of it, and in the receptacle of the winds.

4 *He showed me* how their spirits were divided; how they were balanced; and how both the springs and the winds were numbered according to the force of their spirit.

5 *He showed me* the power of the moon's light, that its power is a just one; as well as the divisions of the stars, according to their respective names;

6 *That* every division is divided; that the lightning flashes;

7 That its troops immediately obey; and that a cessation takes place during thunder in continuance of its sound. Nor are the thunder and the lightning separated; neither do both of them move with one spirit; yet are they not separated.

8 For when the lightning lightens, the thunder sounds, and the spirit at a proper period pauses, making an equal division between them; for the receptacle, upon which their periods depend, is *loose* as sand. Each of them at a proper season is restrained with a bridle; and turned by the power of the spirit, which thus propels *them* according to the spacious extent of the earth.

9 The spirit likewise of the sea is potent and strong; and as a strong power causes it to ebb, so is it driven forwards, and scattered against the mountains of the earth. The spirit of the frost has its angel; in the spirit of hail there is a good angel; the spirit of snow ceases in its strength, and a solitary spirit is in it, which ascends from it like vapour, and is called refrigeration.

10 The spirit also of mist dwells with them in their receptacle; but it has a receptacle to itself; for its progress is in splendour,

11 In light, and in darkness, in winter and in summer. Its receptacle is bright, and an angel is *in it*.

12 The spirit of dew *has* its abode in the extremities of heaven, in connection with the receptacle of rain; and its progress is in winter and in summer. The cloud produced by it, and the cloud of the mist, become united; one gives to the other; and when the spirit of rain is in motion from its receptacle, angels come, and opening its receptacle, bring it forth.

13 When likewise it is sprinkled over all the earth, it forms an union with every kind of water on the ground; for the waters remain on the ground, because *they afford* nourishment to the earth from the Most High, who is in heaven.

14 Upon this account therefore there is a regulation in the quantity of rain, which the angels receive.

15 These things I saw; all of them, even paradise.

CHAPTER 60

1 In those days I beheld long ropes given to those angels; who took to their wings, and fled, advancing towards the north.

2 And I inquired of the angel, saying, Wherefore have they taken those long ropes, and gone forth? He said, They are gone forth to measure.

3 The angel, who proceeded with me, said, These are the measures of the righteous; and cords shall the righteous bring, that they may trust in the name of the Lord of spirits for ever and ever.

4 The elect shall begin to dwell with the elect.

5 And these are the measures which shall be given to faith, and *which* shall strengthen the words of righteousness.

6 These measures shall reveal all the secrets in the depth of the earth.

7 And *it shall be,* that those who have been destroyed in the desert, and who have been devoured by the fish of the sea, and by wild beasts, shall return, and trust in the day of the Elect One; for none shall perish in the presence of the Lord of spirits, nor shall any be capable of perishing.

8 Then they received the commandment, all *who were* in the heavens above; to whom a combined power, voice, and splendour, like fire, were given.

9 And first, with *their* voice, they blessed him, they exalted him, they glorified him with wisdom, and

ascribed to him wisdom with the word, and with the breath of life.

10 Then the Lord of spirits seated upon the throne of his glory the Elect One;

11 Who shall judge all the works of the holy, in heaven above, and in a balance shall he weigh their actions. And when he shall lift up his countenance to judge their secret ways in the word of the name of the Lord of spirits, and their progress in the path of the righteous judgment of God most high;

12 They shall all speak with united voice; and bless, glorify, exalt, and praise, in the name of the Lord of spirits.

13 He shall call to every power of the heavens, to all the holy above, and to the power of God. The Cherubim, the Seraphim, and the Ophanin, all the angels of power, and all the angels of the Lords, namely, of the Elect One, and of the other Power, who *was* upon earth over the water on that day,

14 Shall raise their united voice; shall bless, glorify, praise, and exalt with the spirit of faith, with the spirit of wisdom and patience, with the spirit of mercy, with the spirit of judgment and peace, and with the spirit of benevolence; all shall say with united voice: Blessed is He; and the name of the Lord of spirits shall be blessed for ever and for ever; all, who sleep not, shall bless it in heaven above.

15 All the holy in heaven shall bless it; all the elect who dwell in the garden of life; and every spirit of light,

who is capable of blessing, glorifying, exalting, and praising thy holy name; and every mortal man,[56] more than the powers *of heaven,* shall glorify and bless thy name for ever and ever.

16 For great is the mercy of the Lord of spirits; long-suffering is he; and all his works, all his power, great as are the things which he has done, has he revealed to the saints and to the elect, in the name of the Lord of spirits.

CHAPTER 61

1 Thus the Lord commanded the kings, the princes, the exalted, and those who dwell on earth, saying, Open your eyes, and lift up your horns, if you are capable of comprehending the Elect One.

2 The Lord of spirits sat upon the throne of his glory.

3 And the spirit of righteousness was poured out over him.

4 The word of his mouth shall destroy all the sinners and all the ungodly, who shall perish at his presence.

5 In that day shall all the kings, the princes, the exalted, and those who possess the earth, stand up, behold, and perceive, that he is sitting on the throne of his glory; that before him the saints shall be judged in righteousness;

6 And that nothing, which shall be spoken before him, shall be *spoken* in vain.

---

56. **Every mortal man.** Literally, "all of flesh" (Laurence, p. 73).

7 Trouble shall come upon them, as upon a woman in travail, whose labour is severe, when her child comes to the mouth of the womb, and she finds it difficult to bring forth.

8 One portion of them shall look upon another. They shall be astonished, and shall humble their countenance;

9 And trouble shall seize them, when they shall behold this Son of woman sitting upon the throne of his glory.

10 Then shall the kings, the princes, and all who possess the earth, glorify him who has dominion over all things, him who was concealed; for from the beginning the Son of man existed in secret, whom the Most High preserved in the presence of his power, and revealed to the elect.

11 He shall sow the congregation of the saints, and of the elect; and all the elect shall stand before him in that day.

12 All the kings, the princes, the exalted, and those who rule over the earth, shall fall down on their faces before him, and shall worship him.

13 They shall fix their hopes on this Son of man, shall pray to him, and petition him for mercy.

14 Then shall the Lord of spirits hasten to expel them from his presence. Their faces shall be full of confusion, and their faces shall darkness cover. The angels shall take them to punishment, that vengeance may be inflicted on those who have oppressed his children and

his elect. And they shall become an example to the saints and to his elect. Through them shall these be made joyful; for the anger of the Lord of spirits shall rest upon them.

15 Then the sword of the Lord of spirits shall be drunk with their blood; but the saints and elect shall be safe in that day; nor the face of the sinners and the ungodly shall they thenceforwards behold.

16 The Lord of spirits shall remain over them:

17 And with this Son of man shall they dwell, eat, lie down, and rise up, for ever and ever.

18 The saints and the elect have arisen from the earth, have left off to depress their countenances, and have been clothed with the garment of life. That garment of life is with the Lord of spirits, in whose presence your garment shall not wax old, nor shall your glory diminish.

CHAPTER 62

1 In those days the kings who possess the earth shall be punished by the angels of his wrath, wheresoever they shall be delivered up, that he may give rest for a short period; and that they may fall down and worship before the Lord of spirits, confessing their sins before him.

2 They shall bless and glorify the Lord of spirits, saying, Blessed is the Lord of spirits, the Lord of kings, the Lord of princes, the Lord of the rich, the Lord of glory, and the Lord of wisdom.

3 He shall enlighten every secret thing.

4 Thy power is from generation to generation; and thy glory for ever and ever.

5 Deep are all thy secrets, and numberless; and thy righteousness cannot be computed.

6 Now we know, that we should glorify and bless the Lord of kings, him who is King over all things.

7 They shall also say, Who has granted us rest to glorify, laud, bless, and confess in the presence of his glory?

8 And now small is the rest we desire; but we do not find *it;* we reject, and do not possess *it.* Light has passed away from before us; and darkness *has covered* our thrones for ever.

9 For we have not confessed before him; we have not glorified the name of the Lord of kings; we have not glorified the Lord in all his works; but we have trusted in the sceptre of our dominion and of our glory.

10 In the day of our suffering and of our trouble he will not save us, neither shall we find rest. We confess that our Lord is faithful in all his works, in all his judgments, and in his righteousness.

11 In his judgments he pays no respect to persons; and we must depart from his presence, on account of our *evil* deeds.

12 All our sins are truly without number.

13 Then shall they say to themselves, Our souls are satiated with the instruments of crime;

14 But that prevents us not from descending

to the flaming womb of hell.

15 Afterwards, their countenances shall be filled with darkness and confusion before the Son of man; from whose presence they shall be expelled, and before whom the sword shall remain to expel them.

16 Thus saith the Lord of spirits, This is the decree and the judgment against the princes, the kings, the exalted, and those who possess the earth, in the presence of the Lord of spirits.

CHAPTER 63

I saw also other countenances in that secret place. I heard the voice of an angel, saying, These are the angels who have descended from heaven to earth, and have revealed secrets to the sons of men, and have seduced the sons of men to the commission of sin.

CHAPTER 64[57]

1 In those days Noah saw that the earth became inclined, and that destruction approached.

2 Then he lifted up his feet, and went to the ends of the earth, to the dwelling of his great-grandfather Enoch.

3 And Noah cried with a bitter voice, Hear me; hear me; hear me: three times. And he said, Tell me what is transacting upon earth; for the earth labours, and is violently shaken. Surely I shall perish with it.

4 After this there was a great perturbation on

---

57. Chapters 64, 65, 66 and the first verse of 67 evidently contain a vision of Noah and not of Enoch (Laurence, p. 78).

earth, and a voice was heard from heaven. I fell down on my face, when my great-grandfather Enoch came and stood by me.

5 He said to me, Why hast thou cried out to me with a bitter cry and lamentation?

6 A commandment has gone forth from the Lord against those who dwell on the earth, that they may be destroyed; for they know every secret of the angels, every oppressive and secret power of the devils,[58] and every power of those who commit sorcery, as well as of those who make molten *images* in the whole earth.

7 *They know* how silver is produced from the dust of the earth, and how on the earth the *metallic* drop exists; for lead and tin are not produced from earth, as the primary fountain of their production.

8 There is an angel standing upon it, and that angel struggles to prevail.

9 Afterwards my great-grandfather Enoch seized me with his hand, raising me up, and saying to me, Go, for I have asked the Lord of spirits respecting this perturbation of the earth; who replied, On account of their impiety have their innumerable judgments been consummated before me. Respecting the moons have they inquired, and they have known that the earth will perish with those who dwell upon it,[59] and that to these there will be *no place of* refuge for ever.

---

58. The devils. Literally, "the Satans" (Laurence, p. 78).
59. Respecting the moons...dwell upon it. Or, "Because of the sorceries which they have searched out and learnt, the earth and those who dwell upon it will be destroyed" (Knibb, p. 155).

10 They have discovered secrets, and *they are* those who have been judged; but not thou, my son. The Lord of spirits knows that thou art pure and good, *free* from the reproach of *discovering* secrets.

11 He, the holy One, will establish thy name in the midst of the saints, and will preserve thee from those who dwell upon the earth. He will establish thy seed in righteousness, with dominion and great glory;[60] and from thy seed shall spring forth righteous and holy men without number for ever.

CHAPTER 65

1 After this he showed me the angels of punishment, who were prepared to come, and to open all the mighty waters under the earth:

2 That they may be for judgment, and for the destruction of all those who remain and dwell upon the earth.

3 And the Lord of spirits commanded the angels who went forth, not to take up the men and preserve *them*.

4 For those angels *presided* over all the mighty waters. Then I went out from the presence of Enoch.

CHAPTER 66

1 In those days the word of God came to me, and said, Noah, behold, thy lot has ascended up to me, a lot void of crime, a lot beloved and upright.

---

60. With dominion...glory. Literally, "for kings, and for great glory" (Laurence, p. 79).

2 Now then shall the angels labour at the trees;[61] but when they proceed to this, I will put my hand upon it, and preserve it.

3 The seed of life shall arise from it, and a change shall take place, that the dry land may not be left empty. I will establish thy seed before me for ever and ever, and the seed of those who dwell with thee on the surface of the earth. It shall be blessed and multiplied in the presence of the earth, in the name of the Lord.

4 And they shall confine those angels who disclosed impiety. In that burning valley *it is, that they shall be confined,* which at first my great-grandfather Enoch showed me in the west, where there were mountains of gold and silver, of iron, of fluid metal, and of tin.

5 I beheld that valley in which there was great perturbation, and *where* the waters were troubled.

6 And when all this was effected, from the fluid mass of fire, and the perturbation which prevailed[62] in that place, there arose a strong smell of sulphur, which became mixed with the waters; and the valley of the angels, who had been guilty of seduction, burned underneath its soil.

7 Through that valley also rivers of fire were flowing, to which those angels shall be condemned, who seduced the inhabitants of the earth.

8 And in those days shall these waters be to kings,

61. **Shall...labour at the trees.** Or, "are making a wooden (structure)" (Knibb, p. 156).
62. **The perturbation which prevailed.** Literally, "troubled them" (Laurence, p. 81).

to princes, to the exalted, and to the inhabitants of the earth, for the healing of the soul and body, and for the judgment of the spirit.

9 Their spirits shall be full of revelry,[63] that they may be judged in their bodies; because they have denied the Lord of spirits, and *although* they perceive their condemnation day by day, they believe not in his name.

10 And as the inflammation of their bodies shall be great, so shall their spirits undergo a change for ever.

11 For no word which is uttered before the Lord of spirits shall be in vain.

12 Judgment has come upon them, because they trusted in their carnal revelry, and denied the Lord of spirits.

13 In those days shall the waters of that valley be changed; for when the angels shall be judged, then shall the heat of those springs of water experience an alteration.

14 And when the angels shall ascend, the water of the springs shall *again* undergo a change, and be frozen. Then I heard holy Michael answering and saying, This judgment, with which the angels shall be judged, shall bear testimony against the kings, the princes, and those who possess the earth.

15 For these waters of judgment shall be for their healing, and for the death[64] of their bodies. But they shall not perceive and believe that the waters will be changed, and become a fire, which shall blaze for ever.

63. Revelry. Or, "lust" (Knibb, p. 157).
64. Death. Or, "lust" (Charles, p. 176; Knibb, p. 158).

CHAPTER 67

1 After this he gave me the characteristical marks[65] of all the secret things in the book of my great-grandfather Enoch, and in the parables which had been given to him; inserting them for me among the words of the book of parables.

2 At that time holy Michael answered and said to Raphael, The power of the spirit hurries me away, and impels me on. The severity of the judgment, of the secret judgment of the angels, who is capable *of beholding*—the endurance of that severe judgment which has taken place and been made permanent—without being melted at the sight of it? Again holy Michael answered and said to holy Raphael, Who is there whose heart is not softened by it, and whose reins are not troubled at this thing?

3 Judgment has gone forth against them by those who have thus dragged them away; and that was, when they stood in the presence of the Lord of spirits.

4 In like manner also holy Rakael said to Raphael, They shall not be before the eye of the Lord;[66] since the Lord of spirits has been offended with them; for like Lords[67] have they conducted themselves. Therefore will he bring upon them a secret judgment for ever and ever.

---

65. **Characteristical marks.** Literally, "the signs" (Laurence, p. 83).
66. **They shall not...eye of the Lord.** Or, "I will not take their part under the eye of the Lord" (Knibb, p. 159).
67. **For like Lords.** Or, "for they act as if they were the Lord" (Knibb, p. 159).

5 For neither shall angel nor man receive a portion of it; but they alone shall receive their own judgment for ever and ever.

CHAPTER 68

1 After this judgment they shall be astonished and irritated; for it shall be exhibited to the inhabitants of the earth.

2 Behold the names of those angels. These are their names. The first of them is Samyaza; the second, Arstikapha; the third, Armen; the fourth, Kakabael; the fifth, Turel; the sixth, Rumyel; the seventh, Danyal; the eighth, Kael; the ninth, Barakel; the tenth, Azazel; the eleventh, Armers; the twelfth, Bataryal; the thirteenth, Basasael; the fourteenth, Ananel; the fifteenth, Turyal; the sixteenth, Simapiseel; the seventeenth, Yetarel; the eighteenth, Tumael; the nineteenth, Tarel; the twentieth, Rumel; the twenty-first, Azazyel.

3 These are the chiefs of their angels, and the names of the leaders of their hundreds, and the leaders of their fifties, and the leaders of their tens.

4 The name of the first is Yekun:[68] he it was who seduced all the sons of the holy angels; and causing them to descend on earth, led astray the offspring of men.

5 The name of the second is Kesabel, who pointed out evil counsel to the sons of the holy angels, and induced them to corrupt their bodies by generating mankind.

---

68. **Yekun** may simply mean "the rebel" (Knibb, p. 160).

6 The name of the third is Gadrel: he discovered every stroke of death to the children of men.

7 He seduced Eve; and discovered to the children of men the instruments of death, the coat of mail, the shield, and the sword for slaughter; every instrument of death to the children of men.

8 From his hand were *these things* derived to them who dwell upon earth, from that period for ever.

9 The name of the fourth is Penemue: he discovered to the children of men bitterness and sweetness;

10 And pointed out to them every secret of their wisdom.

11 He taught men to understand writing, and *the use of* ink and paper.

12 Therefore numerous have been those who have gone astray from every period of the world, even to this day.

13 For men were not born for this, thus with pen and with ink to confirm their faith;

14 Since they were not created, except that, like the angels, they might remain righteous and pure.

15 Nor would death, which destroys everything, have affected them;

16 But by this their knowledge they perish, and by this also *its* power consumes *them*.

17 The name of the fifth is Kasyade: he discovered to the children of men every wicked stroke of spirits and of demons:

18 The stroke of the embryo in the womb, to

diminish *it*;[69] the stroke of the spirit *by* the bite of the serpent, and the stroke which is *given* in the mid-day *by* the offspring of the serpent, the name of which is Tabaet.[70]

19 This is the number of the Kesbel; the principal part of the oath which the Most High, dwelling in glory, revealed to the holy ones.

20 Its name is Beka. He spoke to holy Michael to discover to them the sacred name, that they might understand that secret name, and thus remember the oath; and that those who pointed out every secret thing to the children of men might tremble at that name and oath.

21 This is the power of that oath; for powerful it is, and strong.

22 And he established this oath of Akae by the instrumentality of the holy Michael.

23 These are the secrets of this oath, and by it were they confirmed.

24 Heaven was suspended *by it* before the world was made, for ever.

25 By it has the earth been founded upon the flood; while from the concealed parts of the hills the agitated waters proceed forth from the creation to the end of the world.

26 By this oath the sea has been formed, and the foundation of it.

---

69. The stroke ... to diminish it. Or, "the blows (which attack) the embryo in the womb so that it miscarries" (Knibb, p. 162).
70. Tabaet. Literally, "male" or "strong" (Knibb p. 162).

27 During the period of *its* fury he has established the sand against it, which continues unchanged for ever; and by this oath the abyss has been made strong; nor is it removable from its station for ever and ever.

28 By this oath the sun and moon complete their progress, never swerving from the command given to them for ever and ever.

29 By this oath the stars complete their progress;

30 And when their names are called, they return an answer, for ever and ever.

31 Thus *in* the heavens *take place* the blowings of the winds: all of them have breathings,[71] and *effect* a complete combination of breathings.

32 There the treasures of thunder are kept, and the splendour of the lightning.

33 There are kept the treasures of hail and of frost, the treasures of snow, the treasures of rain and of dew.

34 All these confess and laud before the Lord of spirits.

35 They glorify with all their power of praise; and he sustains them in all that *act of* thanksgiving; while they laud, glorify, and exalt the name of the Lord of spirits for ever and ever.

36 And with them he establishes this oath, by which they and their paths are preserved; nor does their progress perish.

37 Great was their joy.

38 They blessed, glorified, and exalted, because the

---

71. Breathings. Or, "spirits" (Laurence, p. 87).

name of the Son of man was revealed to them.

39 He sat upon the throne of his glory; and the principal part of the judgment was assigned to him, the Son of man. Sinners shall disappear and perish from the face of the earth, while those who seduced them shall be bound with chains for ever.

40 According to their ranks of corruption shall they be imprisoned, and all their works shall disappear from the face of the earth; nor thenceforward shall there be any to corrupt; for the Son of man has been seen, sitting on the throne of his glory.

41 Everything wicked shall disappear, and depart from before his face; and the word of the Son of man shall become powerful in the presence of the Lord of spirits.

42 This is the third parable of Enoch.

CHAPTER 69

1 After this the name of the Son of man, living with the Lord of spirits, was exalted by the inhabitants of the earth.

2 It was exalted in the chariots of the Spirit; and the name went forth in the midst of them.

3 From that time I was not drawn in the midst of them; but he seated me between two spirits, between the north and the west, where the angels received their ropes, to measure out a place for the elect and the righteous.

4 There I beheld the fathers of the first men, and the saints, who dwell in that place for ever.

CHAPTER 70

1 Afterwards my spirit was concealed, ascending into the heavens. I beheld the sons of the holy angels treading on flaming fire, whose garments and robes were white, and whose countenances were transparent as crystal.

2 I saw two rivers of fire glittering like the hyacinth.

3 Then I fell on my face before the Lord of spirits.

4 And Michael, one of the archangels, took me by my right hand, raised me up, and brought me out *to* where *was* every secret *of* mercy and secret *of* righteousness.

5 He showed me all the hidden things of the extremities of heaven, all the receptacles of the stars, and the splendours of all, from whence they went forth before the face of the holy.

6 And he concealed the spirit of Enoch in the heaven of heavens.

7 There I beheld, in the midst of that light, a building raised with stones of ice;

8 And in the midst of these stones vibrations[72] of living fire. My spirit saw around the circle of this flaming habitation, on one of its extremities, *that there were* rivers full of living fire, which encompassed it.

9 Then the Seraphim, the Cherubim, and Ophanin[73]

---

72. **Vibrations.** Literally, "tongues" (Laurence, p. 90).
73. **Ophanin.** The "wheels" of Ezek. 1:15–21 (Charles, p. 162).

surrounded *it:* these are those who never sleep, but watch the throne of his glory.

10 And I beheld angels innumerable, thousands of thousands, and myriads of myriads, who surrounded that habitation.

11 Michael, Raphael, Gabriel, Phanuel, and the holy angels who were in the heavens above, went in and out of it. Michael, Raphael, and Gabriel went out of that habitation, and holy angels innumerable.

12 With them *was* the Ancient of days, whose head *was* white as wool, and pure, and his robe *was* indescribable.

13 Then I fell upon my face, while all my flesh was dissolved, and my spirit became changed.

14 I cried out with a loud voice, with a powerful spirit, blessing, glorifying, and exalting.

15 And those blessings, which proceeded from my mouth, became acceptable in the presence of the Ancient of days.

16 The Ancient of days came with Michael and Gabriel, Raphael and Phanuel, with thousands of thousands, and myriads of myriads, which could not be numbered.

17 Then that angel came to me, and with his voice saluted me, saying, Thou art the Son of man,[74] who art born for righteousness, and righteousness has rested on thee.

74, 75. **Son of man.** Laurence's original translation renders this phrase "offspring of man." Knibb (p. 166) and Charles (p. 185) in-

18 The righteousness of the Ancient of days shall not forsake thee.

19 He said, On thee shall he confer peace in the name of the existing world; for from thence has peace gone forth since the world was created.

20 And thus shall it happen to thee for ever and ever.

21 All who shall exist, and who shall walk in thy path of righteousness, shall not forsake thee for ever.

22 With thee shall be their habitations, with thee their lot; nor from thee shall they be separated for ever and ever.

23 And thus shall length of days be with the Son of man.[75]

24 Peace shall be to the righteous; and the path of integrity shall the righteous pursue, in the name of the Lord of spirits, for ever and ever.

CHAPTER 71

1 The book of the revolutions of the luminaries of heaven, according to their respective classes, their respective powers, their respective periods, their respective names, the places where they commence their progress, and their respective months, which Uriel, the holy angel who was with me, explained to me; he who conducts them. The whole account of them, according to every year of the world for ever, until a new work

dicate that it should be "Son of man," consistent with the other occurrences of that term in the Book of Enoch. (See "Forbidden Mysteries of Enoch," p. 21.)

shall be effected, which will be eternal.

2 This is the first law of the luminaries. The sun *and* the light arrive at the gates of heaven, which are on the east, and on the west of it at the western gates of heaven.

3 I beheld the gates whence the sun goes forth; and the gates where the sun sets;

4 In which gates also the moon rises and sets; and I *beheld* the conductors of the stars, among those who precede them; six *gates were* at the rising, and six at the setting of the sun.

5 All these respectively, one after another, are on a level; and numerous windows are on the right and on the left sides of those gates.

6 First proceeds forth that great luminary, which is called the sun; the orb of which is as the orb of heaven, the whole of it being replete with splendid and flaming fire.

7 Its chariot, where it ascends, the wind blows.

8 The sun sets in heaven, and, returning by the north, to proceed towards the east, is conducted so as to enter by that gate, and illuminate the face of heaven.

9 In the same manner it goes forth in the first month by a great gate.

10 It goes forth through the fourth of those six gates, which are at the rising of the sun.

11 And in the fourth gate, through which the sun with the moon proceeds, in the first part of it,[76] there

---

76. **Through which...part of it.** Or, "from which the sun rises in the first month" (Knibb, p. 168).

are twelve open windows, from which issues out a flame, when they are opened at their proper periods.

12 When the sun rises in heaven, it goes forth through this fourth gate thirty days, and by the fourth gate in the west of heaven on a level with it descends.

13 During that period the day is lengthened from the day, and the night curtailed from the night for thirty days. And then the day is longer by two parts than the night.

14 The day is precisely ten parts, and the night is eight.

15 The sun goes forth through this fourth gate, and sets in it, and turns to the fifth gate during thirty days; after which it proceeds from, and sets in, the fifth gate.

16 Then the day becomes lengthened by a second portion, so that it is eleven parts: while the night becomes shortened, and is only seven parts.

17 The sun *now* returns to the east, entering into the sixth gate, and rising and setting in the sixth gate thirty-one days, on account of its signs.

18 At that period the day is longer than the night, being twice *as long as* the night; and becomes twelve parts;

19 But the night is shortened, and becomes six parts. Then the sun rises up, that the day may be shortened, and the night lengthened.

20 And the sun returns towards the east, entering into the sixth gate, where it rises and sets for thirty days.

21 When that period is completed, the day becomes

shortened precisely one part, so that it is eleven parts, while the night is seven parts.

22 Then the sun goes from the west, from that sixth gate, and proceeds eastwards, rising in the fifth gate for thirty days, and setting again westwards in the fifth gate of the west.

23 At that period the day becomes shortened two parts; and is ten parts, while the night is eight parts.

24 Then the sun goes from the fifth gate, as it sets in the fifth gate of the west; and rises in the fourth gate for thirty-one days, on account of its signs, setting in the west.

25 At that period the day is made equal with the night; and, being equal with it, the night becomes nine parts, and the day nine parts.

26 Then the sun goes from that gate, as it sets in the west; and returning to the east proceeds by the third gate for thirty days, setting in the west at the third gate.

27 At that period the night is lengthened from the day during thirty mornings, and the day is curtailed from the day during thirty days; the night being ten parts precisely, and the day eight parts.

28 The sun now goes from the third gate, as it sets in the third gate in the west; but returning to the east, it proceeds by the second gate of the east for thirty days.

29 In like manner also it sets in the second gate in the west of heaven.

30 At that period the night is eleven parts, and the day seven parts.

31 Then the sun goes at that time from the second gate, as it sets in the second gate in the west; but returns to the east, *proceeding* by the first gate, for thirty-one days.

32 And sets in the west in the first gate.

33 At that period the night is lengthened as much again as the day.

34 It is twelve parts precisely, while the day is six parts.

35 The sun has *thus* completed its beginnings, and a second time goes round from these beginnings.

36 Into that [first] gate it enters for thirty days, and sets in the west, in the opposite part *of heaven*.

37 At that period the night is contracted in its length a fourth part, that is, one portion, and becomes eleven parts.

38 The day is seven parts.

39 Then the sun returns, and enters into the second gate of the east.

40 It returns by these beginnings thirty days, rising and setting.

41 At that period the night is contracted in its length. It becomes ten parts, and the day eight parts. Then the sun goes from that second gate, and sets in the west; but returns to the east, and rises in the east, in the third gate, thirty-one days, setting in the west of heaven.

42 At that period the night becomes shortened. It is nine parts. And the night is equal with the day. The year is precisely three hundred and sixty-four days.

43 The lengthening of the day and night, and the contraction of the day and night, are made to differ from each other by the progress of the sun.

44 By means of this progress the day is daily lengthened, and the night greatly shortened.

45 This is the law and progress of the sun, and its turning when it turns back, turning during sixty days,[77] and going forth. This is the great everlasting luminary, that which he names the sun for ever and ever.

46 This also is that which goes forth a great luminary, and which is named after its peculiar kind, as God commanded.

47 And thus it goes in and out, neither slackening nor resting; but running on in its chariot by day and by night. It shines with a seventh portion of light from the moon;[78] but the dimensions of both are equal.

CHAPTER 72

1 After this law I beheld another law of an inferior luminary, the name of which is the moon, and the orb of which is as the orb of heaven.

2 Its chariot, *which* it secretly ascends, the wind blows; and light is given to it by measure.

---

77. That is, it is sixty days in the same gates, viz. thirty days twice every year (Laurence, p. 97).

78. It shines with … from the moon. Or, "Its light is seven times brighter than that of the moon" (Knibb, p. 171). The Aramaic texts more clearly describe how the moon's light waxes and wanes by a half of a seventh part each day. Here in the Ethiopic version, the moon is thought of as two halves, each half being divided into seven parts. Hence, the "fourteen portions" of 72:9–10 (Knibb, p. 171).

3 Every month at its exit and entrance it becomes changed; and its periods are as the periods of the sun. And when in like manner its light is to exist,[79] its light is a seventh portion from the light of the sun.

4 Thus it rises, and at its commencement towards the east goes forth for thirty days.

5 At that time it appears, and becomes to you the beginning of the month. Thirty days *it is* with the sun in the gate from which the sun goes forth.

6 Half of it is in extent seven portions, one *half;* and the whole of its orb is void of light, except a seventh portion out of the fourteen portions of its light. And in a day it receives a seventh portion, or half *that portion,* of its light. Its light is by sevens, by one portion, and by the half *of a portion.* It sets with the sun.

7 And when the sun rises, the moon rises with it; receiving half a portion of light.

8 On that night, when it commences its period, previously to the day of the month, the moon sets with the sun.

9 And on that night it is dark *in* its fourteen portions, that is, *in each* half; but it rises on that day with one seventh portion precisely, and in its progress declines from the rising of the sun.

10 During the remainder of its period its light increases to fourteen portions.

---

79. And when in...is to exist. I.e., when the moon is full (Knibb, p. 171).

CHAPTER 73

1 Then I saw another progress and regulation which He effected in the law of the moon. The progress of the moons, and everything *relating to them*, Uriel showed me, the holy angel who conducted them all.

2 Their stations I wrote down as he showed them to me.

3 I wrote down their months, as they occur, and the appearance of their light, until it is completed in fifteen days.

4 In each of its two seven portions it completes all its light at rising and at setting.

5 On stated months it changes *its* settings; and on stated months it makes its progress *through* each *gate*. In two *gates* the moon sets with the sun, *viz.* in those two gates which are in the midst, in the third and fourth gate. *From the third gate* it goes forth for seven days, and makes its circuit.

6 Again it returns to the gate whence the sun goes forth, and in that completes the whole of its light. Then it declines from the sun, and enters in eight days into the sixth gate, *and returns in seven days to the third gate,* from which the sun goes forth.

7 When the sun proceeds to the fourth gate, the *moon* goes forth for seven days, until it passes from the fifth *gate*.

8 Again it returns in seven days to the fourth gate, and completing all its light, declines, and passes on by the first gate in eight days;

9 And returns in seven days to the fourth gate, from which the sun goes forth.

10 Thus I beheld their stations, as according to the fixed order of the months the sun rises and sets.

11 At those times there is an excess of thirty days belonging to the sun in five years; all the days belonging to each year of the five years, when completed, amount to three hundred and sixty-four days; and to the sun and stars belong six days; six days in each of the five years; *thus* thirty days belong to them;

12 So that the moon has thirty days less than the sun and stars.

13 The moon brings on all the years exactly, that their stations may come neither too forwards nor too backwards a single day; but that the years may be changed with correct precision in three hundred and sixty-four days. In three years the days are one thousand and ninety-two; in five years they are one thousand eight hundred and twenty; and in eight years two thousand nine hundred and twelve days.

14 To the moon alone belong in three years one thousand and sixty-two days; in five years it has fifty days less *than the sun,* for an addition being made to the *one thousand and* sixty-two days, in five years there are one thousand seven hundred and seventy days; and the days of the moon in eight years are two thousand eight hundred and thirty-two days.

15 For its days in eight years are less *than those of the sun by* eighty days, which eighty days are its

diminution in eight years.

16 The year then becomes truly complete according to the station of the moons, and the station of the sun; which rise in the *different* gates; which rise and set in them for thirty days.

CHAPTER 74

1 *These are* the leaders of the chiefs of the thousands, *those* which *preside* over all creation, and over all the stars; with the four *days* which are added and never separated from the place allotted them, according to the complete computation of the year.

2 And these serve four days, which are not computed in the computation of the year.

3 Respecting them, men greatly err, for these luminaries truly serve, in the mansion of the world, one *day* in the first gate, one in the third gate, one in the fourth, and one in the sixth gate.

4 And the harmony of the world becomes complete every three hundred and sixty-fourth state of it. For the signs,

5 The seasons,

6 The years,

7 And the days, Uriel showed me; the angel whom the Lord of glory appointed over all the luminaries.

8 Of heaven in heaven, and in the world; that they might rule in the face of the sky, and appearing over the earth, become

9 Conductors of the days and nights: the sun, the

moon, the stars, and all the ministers of heaven, which make their circuit with all the chariots of heaven.

10 Thus Uriel showed me twelve gates open for the circuit of the chariots of the sun in heaven, from which the rays of the sun shoot forth.

11 From these proceed heat over the earth, when they are opened in their stated seasons. They are for the winds, and the spirit of the dew, when in their seasons they are opened; opened in heaven at *its* extremities.

12 Twelve gates I beheld in heaven, at the extremities of the earth, through which the sun, moon, and stars, and all the works of heaven, proceed at their rising and setting.

13 Many windows also are open on the right and on the left.

14 One window at a *certain* season grows extremely hot. So also are there gates from which the stars go forth as they are commanded, and in which they set according to their number.

15 I saw likewise the chariots of heaven, running in the world above to those gates in which the stars turn, which never set. One of these is greater than all, which goes round the whole world.

CHAPTER 75

1 And at the extremities of the earth I beheld twelve gates open for all the winds, from which they proceed and blow over the earth.

2 Three of them are open in the front of heaven,

three in the west, three on the right side of heaven, and three on the left. The first three are those which are towards the east, three are towards the north, three behind those which are upon the left, towards the south, and three on the west.

3 From four of them proceed winds of blessing, and of health; and from eight proceed winds of punishment; when they are sent to destroy the earth, and the heaven above it, all its inhabitants, and all which are in the waters, or on dry land.

4 The first of these winds proceeds from the gate termed the eastern, through the first gate on the east, which inclines southwards. From this goes forth destruction, drought, heat, and perdition.

5 From the second gate, the middle one, proceeds equity. There issue from it rain, fruitfulness, health, and dew; and from the third gate northwards, proceed cold and drought.

6 After these proceed the south winds through three principal gates; through their first gate, which inclines eastwards, proceeds a hot wind.

7 But from the middle gate proceed grateful odour, dew, rain, health, and life.

8 From the third gate, which is westwards, proceed dew, rain, blight, and destruction.

9 After these are the winds to the north, which is called the sea. *They proceed* from three gates. The first[80] gate *is that* which is on the east, inclining south-

80. First. Or, "seventh" (Knibb, p. 178).

wards; from this proceed dew, rain, blight, and destruction. From the middle direct gate proceed rain, dew, life, and health. And from the third gate, which is westwards, inclining towards the south, proceed mist, frost, snow, rain, dew, and blight.

10 After these *in the* fourth *quarter* are the winds to the west. From the first gate, inclining northwards, proceed dew, rain, frost, cold, snow, and chill; from the middle gate proceed rain, health, and blessing;

11 And from the last gate, which is southwards, proceed drought, destruction, scorching, and perdition.

12 The *account of the* twelve gates of the four quarters of heaven is ended.

13 All their laws, all their *infliction* of punishment, and the health *produced* by them, have I explained to thee, my son Mathusala.[81]

CHAPTER 76

1 The first wind is called the eastern, because it is the first.

2 The second is called the south, because the Most High there descends, and frequently there descends *he who* is blessed for ever.

3 The western wind has the name of diminution, because there all the luminaries of heaven are diminished, and descend.

4 The fourth wind, which is named the north, is divided into three parts; one of which is for the habi-

---

81. Mathusala. Enoch's son, Methuselah. Cp. Gen. 5:21.

tation of man; another for seas of water, with valleys, woods, rivers, shady places, and snow; and the third part *contains* paradise.

5 Seven high mountains I beheld, higher than all the mountains of the earth, from which frost proceeds; while days, seasons, and years depart and pass away.

6 Seven rivers I beheld upon earth, greater than all rivers, one of which takes its course from the west; into a great sea its water flows.

7 Two come from the north to the sea, their waters flowing into the Erythraean sea,[82] on the east. And with respect to the remaining four, they take their course in the cavity of the north, *two* to their sea, the Erythraean sea, and two are poured into a great sea, where also it is said *there is* a desert.

8 Seven great islands I saw in the sea and on the earth. Seven in the great sea.

CHAPTER 77

1 The names of the sun are these: one Aryares, the other Tomas.

2 The moon has four names. The first is Asonya; the second, Ebla; the third, Benase; and the fourth, Erae.

3 These are the two great luminaries, whose orbs are as the orbs of heaven; and the dimensions of both are equal.

4 In the orb of the sun *there is* a seventh portion

---

82. The Red Sea.

of light, which is added to it from the moon.[83] By measure it is put in, until a seventh portion of *the light of* the sun is departed. They set, enter into the western gate, circuit by the north, and through the eastern gate go forth over the face of heaven.

5 When the moon rises, it appears in heaven; and the half of a seventh portion of light is all *which is* in it.

6 In fourteen *days* the whole of its light is completed.

7 *By* three quintuples light is put into it, until *in* fifteen *days* its light is completed, according to the signs of the year; it has three quintuples.

8 The moon has the half of a seventh portion.

9 During its diminution on the first day its light decreases a fourteenth part; on the second day it decreases a thirteenth part; on the third day a twelfth part; on the fourth day an eleventh part; on the fifth day a tenth part; on the sixth day a ninth part; on the seventh day it decreases an eighth part; on the eighth day it decreases a seventh part; on the ninth day it decreases a sixth part; on the tenth day it decreases a fifth part; on the eleventh day it decreases a fourth part; on the twelfth day it decreases a third part; on the thirteenth day it decreases a second part; on the fourteenth day it decreases a half of its seventh part; and on the fifteenth day the whole remainder of its light is consumed.

10 On stated months the moon has twenty-nine days.

---

83. **A seventh portion...from the moon.** Or, "seven parts of light which are added to it more than to the moon" (Knibb, p. 182).

11 It also has a period of twenty-eight days.

12 Uriel likewise showed me another regulation, when light is poured into the moon, how it is poured into it from the sun.

13 All the time that the moon is in progress with its light, it is poured *into it* in the presence of the sun, until *its* light is in fourteen days completed in heaven.

14 And when it is wholly extinguished, its light is consumed in heaven; and on the first day it is called the new moon, for on that day light is received into it.

15 It becomes precisely completed on the day that the sun descends into the west, while the moon ascends at night from the east.

16 The moon then shines all the night, until the sun rises before it; when the moon disappears in turn before the sun.

17 Where light comes to the moon, there again it decreases, until all its light is extinguished, and the days of the moon pass away.

18 Then its orb remains solitary without light.

19 During three months it effects in thirty days *each month* its period; and during three *more* months it effects it in twenty-nine days each. *These are the times* in which it effects its decrease in its first period, and in the first gate, *namely,* in one hundred and seventy-seven days.

20 And at the time of its going forth during three months it appears thirty days each, and during three *more* months it appears twenty-nine days each.

21 In the night it appears for each twenty *days* as *the face of* a man, and in the day as heaven; for it is nothing else except its light.

CHAPTER 78

1 And now, my son Mathusala, I have shown thee everything; and *the account of* every ordinance of the stars of heaven is finished.

2 He showed me every ordinance respecting these, which *takes place* at all times and in all seasons under every influence, in all years, at the arrival and under the rule of each, during every month and every week. *He showed me* also the decrease of the moon, which is effected in the sixth gate; for in that sixth gate is its light consumed.

3 From this is the beginning of the month; and its decrease is effected in the sixth gate in its period, until a hundred and seventy-seven days are completed; according to the mode of computation by weeks, twenty-five *weeks* and two days.

4 *Its period* is less than that of the sun, according to the ordinance of the stars, by five days in one half year[84] precisely.

5 When that *their* visible situation is completed. Such is the appearance and likeness of every luminary, which Uriel, the great angel who conducts them, showed to me.

---

84. **In one half year.** Literally, "in one time" (Laurence, p. 110).

CHAPTER 79

1 In those days Uriel answered and said to me, Behold, I have showed thee all things, O Enoch;

2 And all things have I revealed to thee. Thou seest the sun, the moon, and those which conduct the stars of heaven, which cause all their operations, seasons, and arrivals to return.

3 In the days of sinners the years shall be shortened.

4 Their seed shall be backward in their prolific soil; and everything done on earth shall be subverted, and disappear in its season. The rain shall be restrained, and heaven shall stand still.

5 In those days the fruits of the earth shall be late, and not flourish in their season; and in their season the fruits of the trees shall be withholden.

6 The moon shall change its laws, and not be seen at its proper period. But in those days shall heaven be seen; and barrenness shall take place in the borders of the great chariots in the west. *Heaven* shall shine more than *when illuminated by* the orders of light; while many chiefs among the stars of authority shall err, perverting their ways and works.

7 Those shall not appear in their season, who command them, and all the classes of the stars shall be shut up against sinners.

8 The thoughts of those who dwell on earth shall transgress within them; and they shall be perverted in all their ways.

9 They shall transgress, and think themselves[85] gods; while evil shall be multiplied among them.

10 And punishment shall come upon them, so that all of them shall be destroyed.

CHAPTER 80

1 He said, O Enoch, look on the book which heaven has gradually dropped down;[86] and, reading that which is written in it, understand every part of it.

2 Then I looked on all which was written, and understood all, reading the book and everything written in it, all the works of man;

3 And of all the children of flesh upon earth, during the generations of the world.

4 Immediately after I blessed the Lord, the King of glory, who has thus for ever formed the whole workmanship of the world.

5 And I glorified the Lord, on account of his longsuffering and blessing towards the children of the world.

6 At that time I said, Blessed is the man, who shall die righteous and good, against whom no catalogue of crime has been written, and with whom iniquity is not found.

7 Then those three holy ones caused me to approach, and placed me on the earth, before the door of my house.

85. Themselves. Or, "them," i.e., the chiefs among the stars (vs. 6) (Knibb, p. 186).
86. The book which...dropped down. Or, "the book of the tablets of heaven" (Knibb, p. 186).

8 And they said unto me, Explain everything to Mathusala thy son; and inform all thy children, that no flesh shall be justified before the Lord; for he is their Creator.

9 During one year we will leave thee with thy children, until thou shalt again recover thy strength, that thou mayest instruct thy family, write these things, and explain them to all thy children. But in another year they shall take thee from the midst of them, and thy heart shall be strengthened; for the elect shall point out righteousness to the elect; the righteous with the righteous shall rejoice, congratulating each other; but sinners with sinners shall die,

10 And the perverted with the perverted shall be drowned.

11 Those likewise who act righteously shall die on account of the works of man, and shall be gathered together on account of the works of the wicked.

12 In those days they finished conversing with me.

13 And I returned to my fellow men, blessing the Lord of worlds.

CHAPTER 81

1 Now, my son Mathusala, all these things I speak unto thee, and write for thee. To thee I have revealed all, and have given thee books of everything.

2 Preserve, my son Mathusala, the books written by thy father; that thou mayest transmit them to future generations.

3 Wisdom have I given to thee, to thy children, and thy posterity, that they may transmit to their children, for generations for ever, this wisdom in their thoughts; and that those who comprehend *it* may not slumber, but hear with their ears; that they may learn this wisdom, and be deemed worthy of eating *this* wholesome food.

4 Blessed are all the righteous; blessed all who walk in *the paths of* righteousness; in whom no crime *is found,* as in sinners, when all their days are numbered.

5 With respect to the progress of the sun in heaven, it enters and goes out of *each* gate for thirty days, with the leaders of the thousand classes of the stars; with four which are added, and appertain to the four quarters of the year, which conduct them, and accompany them at four periods.

6 Respecting these, men greatly err, and do not compute them in the computation of every age; for they greatly err respecting them; nor do men know accurately that they are in the computation of the year. But indeed these are marked down for ever; one in the first gate, one in the third, one in the fourth, and one in the sixth:

7 So that the year is completed in three hundred and sixty-four days.

8 Truly has been stated, and accurately has been computed that which is marked down; for the luminaries, the months, the fixed periods, the years, and the days, Uriel has explained to me, and communicated to

me; whom the Lord of all creation, on my account, commanded (according to the might of heaven, and the power which it possesses both by night and by day) to explain *the laws of* light to man, of the sun, moon, and stars, and of all the powers of heaven, which are turned with their respective orbs.

9 This is the ordinance of the stars, which set in their places, in their seasons, in their periods, in their days, and in their months.

10 These are the names of those who conduct them, who watch and enter in their seasons, according to their ordinance in their periods, in their months, in *the times of* their influence, and in their stations.

11 Four conductors of them first enter, who separate the four quarters of the year. After these, twelve conductors of their classes, who separate the months and the year *into* three hundred and sixty-four *days,* with the leaders of a thousand, who distinguish between the days, as well as between the four additional ones; which, *as* conductors, divide the four quarters of the year.

12 These leaders of a thousand are in the midst of the conductors, and the conductors are added each behind his station, and their conductors make the separation. These are the names of the conductors, who separate the four quarters of the year, who are appointed *over them:* Melkel, Helammelak,

13 Meliyal, and Narel.

14 And the names of those who conduct them are

Adnarel, Jyasusal, and Jyelumeal.

15 These are the three who follow after the conductors of the classes *of stars;* each following after the three conductors of the classes, which themselves follow after those conductors of the stations, who divide the four quarters of the year.

16 In the first part of the year rises and rules Melkyas, who is named Tamani, and Zahay.[87]

17 All the days of his influence, *during* which he rules, are ninety-one days.

18 And these are the signs of the days which are seen upon earth. In the days of his influence *there is* perspiration, heat, and trouble. All the trees become fruitful; the leaf of every tree comes forth; the corn is reaped; the rose and every species of flowers blossoms in the field; and the trees of winter are dried up.

19 These are the names of the conductors who are under them: Barkel, Zelsabel; and another additional conductor of a thousand is named Heloyalef, the days of whose influence have been completed. The other conductor next after them *is* Helemmelek, whose name they call the splendid Zahay.[88]

20 All the days of his light are ninety-one days.

21 These are the signs of the days upon earth, heat and drought; while the trees bring forth their fruits, warmed and concocted, and give their fruits to dry.

22 The flocks follow and yean.[89] All the fruits of

---

87. Tamani, and Zahay. Or, "the southern sun" (Knibb, p. 190).
88. Zahay. Or, "sun" (Knibb, p. 191).
89. Follow and yean. Mate and bear young.

the earth are collected, with everything in the fields, and the vines are trodden. This takes place during the time of his influence.

23 These are their names and orders, and *the names* of the conductors who are under them, of those who are chiefs of a thousand: Gedaeyal, Keel, Heel.

24 And the name of the additional leader of a thousand is Asphael.

25 The days of his influence have been completed.

CHAPTER 82

1 And now I have shown thee, my son Mathusala, every sight which I saw prior to thy birth. I will relate another vision, which I saw before I was married; they resemble each other.

2 The first was when I was learning a book; and the other before I was married to thy mother. I saw a potent vision;

3 And on account of these things besought the Lord.

4 I was lying down in the house of my grandfather Malalel, *when* I saw in a vision heaven purifying, and snatched away.[90]

5 And falling to the earth,[91] I saw likewise the earth absorbed by a great abyss; and mountains suspended over mountains.

6 Hills were sinking upon hills, lofty trees were

90. Purifying, and snatched away. Or, "was thrown down and removed" (Knibb, p. 192).

91. And falling to the earth. Or, "and when it fell upon the earth" (Knibb, p. 192).

gliding off from their trunks, and were in the act of being projected, and of sinking into the abyss.

7 *Being alarmed* at these things, my voice faltered.[92] I cried out and said, The earth is destroyed. Then my grandfather Malalel raised me up, and said to me: Why dost thou thus cry out, my son? and wherefore dost thou thus lament?

8 I related to him the whole vision which I had seen. He said to me, Confirmed is that which thou hast seen, my son;

9 And potent the vision of thy dream respecting every secret sin of the earth. Its substance shall sink into the abyss, and a great destruction take place.

10 Now, my son, rise up; and beseech the Lord of glory (for thou art faithful), that a remnant may be left upon earth, and that he would not wholly destroy it. My son, all this *calamity* upon earth comes down from heaven; upon earth shall there be a great destruction.

11 Then I arose, prayed, and entreated; and wrote down my prayer for the generations of the world, explaining everything to my son Mathusala.

12 When I went out below, and looking up to heaven, beheld the sun proceeding from the east, the moon descending to the west, a few *scattered* stars, and everything which God has known from the beginning, I blessed the Lord of judgment, and magnified him: because he hath sent forth the sun from the chambers[93]

92. **My voice faltered.** Literally, "the word fell down in my mouth" (Laurence, p. 118).
93. **Chambers.** Literally, "windows" (Laurence, p. 119).

of the east; that, ascending and rising in the face of heaven, it might spring up, and pursue the path which has been pointed out to it.

CHAPTER 83

1 I lifted up my hands in righteousness, and blessed the holy, and the Great One. I spoke with the breath of my mouth, and with a tongue of flesh, which God has formed for all the sons of mortal men, that with it they may speak; giving them breath, a mouth, and a tongue to converse with.

2 Blessed art thou, O Lord, the King, great and powerful in thy greatness, Lord of all the creatures of heaven, King of kings, God of the whole world, whose reign, whose kingdom, and whose majesty endure for ever and ever.

3 From generation to generation shall thy dominion *exist*. All the heavens are thy throne for ever, and all the earth thy footstool for ever and for ever.

4 For thou hast made *them*, and over all thou reignest. No act whatsoever exceeds thy power. With thee wisdom is unchangeable; nor from thy throne and from thy presence is it ever averted. Thou knowest all things, seest and hearest them; nor is anything concealed from thee; for thou perceivest all things.

5 The angels of thy heavens have transgressed; and on mortal flesh shall thy wrath remain, until the day of the great judgment.

6 Now then, O God, Lord and mighty King,

I entreat thee, and beseech thee to grant my prayer, that a posterity may be left to me on earth, and that the whole human race may not perish;

7 That the earth may not be left destitute, and destruction take place for ever.

8 O my Lord, let the race perish from off the earth which has offended thee, but a righteous and upright race establish for a posterity[94] for ever. Hide not thy face, O Lord, from the prayer of thy servant.

CHAPTER 84

1 After this I saw another dream, and explained it all to thee, my son. Enoch arose and said to his son Mathusala, To thee, my son, will I speak. Hear my word; and incline thine ear to the visionary dream of thy father. Before I married thy mother Edna, I saw a vision on my bed;[95]

2 And behold, a cow sprung forth from the earth;

3 And this cow was white.

4 Afterwards a female heifer sprung forth; and with it another heifer:[96] one of them was black, and one was red.[97]

---

94. **For a posterity.** Literally, "for the plant of a seed" (Laurence, p. 121).

95. This second vision of Enoch seems to portray in symbolic language the complete history of the world from the time of Adam down to the final judgment and the establishment of the Messianic Kingdom (Charles, p. 227).

96. **Another heifer.** The sense seems to require that the passage should read, "two other heifers" (Laurence, p. 121).

97. Cain and Abel.

5 The black heifer then struck the red one, and pursued it over the earth.

6 From that period I could see nothing more of the red heifer; but the black one increased in bulk, and a female heifer came with him.

7 After this I saw that many cows proceeded forth, resembling him, and following after him.

8 The first female young one also went out in the presence of the first cow; and sought the red heifer; but found him not.

9 And she lamented with a great lamentation, while she was seeking him.

10 Then I looked until that first *cow* came to her, from which time she became silent, and ceased to lament.

11 Afterwards she calved another white cow.

12 And again calved many cows and black heifers.

13 In my sleep also I perceived a white bull, which in like manner grew, and became a large white bull.

14 After him many white cows came forth, resembling him.

15 And they began to calve many *other* white cows, which resembled them and followed each other.

CHAPTER 85

1 Again I looked attentively, while sleeping, and surveyed heaven above.

2 And behold a single star fell from heaven.

3 Which being raised up, ate and fed among those cows.

4 After that I perceived *other* large and black cows; and behold all of them changed their stalls and pastures, while their young began to lament one with another. Again I looked in *my* vision, and surveyed heaven; when behold I saw many stars which descended, and projected themselves from heaven to where the first star was,

5 Into the midst of those young ones; while the cows were with them, feeding in the midst of them.

6 I looked at and observed them; when behold, they all acted after the manner of horses, and began to approach the young cows, all of whom became pregnant, and brought forth elephants, camels, and asses.

7 At these all the cows were alarmed and terrified; when they began biting with their teeth, swallowing, and striking with their horns.

8 They began also to devour the cows; and behold all the children of the earth trembled, shook with terror at them, and suddenly fled away.

CHAPTER 86

1 Again I perceived them, when they began to strike and to swallow each other; and the earth cried out. Then I raised my eyes a second time towards heaven, and saw in a vision, that, behold, there came forth from heaven as it were the likeness of white men. One came forth from thence, and three with him.

2 Those three, who came forth last, seized me by my hand; and raising me up from the generations of

the earth, elevated me to a high station.

3 Then they showed me a lofty tower on the earth, while every hill became diminished. And they said, Remain here, until thou perceivest what shall come upon those elephants, camels, and asses, upon the stars, and upon all the cows.

CHAPTER 87

1 Then I looked at that one of the four *white men*, who came forth first.

2 He seized the first star which fell down from heaven.

3 And, binding it hand and foot, he cast it into a valley; a valley narrow, deep, stupendous, and gloomy.

4 Then one of them drew his sword, and gave it to the elephants, camels, and asses, who began to strike each other. And the whole earth shook on account of them.

5 And when I looked in the vision, behold, one of those four angels, who came forth, hurled from heaven, collected together, and took all the great stars, whose form partly resembled that of horses; and binding them all hand and foot, cast them into the cavities of the earth.

CHAPTER 88

1 Then one of those four went to the white cows, and taught them a mystery. While the cow was trembling, it was born, and became a man,[98] and fabricated for himself a large ship. In this he dwelt, and three

---

98. Noah.

cows[99] dwelt with him in that ship, which covered them.

2 Again I lifted up my eyes towards heaven, and saw a lofty roof. Above it were seven cataracts, which poured forth on a certain village much water.

3 Again I looked, and behold there were fountains open on the earth in that large village.

4 The water began to boil up, and rose over the earth; so that the village was not seen, while its whole soil was covered with water.

5 Much water was over it, darkness, and clouds. Then I surveyed the height of this water; and it was elevated above the village.

6 It flowed over the village, and stood higher than the earth.

7 Then all the cows which were collected there, while I looked on them, were drowned, swallowed up, and destroyed in the water.

8 But the ship floated above it. All the cows, the elephants, the camels, and the asses, were drowned on the earth, and all cattle. Nor could I perceive them. Neither were they able to get out, but perished, and sunk into the deep.

9 Again I looked in the vision until those cataracts from that lofty roof were removed, and the fountains of the earth became equalized, while other depths were opened;

10 Into which the water began to descend, until the dry ground appeared.

---

99. Shem, Ham, and Japheth.

11 The ship remained on the earth; the darkness receded; and it became light.

12 Then the white cow, which became a man, went out of the ship, and the three cows with him.

13 One of the three cows was white, resembling that cow; one of them was red as blood; and one of them was black. And the white cow left them.

14 Then began wild beasts and birds to bring forth.

15 Of all these the different kinds assembled together, lions, tigers, wolves, dogs, wild boars, foxes, rabbits, and the hanzar,

16 The siset, the avest, kites, the phonkas, and ravens.

17 Then a white cow[100] was born in the midst of them.

18 And they began to bite each other; when the white cow, which was born in the midst of them, brought forth a wild ass and a white cow at the same time, and *after that* many wild asses. Then the white cow,[101] which was born, brought forth a black wild sow and a white sheep.[102]

19 That wild sow also brought forth many swine;

20 And that sheep brought forth twelve sheep.[103]

21 When those twelve sheep grew up, they delivered one of them[104] to the asses.[105]

---

100. Abraham.
101. Isaac.
102. Esau and Jacob.
103. The twelve patriarchs.
104. Joseph.
105. The Midianites.

22 Again those asses delivered that sheep to the wolves,[106]

23 And he grew up in the midst of them.

24 Then the Lord brought the eleven *other* sheep, that they might dwell and feed with him in the midst of the wolves.

25 They multiplied, and there was abundance of pasture for them.

26 But the wolves began to frighten and oppress them, while they destroyed their young ones.

27 And they left their young in torrents of deep water.

28 Now the sheep began to cry out on account of their young, and fled for refuge to their Lord. One[107] however, which was saved, escaped, and went away to the wild asses.

29 I beheld the sheep moaning, crying, and petitioning their Lord,

30 With all their might, until the Lord of the sheep descended at their voice from *his* lofty habitation; went to them; and inspected them.

31 He called to that sheep which had secretly stolen away from the wolves, and told him to make the wolves understand that they were not to touch the sheep.

32 Then that sheep went to the wolves with the word of the Lord, when another met him,[108] and proceeded with him.

---

106. The Egyptians.
107. Moses.
108. Aaron.

33 Both of them together entered the dwelling of the wolves; and conversing with them made them understand, that from thenceforwards they were not to touch the sheep.

34 Afterwards I perceived the wolves greatly prevailing over the sheep with their whole force. The sheep cried out; and their Lord came to them.

35 He began to strike the wolves, who commenced a grievous lamentation; but the sheep were silent, nor from that time did they cry out.

36 I then looked at them, until they departed from the wolves. The eyes of the wolves were blind, who went out and followed them with all their might. But the Lord of the sheep proceeded with them, and conducted them.

37 All his sheep followed him.

38 His countenance *was* terrific and splendid, and glorious was his aspect. Yet the wolves began to follow the sheep, until they overtook them in a certain lake of water.[109]

39 Then that lake became divided; the water standing up on both sides before their face.

40 And while their Lord was conducting them, he placed himself between them and the wolves.

41 The wolves however perceived not the sheep, but went into the midst of the lake, following them, and running after them into the lake of water.

42 But when they saw the Lord of the sheep, they

---
109. The Red Sea.

turned to fly from before his face.

43 Then the water of the lake returned, and that suddenly, according to its nature. It became full, and was raised up, until it covered the wolves. And I saw that all of them which had followed the sheep perished, and were drowned.

44 But the sheep passed over this water, proceeding to a wilderness, which was without both water and grass. And they began to open their eyes and to see.

45 Then I beheld the Lord of the sheep inspecting them, and giving them water and grass.

46 The sheep *already mentioned* was proceeding *with them,* and conducting them.

47 And when he had ascended the top of a lofty rock, the Lord of the sheep sent him to them.

48 Afterwards I perceived their Lord standing before them, with an aspect terrific and severe.

49 And when they all beheld him, they were frightened at his countenance.

50 All of them were alarmed, and trembled. They cried out after that sheep; and to the other sheep who had been with him, and who was in the midst of them, *saying,* We are not able to stand before our Lord, or to look upon him.

51 Then that sheep who conducted them went away, and ascended the top of the rock;

52 When the *rest of the* sheep began to grow blind, and to wander from the path which he had shown them; but he knew it not.

53 Their Lord however was moved with great indignation against them; and when that sheep had learned *what had happened,*

54 He descended from the top of the rock, and coming to them, found that there were many,

55 Which had become blind;

56 And had wandered from his path. As soon as they beheld him, they feared, and trembled at his presence;

57 And became desirous of returning to their fold.

58 Then that sheep, taking with him other sheep, went to those which had wandered.

59 And afterwards began to kill them. They were terrified at his countenance. Then he caused those which had wandered to return; who went back to their fold.

60 I likewise saw there in the vision, that this sheep became a man, built an house[110] for the Lord of the sheep, and made them all stand in that house.

61 I perceived also that the sheep which proceeded to meet this sheep, their conductor, died. I saw, too, that all the great sheep perished, while smaller ones rose up in their place, entered into a pasture, and approached a river of water.[111]

62 Then that sheep, their conductor, who became a man, was separated from them, and died.

63 All the sheep sought after him, and cried for him with bitter lamentation.

64 I saw likewise that they ceased to cry after that

---

110. **An house.** A tabernacle (Milik, p. 205).

111. The river Jordan.

sheep, and passed over the river of water.

65 And that there arose other sheep, all of whom conducted them,[112] instead of those who were dead, and who had *previously* conducted them.

66 Then I saw that the sheep entered into a goodly place, and a territory delectable and glorious.

67 I saw also that they became satiated; that their house was in the midst of a delectable territory: and that sometimes their eyes were opened, and that sometimes they were blind; until another sheep[113] arose and conducted them. He brought them all back; and their eyes were opened.

68 Then dogs, foxes, and wild boars began to devour them, until *again* another sheep[114] arose, the master of the flock, one of themselves, a ram, to conduct them. This ram began to butt on every side those dogs, foxes, and wild boars, until they all perished.

69 But the *former* sheep opened his eyes, and saw the ram in the midst of them, who had laid aside his glory.

70 And he began to strike the sheep, treading upon them, and behaving himself without dignity.

71 Then their Lord sent the *former* sheep *again* to a still different sheep,[115] and raised him up to be a ram, and to conduct them instead of that sheep who had laid aside his glory.

---

112. The Judges of Israel.
113. Samuel.
114. Saul.
115. David.

72 Going therefore to him, and conversing with him alone, he raised up that ram, and made him a prince and leader of the flock. All the time that the dogs[116] troubled the sheep,

73 The first ram paid respect to this latter ram.

74 Then the latter ram arose, and fled away from before his face. And I saw that those dogs caused the first ram to fall.

75 But the latter ram arose, and conducted the smaller sheep.

76 That ram likewise begat many sheep, and died.

77 Then there was a smaller sheep,[117] a ram, instead of him, which became a prince and leader, conducting the flock.

78 And the sheep increased in size, and multiplied.

79 And all the dogs, foxes, and wild boars feared, and fled away from him.

80 That ram also struck and killed all the wild beasts, so that they could not again prevail in the midst of the sheep, nor at any time ever snatch them away.

81 And that house was made large and wide; a lofty tower being built upon it by the sheep, for the Lord of the sheep.

82 The house was low, but the tower was elevated and very high.

83 Then the Lord of the sheep stood upon that tower, and caused a full table to approach before him.

116. The Philistines.
117. Solomon.

84 Again I saw that those sheep wandered, and went various ways, forsaking that their house;

85 And that their Lord called to some among them, whom he sent[118] to them.

86 But these the sheep began to kill. And when one of them was saved from slaughter[119] he leaped, and cried out against those who were desirous of killing him.

87 But the Lord of the sheep delivered him from their hands, and made him ascend to him, and remain with him.

88 He sent also many others to them, to testify, and with lamentations to exclaim against them.

89 Again I saw, when some of them forsook the house of their Lord, and his tower; wandering on all sides, and growing blind,

90 I saw that the Lord of the sheep made a great slaughter among them in their pasture, until they cried out to him in consequence of that slaughter. Then he departed from the place *of his habitation,* and left them in the power of lions, tigers, wolves, and the zeebt,[120] and in the power of foxes, and of every beast.

91 And the wild beasts began to tear them.

92 I saw, too, that he forsook the house of their fathers, and their tower; giving them all into the power of lions to tear and devour them; into the power of every beast.

---

118. The prophets.
119. Elijah.
120. **Zeebt.** Hyenas (Knibb, p. 209).

93 Then I began to cry out with all my might, imploring the Lord of the sheep, and showing him how the sheep were devoured by all the beasts of prey.

94 But he looked on in silence, rejoicing that they were devoured, swallowed up, and carried off; and leaving them in the power of every beast for food. He called also seventy shepherds, and resigned to them *the care of* the sheep, that they might overlook them;

95 Saying to them and to their associates, Every one of you henceforwards overlook the sheep, and whatsoever I command you, do; and I will deliver *them* to you numbered.

96 I will tell you which of them shall be slain; these destroy. And he delivered the sheep to them.

97 Then he called to another, and said, Understand, and watch everything which the shepherds shall do to these sheep; for many more of them shall perish than I have commanded.

98 Of every excess and slaughter, which the shepherds shall commit, *there shall be* an account; as, how many may have perished by my command, and how many they may have destroyed of their own heads.

99 Of all the destruction *brought about by* each of the shepherds there shall be an account; and according to the number I will cause a recital to be made before me, how many they have destroyed of their own heads, and how many they have delivered up to destruction, that I may have this testimony against them; that I may know all their proceedings; and that, delivering *the*

sheep to them, I may see what they will do; whether they will act as I have commanded them, or not.

100 *Of this*, however, they shall be ignorant; neither shalt thou make any explanation to them, neither shalt thou reprove them; but there shall be an account of all the destruction *done* by them in their respective seasons. Then they began to kill, and destroy more than it was commanded them.

101 And they left the sheep in the power of lions, so that very many of them were devoured and swallowed up by lions and tigers; and wild boars preyed upon them. That tower they burnt, and overthrew that house.

102 Then I grieved extremely on account of the tower, and because the house of the sheep was overthrown.

103 Neither was I afterwards able to perceive whether they *again* entered that house.

104 The shepherds likewise, and their associates, delivered them to all the wild beasts, that they might devour them. Each of them in his season, according to his number, was delivered up; each of them, one with another, was described in a book, how many of them, one with another, were destroyed, in a book.

105 More, however, than was ordered, every *shepherd* killed and destroyed.

106 Then I began to weep, and was greatly indignant, on account of the sheep.

107 In like manner also I saw in the vision him who

wrote, how he wrote down one, destroyed by the shepherds, every day. He ascended, remained, and exhibited each of his books to the Lord of the sheep, *containing* all which they had done, and all which each of them had made away with;

108 And all which they had delivered up to destruction.

109 He took the book up in his hands, read it, sealed it, and deposited it.

110 After this, I saw shepherds overlooking for twelve hours.

111 And behold three of the sheep[121] departed, arrived, went in; and began building all which was fallen down of that house.

112 But the wild boars[122] hindered them, although they prevailed not.

113 Again they began to build as before, and raised up that tower, which was called a lofty tower.

114 And again they began to place before the tower a table, with every impure and unclean kind of bread upon it.

115 Moreover also all the sheep were blind, and could not see; as were the shepherds likewise.

116 Thus were they delivered up to the shepherds for a great destruction, who trod them under foot, and devoured them.

117 Yet was their Lord silent, until all the sheep in

---

121. Zerubbabel, Joshua, and Nehemiah.
122. The Samaritans.

the field were destroyed. The shepherds and the sheep were all mixed together; but they did not save them from the power of the beasts.

118 Then he who wrote the book ascended, exhibited it, and read it at the residence of the Lord of the sheep. He petitioned him for them, and prayed, pointing out every act of the shepherds, and testifying before him against them all. Then taking the book, he deposited it with him, and departed.

CHAPTER 89

1 And I observed during the time, that thus thirty-seven[123] shepherds were overlooking, all of whom finished in their respective periods as the first. Others then received them into their hands, that they might overlook them in their respective periods, every shepherd in his own period.

2 Afterwards I saw in the vision, that all the birds of heaven arrived; eagles, the avest, kites and ravens. The eagle instructed them all.

3 They began to devour the sheep, to peck out their eyes, and to eat up their bodies.

4 The sheep then cried out; for their bodies were devoured by the birds.

5 I also cried out, and groaned in my sleep against that shepherd which overlooked the flock.

6 And I looked, while the sheep were eaten up by

---

123. **Thirty-seven.** An apparent error for *thirty-five* (see verse 7). The kings of Judah and Israel (Laurence, p. 139).

the dogs, by the eagles, and by the kites. They neither left them their body, nor their skin, nor their muscles, until their bones alone remained; until their bones fell upon the ground. And the sheep became diminished.

7 I observed likewise during the time, that twenty-three shepherds[124] were overlooking; who completed in their respective periods fifty-eight periods.

8 Then were small lambs born of those white sheep; who began to open their eyes and to see, crying out to the sheep.

9 The sheep, however, cried not out to them, neither did they hear what they uttered to them; but were deaf, blind, and obdurate in the greatest degrees.

10 I saw in the vision that ravens flew down upon those lambs;

11 That they seized one of them; and that tearing the sheep in pieces, they devoured them.

12 I saw also, that horns grew upon those lambs; and that the ravens lighted down upon their horns.

13 I saw, too, that a large horn sprouted out on an animal among the sheep, and that their eyes were opened.

14 He looked at them. Their eyes were wide open; and he cried out to them.

15 Then the dabela[125] saw him; all of whom ran to him.

---

124. The kings of Babylon, etc., during and after the captivity. The numbers thirty-*five* and twenty-three make fifty-eight; and not thirty-*seven*, as erroneously put in the first verse (Laurence, p. 139).
125. **Dabela.** The ibex, probably symbolizing Alexander the Great (Laurence, p. 140).

16 And besides this, all the eagles, the avest, the ravens and the kites, were still carrying off the sheep, flying down upon them, and devouring them. The sheep were silent, but the dabela lamented and cried out.

17 Then the ravens contended, and struggled with them.

18 They wished among them to break his horn; but they prevailed not over him.

19 I looked on them, until the shepherds, the eagles, the avest, and the kites came.

20 Who cried out to the ravens to break the horn of the dabela; to contend with him; and to kill him. But he struggled with them, and cried out, that help might come to him.

21 Then I perceived that the man came who had written down the names of the shepherds, and who ascended up before the Lord of the sheep.

22 He brought assistance, and caused every one to see him descending to the help of the dabela.

23 I perceived likewise that the Lord of the sheep came to them in wrath, while all those who saw him fled away; all fell down in his tabernacle before his face; while all the eagles, the avest, ravens, and kites assembled, and brought with them all the sheep of the field.

24 All came together, and strove to break the horn of the dabela.

25 Then I saw, that the man, who wrote the book at the word of the Lord, opened the book of destruc-

tion, of that destruction which the last twelve shepherds[126] wrought; and pointed out before the Lord of the sheep, that they destroyed more than those who preceded them.

26 I saw also that the Lord of the sheep came to them, and taking in his hand the sceptre of his wrath seized the earth, which became rent asunder; while all the beasts and birds of heaven fell from the sheep, and sunk into the earth, which closed over them.

27 I saw, too, that a large sword was given to the sheep, who went forth against all the beasts of the field to slay them.

28 But all the beasts and birds of heaven fled away from before their face.

29 And I saw a throne erected in a delectable land;

30 Upon this sat the Lord of the sheep, who received all the sealed books;

31 Which were open before him.

32 Then the Lord called the first seven white ones, and commanded them to bring before him the first of the first stars, which preceded the stars whose form partly resembled that of horses; the first star, which fell down first; and they brought them all before him.

33 And he spoke to the man who wrote in his presence, who was one of the seven white ones, saying, Take those seventy shepherds, to whom I delivered up the sheep, and *who* receiving them killed more of them

126. The native princes of Judah after its delivery from the Syrian yoke.

than I commanded. Behold, I saw them all bound, and all standing before him. First came on the trial of the stars, which, being judged, and found guilty, went to the place of punishment. They thrust them into *a place*, deep, and full of flaming fire, and full of pillars of fire. Then the seventy shepherds were judged, and being found guilty, were thrust into the flaming abyss.

34 At that time likewise I perceived, that one abyss was thus opened in the midst of the earth, which was full of fire.

35 And to this were brought the blind sheep; which being judged, and found guilty, were all thrust into that abyss of fire on the earth, and burnt.

36 The abyss was on the right of that house.

37 And I saw the sheep burning, and their bones consuming.

38 I stood beholding him immerge that ancient house, while they brought out its pillars, every plant in it, and the ivory infolding it. They brought it out, and deposited it in a place on the right side of the earth.

39 I also saw, that the Lord of the sheep produced a new house, great, and loftier than the former, which he bounded by the former circular spot. All its pillars were new, and its ivory new, as well as more abundant than the former ancient *ivory*, which he had brought out.

40 And while all the sheep which were left were in the midst of it, all the beasts of the earth, and all the birds of heaven, fell down and worshipped them, petitioning them, and obeying them in everything.

41 Then those three, who were clothed in white, and who, holding me by my hand, had before caused me to ascend, while the hand of him *who* spoke held me; raised me up, and placed me in the midst of the sheep, before the judgment took place.

42 The sheep were all white, with wool long and pure. Then all who had perished, and had been destroyed, every beast of the field, and every bird of heaven, assembled in that house: while the Lord of the sheep rejoiced with great joy, because all were good, and had come back again to his dwelling.

43 And I saw that they laid down the sword which had been given to the sheep, and returned it to his house, sealing it up in the presence of the Lord.

44 All the sheep would have been inclosed in that house, had it been capable of containing them; and the eyes of all were open, gazing on the good One; nor was there one among them who did not behold him.

45 I likewise perceived that the house was large, wide, and extremely full. I saw, too, that a white cow was born, whose horns were great; and that all the beasts of the field, and all the birds of heaven, were alarmed at him, and entreated him at all times.

46 Then I saw that the nature of all of them was changed, and that they became white cows;

47 And that the first, *who* was in the midst of them, spoke, when that word became[127] a large beast, upon

___

127. Spoke, when that word became. Or, "was a wild-ox, and that wild-ox was..." (Knibb, p. 216).

the head of which were great and black horns;

48 While the Lord of the sheep rejoiced over them, and over all the cows.

49 I lay down in the midst of them: I awoke; and saw the whole. This is the vision which I saw, lying down and waking. Then I blessed the Lord of righteousness, and gave glory to Him.

50 Afterwards I wept abundantly, nor did my tears cease, so that I became incapable of enduring it. While I was looking on, they flowed on account of what I saw; for all was come and gone by; every individual circumstance respecting the conduct of mankind was seen by me.

51 In that night I remembered my former dream; and therefore wept and was troubled, because I had seen that vision.

CHAPTER 90

1 And now, my son Mathusala, call to me all thy brethren, and assemble for me all the children of thy mother; for a voice calls me, and the spirit is poured out upon me, that I may show you everything which shall happen to you for ever.

2 Then Mathusala went, called to him all his brethren, and assembled his kindred.

3 And conversing with all his children in truth,

4 *Enoch* said, Hear, my children, every word of your father, and listen in uprightness to the voice of my mouth; for I would gain your attention, while I address you. My beloved, be attached to integrity, and walk in it.

5 Approach not integrity with a double heart; nor be associated with double-minded men: but walk, my children, in righteousness, which will conduct you in good paths; and be truth your companion.

6 For I know, that oppression will exist and prevail on earth; that on earth great punishment shall in the end take place; and that there shall be a consummation of all iniquity, which shall be cut off from its root, and every fabric *raised by* it shall pass away. Iniquity, however, shall again be renewed, and consummated on earth. Every act of crime, and every act of oppression and impiety, shall be a second time embraced.

7 When therefore iniquity, sin, blasphemy, tyranny, and every *evil* work, shall increase, and *when* transgression, impiety, and uncleanness also shall increase, *then* upon them all shall great punishment be inflicted from heaven.

8 The holy Lord shall go forth in wrath, and upon them all shall great punishment from heaven be inflicted.

9 The holy Lord shall go forth in wrath, and with punishment, that he may execute judgment upon earth.

10 In those days oppression shall be cut off from its roots, and iniquity with fraud shall be eradicated, perishing from under heaven.

11 Every place of strength[128] shall be surrendered with its inhabitants; with fire shall it be burnt. They

128. Every place of strength. Or, "all the idols of the nations" (Knibb, p. 218).

shall be brought from every part of the earth, and be cast into a judgment of fire. They shall perish in wrath, and by a judgment overpowering them for ever.

12 Righteousness shall be raised up from slumber; and wisdom shall be raised up, and conferred upon them.

13 Then shall the roots of iniquity be cut off; sinners perish by the sword; and blasphemers be annihilated everywhere.

14 Those who meditate oppression, and those who blaspheme, by the sword shall perish.

15 And now, my children, I will describe and point out to you the path of righteousness and the path of oppression.

16 I will again point them out to you, that you may know what is to come.

17 Hear now, my children, and walk in the path of righteousness, but shun that of oppression; for all who walk in the path of iniquity shall perish for ever.

CHAPTER 91

1 That which was written by Enoch. He wrote all this instruction of wisdom for every man of dignity, and every judge of the earth; for all my children who shall dwell upon earth, and for subsequent generations, conducting themselves uprightly and peaceably.

2 Let not your spirit be grieved on account of the times; for the holy, the Great One, has prescribed a period to all.

3 Let the righteous man arise from slumber; let him arise, and proceed in the path of righteousness, in all its paths; and let him advance in goodness and in eternal clemency. Mercy shall be showed to the righteous man; upon him shall be conferred integrity and power for ever. In goodness and in righteousness shall he exist, and shall walk in everlasting light; but sin shall perish in eternal darkness, nor be seen from this time forward for evermore.

CHAPTER 92

1 After this, Enoch began to speak from a book.

2 And Enoch said, Concerning the children of righteousness, concerning the elect of the world, and concerning the plant of righteousness and integrity.

3 *Concerning* these things will I speak, and *these things* will I explain to you, my children: I *who* am Enoch. In consequence of that which has been shown to me, from my heavenly vision and from the voice of the holy angels[129] have I acquired knowledge; and from the tablet of heaven have I acquired understanding.

4 Enoch then began to speak from a book, and said, I have been born the seventh in the first week, while judgment and righteousness wait with patience.

5 But after me, in the second week, great wicked-

---

129. **Holy angels.** A Qumran text reads, "Watchers and Holy Ones," clearly denoting heavenly Watchers who did not fall along with the wicked ones (Milik, p. 264). See also Dan. 4:13, "a watcher and an holy one came down from heaven"; 4:17, "watchers, and...holy ones."

ness shall arise, and fraud shall spring forth.

6 In that week the end of the first shall take place, in which mankind shall be safe.[130]

7 But when *the first* is completed, iniquity shall grow up; and he shall execute the decree upon sinners.[131]

8 Afterwards, in the third week, during its completion, a man[132] of the plant of righteous judgment shall be selected; and after him the plant of righteousness shall come for ever.

9 Subsequently, in the fourth week, during its completion, the visions of the holy and the righteous shall be seen, the order of generation after generation *shall take place,* and an habitation shall be made for them. Then in the fifth week, during its completion, the house of glory and of dominion[133] shall be erected for ever.

10 After that, in the sixth week, all those who are in it shall be darkened, the hearts of all of them shall be forgetful of wisdom, and in it shall a man[134] ascend.

11 And during its completion he shall burn the house of dominion with fire, and all the race of the elect root shall be dispersed.[135]

12 Afterwards, in the seventh week, a perverse generation shall arise; abundant shall be its deeds, and all

130. Mankind shall be safe. Or, "a man will be saved" (Knibb, p. 224).
131. The Deluge.
132. Abraham.
133. Temple of Solomon.
134. Nebuchadnezzar.
135. Babylonian captivity.

its deeds perverse. During its completion, the righteous shall be selected from the everlasting plant of righteousness; and to them shall be given the sevenfold doctrine of his whole creation.

13 Afterwards there shall be another week, the eighth of righteousness, to which shall be given a sword to execute judgment and justice upon all oppressors.

14 Sinners shall be delivered up into the hands of the righteous, who during its completion shall acquire habitations by their righteousness; and the house of the great King shall be established for celebrations for ever. After this, in the ninth week, shall the judgment of righteousness be revealed to the whole world.

15 Every work of the ungodly shall disappear from the whole earth; the world shall be marked for destruction; and all men shall be on the look out for the path of integrity.

16 And after this, on the seventh day of the tenth week, there shall be an everlasting judgment, which shall be executed upon the Watchers; and a spacious eternal heaven shall spring forth in the midst of the angels.

17 The former heaven shall depart and pass away; a new heaven shall appear; and all the celestial powers shine with sevenfold splendour for ever. Afterwards likewise shall there be many weeks, which shall externally exist in goodness and in righteousness.

18 Neither shall sin be named there for ever and for ever.

19 Who is there of all the children of men, capable of hearing the voice of the Holy One without emotion?

20 Who is there capable of thinking his thoughts? Who capable of contemplating all the workmanship of heaven? Who of comprehending the deeds of heaven?

21 He may behold its animation, but not its spirit. He may be capable of conversing *respecting it,* but not of ascending *to it.* He may see all the boundaries of these things, and meditate upon them; but he can make nothing like them.

22 Who of all men is able to understand the breadth and length of the earth?

23 By whom have been seen the dimensions of all these things? Is it every man who is capable of comprehending the extent of heaven; what its elevation is, and by what it is supported?

24 How many are the numbers of the stars; and where all the luminaries remain at rest?

CHAPTER 93

1 And now let me exhort you, my children, to love righteousness, and to walk in it; for the paths of righteousness are worthy of acceptation; but the paths of iniquity shall suddenly fail, and be diminished.

2 To men of note in their generation the paths of oppression and death are revealed; but they keep far from them, and do not follow them.

3 Now, too, let me exhort you *who are* righteous, not to walk in the paths of evil and oppression, nor in

the paths of death. Approach them not, that you may not perish; but covet,

4 And choose for yourselves righteousness, and a good life.

5 Walk in the paths of peace, that you may live, and be found worthy. Retain my words in your inmost thoughts, and obliterate them not from your hearts; for I know that sinners counsel men to commit crime craftily. They are not found in every place, nor does every counsel possess a little of them.[136]

6 Woe to those who build up iniquity and oppression, and who lay the foundation of fraud; for suddenly shall they be subverted, and never obtain peace.

7 Woe to those who build up their houses with crime; for from their very foundations shall their houses be demolished, and by the sword shall they *themselves* fall. Those, too, who acquire gold and silver, shall justly and suddenly perish. Woe to you who are rich, for in your riches have you trusted; but from your riches you shall be removed; because you have not remembered the Most High in the days of your prosperity: [you shall be removed, because you have not remembered the Most High in the days of your prosperity.[137]]

8 You have committed blasphemy and iniquity; and are destined to the day of the effusion of blood, to

---

136. They are not found…them. I.e., his words.

137. These lines are evidently a repetition of the preceding, from an error in the transcription (Laurence, p. 154).

the day of darkness, and to the day of the great judgment.

9 This I declare and point out to you, that he who created you will destroy you.

10 When you fall, he will not show you mercy; but your Creator will rejoice in your destruction.

11 Let those, then, who shall be righteous among you in those days, detest sinners, and the ungodly.

CHAPTER 94

1 O that my eyes were clouds of water, that I might weep over you, and pour forth my tears like rain, and rest from the sorrow of my heart!

2 Who has permitted you to hate and to transgress? Judgment shall overtake you, ye sinners.

3 The righteous shall not fear the wicked; because God will again bring them into your power, that you may avenge yourselves of them according to your pleasure.

4 Woe to you who shall be so bound by execrations, that you cannot be released from them; the remedy being far removed from you on account of your sins. Woe to you who recompense your neighbour with evil; for you shall be recompensed according to your works.

5 Woe to you, ye false witnesses, you who aggravate iniquity; for you shall suddenly perish.

6 Woe to you, ye sinners; for you reject the righteous; for you receive or reject *at pleasure* those who *commit* iniquity; and their yoke shall prevail over you.

CHAPTER 95

1 Wait in hope, ye righteous; for suddenly shall sinners perish from before you, and you shall exercise dominion over them, according to your will.

2 In the day of the sufferings of sinners your off-spring shall be elevated, and lifted up like eagles. Your nest shall be more exalted than that of the avest; you shall ascend, and enter into the cavities of the earth, and into the clefts of the rocks for ever, like conies, from the sight of the ungodly;

3 Who shall groan over you, and weep like sirens.

4 You shall not fear those who trouble you; for restoration shall be yours; a splendid light shall shine around you, and the voice of tranquillity shall be heard from heaven. Woe to you, sinners; for your wealth makes you resemble saints, but your hearts reproach you, *knowing* that you are sinners. This word shall testify against you, for the remembrance of crime.

5 Woe to you who feed upon the glory of the corn, and drink the strength of the deepest spring, and in *the pride of* your power tread down the humble.

6 Woe to you who drink water at pleasure; for suddenly shall you be recompensed, consumed, and withered, because you have forsaken the fountain of life.

7 Woe to you who act iniquitously, fraudulently, and blasphemously; there shall be a remembrance against you for evil.

8 Woe to you, ye powerful, who with power strike

down righteousness; for the day of your destruction shall come; *while* at that very time many and good days shall be the portion of the righteous, *even* at the period of your judgment.

CHAPTER 96

1 The righteous are confident that sinners will be disgraced, and perish in the day of iniquity.

2 You shall yourselves be conscious of it; for the Most High will remember your destruction, and the angels shall rejoice over it. What will you do ye sinners, and where will you fly in the day of judgment, when you shall hear the words of the prayer of the righteous?

3 You are not like them who in this respect witness against you; you are associates of sinners.

4 In those days shall the prayers of the righteous come up before the Lord. When the day of your judgment shall arrive; and every circumstance of your iniquity be related before the great and the holy One;

5 Your faces shall be covered with shame; while every deed, strengthened by crime, shall be rejected.

6 Woe unto you, sinners, who in the midst of the sea, and on dry land, are those against whom an evil record exists. Woe to you who squander silver and gold, not obtained in righteousness, and say, We are rich, possess wealth, and have acquired everything which we can desire.

7 Now then will we do whatsoever we are disposed to do; for we have amassed silver; our barns are

full, and the husbandmen of our families are like overflowing water.

8 Like water shall your falsehood pass away; for your wealth will not be permanent, but shall suddenly ascend from you, because you have obtained it all iniquitously; to extreme malediction shall you be delivered up.

9 And now I swear to you, ye crafty, as well as simple ones; that you, often contemplating the earth, you *who are* men, clothe yourselves more elegantly than married women, and both together more so than unmarried ones,[138] everywhere *arraying yourselves* in majesty, in magnificence, in authority, and in silver: but gold, purple, honour, and wealth, like water, flow away.

10 Erudition therefore and wisdom are not theirs. Thus shall they perish, together with their riches, with all their glory, and with their honours;

11 While with disgrace, with slaughter, and in extreme penury, shall their spirits be thrust into a furnace of fire.

12 I have sworn to you, ye sinners, that neither mountain nor hill has been or shall be subservient[139] to woman.

13 Neither in this way has crime been sent down to us upon earth, but men of their own heads have

---

138. Than married women...unmarried ones. Or, "than a woman and more coloured (garments) than a girl..." (Knibb, p. 230).

139. Subservient. Literally, "a servant." Perhaps in furnishing them with treasures for ornaments (Laurence, p. 159).

invented it; and greatly shall those who give it efficiency be execrated.

14 Barrenness shall not be *previously* inflicted on woman; but on account of the work of her hands shall she die childless.

15 I have sworn to you, ye sinners, by the holy and the Great One, that all your evil deeds are disclosed in the heavens; and that none of your oppressive acts are concealed and secret.

16 Think not in your minds, neither say in your hearts, that every crime is not manifested and seen. In heaven it is daily written down before the Most High. Henceforwards shall it be manifested; for every act of oppression which you commit shall be daily recorded, until the period of your condemnation.

17 Woe to you, ye simple ones, for you shall perish in your simplicity. To the wise you will not listen, and that which is good you shall not obtain.

18 Now therefore know that you are destined to the day of destruction; nor hope that sinners shall live; but in process of time you shall die; for you are not marked for redemption;

19 But are destined to the day of the great judgment, to the day of distress, and the extreme ignominy of your souls.

20 Woe to you, ye obdurate in heart, who commit crime, and feed on blood. Whence *is it that* you feed on good things, drink, and are satiated? Is it not because our Lord, the Most High, has abundantly supplied every

good thing upon earth? To you there shall not be peace.

21 Woe to you who love the deeds of iniquity. Why do you hope for that which is good? Know that you shall be given up into the hands of the righteous; who shall cut off your necks, slay you, and show you no compassion.

22 Woe to you who rejoice in the trouble of the righteous; for a grave shall not be dug for you.

23 Woe to you who frustrate the word of the righteous; for to you there shall be no hope of life.

24 Woe to you who write down the word of falsehood, and the word of the wicked; for their falsehood they record, that they may hear and not forget folly.

25 To them there shall be no peace; but they shall surely die suddenly.

CHAPTER 97

1 Woe to them who act impiously, who laud and honour the word of falsehood. You have been lost in perdition; and have never led a virtuous life.

2 Woe to you who change the words of integrity. They transgress against the everlasting decree;[140]

3 And cause the heads of those who are not sinners to be trodden down upon the earth.

4 In those days you, O ye righteous, shall have been deemed worthy of having your prayers rise up in remembrance; and shall have deposited them in testi-

---

140. They transgress...the everlasting decree. Or, "they distort the eternal law" (Knibb, p. 232).

mony before the angels, that they might record the sins of sinners in the presence of the Most High.

5 In those days the nations shall be overthrown; but the families of the nations shall rise again in the day of perdition.

6 In those days they who become pregnant shall go forth, carry off their children, and forsake them. Their offspring shall slip from them, and while suckling them shall they forsake them; they shall never return to them, and never instruct their beloved.

7 Again I swear to you, ye sinners, that crime has been prepared for the day of blood, which never ceases.

8 They shall worship stones, and engrave golden, silver, and wooden images. They shall worship impure spirits, demons, and every idol, in temples; but no help shall be obtained for them. Their hearts shall become impious through their folly, and their eyes be blinded with mental superstition.[141] In their visionary dreams shall they be impious and superstitious, lying in all their actions, and worshipping a stone. Altogether shall they perish.

9 But in those days blessed shall they be, to whom the word of wisdom is delivered; who point out and pursue the path of the Most High; who walk in the way of righteousness, and who act not impiously with the impious.

10 They shall be saved.

---

141. **Mental superstition.** Literally, "with the fear of their hearts" (Laurence, p. 162).

11 Woe to you who expand the crime of your neighbour; for in hell shall you be slain.

12 Woe to you who lay the foundation of sin and deceit, and who are bitter on earth; for on it shall you be consumed.

13 Woe to you who build your houses by the labour of others, every part of which is constructed with brick, and with the stone of crime; I tell you, that you shall not obtain peace.

14 Woe to you who despise the extent of the everlasting inheritance of your fathers, while your souls follow after idols; for to you there shall be no tranquillity.

15 Woe to them who commit iniquity, and give aid to blasphemy, who slay their neighbour until the day of the great judgment; for your glory shall fall; malevolence shall He put into your hearts, and the spirit of his wrath shall stir *you* up, that every one of you may perish by the sword.

16 Then shall all the righteous and the holy remember your crimes.

CHAPTER 98

1 In those days shall fathers be struck down with their children in the presence of each other; and brethren with their brethren shall fall dead: until a river shall flow from their blood.

2 For a man shall not restrain his hand from his children, nor from his children's children; his mercy will be to kill them.

3 Nor shall the sinner restrain his hand from his honoured brother. From the dawn of day to the setting sun shall the slaughter continue. The horse shall wade up to his breast, and the chariot shall sink to its axle, in the blood of sinners.

CHAPTER 99

1 In those days the angels shall descend into places of concealment, and gather together in one spot all who have assisted in crime.

2 In that day shall the Most High rise up to execute the great judgment upon all sinners, and to commit the guardianship of all the righteous and holy to the holy angels, that they may protect them as the apple of an eye, until every evil and every crime be annihilated.

3 Whether *or not* the righteous sleep securely, wise men shall then truly perceive.

4 And the sons of the earth shall understand every word of that book, knowing that their riches cannot save them in the ruin of their crimes.

5 Woe to you, ye sinners, when you shall be afflicted on account of the righteous in the day of the great trouble; shall be burnt in the fire; and be recompensed according to your deeds.

6 Woe to you, ye perverted in heart, who are watchful to obtain an accurate knowledge of evil, and to discover terrors. No one shall assist you.

7 Woe to you, ye sinners; for with the words of your mouths, and with the work of your hands, have

you acted impiously; in the flame of a blazing fire shall you be burnt.

8 And now know ye, that the angels shall inquire into your conduct in heaven; of the sun, the moon, and the stars, *shall they inquire* respecting your sins; for upon earth you exercise jurisdiction over the righteous.

9 Every cloud shall bear witness against you, the snow, the dew, and the rain: for all of them shall be withholden from you, that they may not descend upon you, nor become subservient to your crimes.

10 Now then bring gifts of salutation to the rain; that, not being withholden, it may descend upon you; and to the dew, if it has received from you gold and silver. But when the frost, snow, cold, every snowy wind, and every suffering belonging to them, fall upon you, in those days you will be utterly incapable of standing before them.

CHAPTER 100

1 Attentively consider heaven, all ye progeny of heaven, and all ye works of the Most High; fear him, nor conduct yourselves criminally before him.

2 If He shut up the windows of heaven, restraining the rain and dew, that it may not descend upon earth on your account, what will you do?

3 And if He send his wrath upon you, and upon all your deeds, you are not they who can supplicate him; you who utter against his righteousness, language proud and powerful. To you there shall be no peace.

4 Do you not see the commanders of ships, how their vessels are tossed about by the waves, torn to pieces by the winds, and exposed to the greatest peril?

5 That they therefore fear, because their whole property is embarked with them on the ocean; and that they forbode evil in their hearts, because it may swallow them up, and they may perish in it?

6 Is not the whole sea, all its waters, and all its commotion, the work of him, the Most High; of him who has sealed up all its exertions, and girded it on every side with sand?

7 *Is it not* at his rebuke dried up, and alarmed; while all its fish with everything *contained* in it die? And will not you, ye sinners, who are on earth, fear him? Is not He the maker of heaven and earth, and of all things which are in them?

8 And who has given erudition and wisdom to all that move *progressive* upon the earth, and over the sea?

9 Are not the commanders of ships terrified at the ocean? And shall not sinners be terrified at the Most High?

(NO CHAPTER 101)

CHAPTER 102

1 In those days, when He shall cast the calamity of fire upon you, whither will you fly, and where will you be safe?

2 And when He sends forth his word against you, are you not spared, and terrified?

3 All the luminaries are agitated with great fear; and all the earth is spared, while it trembles, and suffers anxiety.

4 All the angels fulfil the commands *received* by them, and are desirous of being concealed from the presence of the great Glory; while the children of the earth are alarmed and troubled.

5 But you, ye sinners, are for ever accursed; to you there shall be no peace.

6 Fear not, ye souls of the righteous; but wait with patient hope for the day of your death in righteousness. Grieve not, because your souls descend in great trouble, with groaning, lamentation, and sorrow, to the receptacle of the dead. In your lifetime your bodies have not received a recompense in proportion to your goodness, but in the period of your existence have sinners existed; in the period of execration and of punishment.

7 And when you die, sinners say concerning you, "As we die, the righteous die. What profit have they in their works? Behold, like us, they expire in sorrow and in darkness. What advantage have they over us? Henceforward are we equal. What will be within their grasp, and what before their eyes for ever? For behold they are dead; and never will they again perceive the light." I say unto you, ye sinners, You have been satiated with meat and drink, with human plunder and rapine, with sin, with the acquisition of wealth and with the sight of good days. Have you not marked the

righteous, how their end is in peace? for no oppression is found in them even to the day of their death. They perish, and are as if they were not, while their souls descend in trouble to the receptacle of the dead.

CHAPTER 103

1 But now I swear to you, ye righteous, by the greatness of his splendour and his glory; by his illustrious kingdom and by his majesty, to you I swear, that I comprehend this mystery; that I have read the tablet of heaven, have seen the writing of the holy Ones, and have discovered what is written and impressed on it concerning you.

2 *I have seen* that all goodness, joy, and glory has been prepared for you, and been written down for the spirits of them who die eminently righteous and good. To you it shall be given in return for your troubles; and your portion *of happiness* shall far exceed the portion of the living.

3 The spirits of you who die in righteousness shall exist and rejoice. Their spirits shall exult; and their remembrance shall be before the face of the mighty One from generation to generation. Nor shall they now fear disgrace.

4 Woe to you, sinners, when you die in your sins; and they, who are like you, say respecting you, Blessed are these sinners. They have lived out their whole period; and now they die in happiness and in wealth. Distress and slaughter they knew not while alive; in

honour they die; nor ever in their lifetime did judgment overtake them.

5 *But* has it not been shown to them, that, *when* to the receptacle of the dead their souls shall be made to descend, their evil deeds shall become their greatest torment? Into darkness, into the snare, and into the flame, which shall burn to the great judgment, shall their spirits enter; and the great judgment shall take effect for ever and for ever.

6 Woe to you; for to you there shall be no peace. Neither can you say to the righteous, and to the good who are alive, "In the days of our trouble have we been afflicted; every *species of* trouble have we seen, and many evil things have suffered.

7 Our spirits have been consumed, lessened, and diminished.

8 We have perished; nor has there been a possibility of help for us in word or in deed: we have found none, but have been tormented and destroyed.

9 We have not expected to live day after day.

10 We hoped indeed to have been the head;

11 But we have become the tail. We have been afflicted, when we have exerted ourselves; but we have been devoured by sinners and the ungodly; their yoke has been heavy upon us.

12 Those have exercised dominion over us who detest and who goad us; and to those who hate us have we humbled our neck; but they have shown no compassion towards us.

13 We have been desirous of escaping from them, that we might fly away and be at rest; but we have found no place to which we could fly, and be secure from them. We have sought an asylum with princes in our distress, and have cried out to those who were devouring us; but our cry has not been regarded, nor have they been disposed to hear our voice;

14 But rather to assist those who plunder and devour us; those who diminish us, and hide their oppression; who remove not their yoke from us, but devour, enervate, and slay us; who conceal our slaughter, nor remember that they have lifted up their hands against us."

CHAPTER 104

1 I swear to you, ye righteous, that in heaven the angels record your goodness before the glory of the mighty One.

2 Wait with patient hope; for formerly you have been disgraced with evil and with affliction; but now shall you shine like the luminaries of heaven. You shall be seen, and the gates of heaven shall be opened to you. Your cries have cried for judgment; and it has appeared to you: for an account of all your sufferings shall be required from the princes, and from every one who has assisted your plunderers.

3 Wait with patient hope; nor relinquish your confidence; for great joy shall be yours, like that of the angels in heaven. Conduct yourselves as you may, still

you shall not be concealed in the day of the great judgment. You shall not be found like sinners; and eternal condemnation shall be far from you, so long as the world exists.

4 And now fear not, ye righteous, when you see sinners flourishing and prosperous in their ways.

5 Be not associates with them; but keep yourselves at a distance from their oppression; be you associated with the host of heaven. You, ye sinners, say, All our transgressions shall not be taken account of, and be recorded. But all your transgressions shall be recorded daily.

6 And be assured by me, that light and darkness, day and night, behold all your transgressions. Be not impious in your thoughts; lie not; surrender not the word of uprightness; lie not against the word of the holy and the mighty One; glorify not your idols; for all your lying and all your impiety is not for righteousness, but for great crime.

7 Now will I point out a mystery: Many sinners shall turn and transgress against the word of uprightness.

8 They shall speak evil things; they shall utter falsehood; execute great undertakings;[142] and compose books in their own words. But when they shall write all my words correctly in their own languages,

9 They shall neither change or diminish them; but shall write them all correctly; all which from the first

---

142. **Execute great undertakings.** Literally, "create a great creation" (Laurence, p. 173).

I have uttered concerning them.[143]

10 Another mystery also I point out. To the righteous and the wise shall be given books of joy, of integrity, and of great wisdom. To them shall books be given, in which they shall believe;

11 And in which they shall rejoice. And all the righteous shall be rewarded, who from these shall acquire the knowledge of every upright path.

CHAPTER 104A

1 In those days, saith the Lord, they shall call to the children of the earth, and make them listen to their wisdom. Show them that you are their leaders;

2 And that remuneration *shall take place* over the whole earth; for I and my Son will for ever hold communion with them in the paths of uprightness, while they are still alive. Peace shall be yours. Rejoice, children of integrity, in the truth.

CHAPTER 105

1 After a time, my son Mathusala took a wife for his son Lamech.

2 She became pregnant by him, and brought forth a child, the flesh of which was as white as snow, and red as a rose; the hair of whose head was white like wool, and long; and whose eyes were beautiful. When

---

143. Despite Enoch's mandate, his book was most certainly "changed" and "diminished" by later editors, though these fragments of it have survived.

he opened them, he illuminated all the house, like the sun; the whole house abounded with light.

3 And when he was taken from the hand of the midwife, opening also his mouth, he spoke to the Lord of righteousness. Then Lamech his father was afraid of him; and flying away came to his own father Mathusala, and said, I have begotten a son, unlike *to other children*. He is not human; but, resembling the offspring of the angels of heaven, is of a different nature *from ours,* being altogether unlike to us.

4 His eyes are *bright* as the rays of the sun; his countenance glorious, and he looks not as if he belonged to me, but to the angels.

5 I am afraid, lest something miraculous should take place on earth in his days.

6 And now, my father, let me entreat and request you to go to our progenitor Enoch, and to learn from him the truth; for his residence is with the angels.

7 When Mathusala heard the words of his son, he came to me at the extremities of the earth; for he had been informed that I was there: and he cried out.

8 I heard his voice, and went to him saying, Behold, I am *here,* my son; since thou art come to me.

9 He answered and said, On account of a great event have I come to thee; and on account of a sight difficult *to be comprehended* have I approached thee.

10 And now, my father, hear me; for to my son Lamech a child has been born, who resembles not him; and whose nature is not like the nature of man. His

colour is whiter than snow; he is redder than the rose; the hair of his head is whiter than white wool; his eyes are like the rays of the sun; and when he opened them he illuminated the whole house.

11 When also he was taken from the hand of the midwife, he opened his mouth, and blessed the Lord of heaven.

12 His father Lamech feared, and fled to me, believing not that *the child* belonged to him, but that he resembled the angels of heaven. And behold I am come to thee, that thou mightest point out to me the truth.

13 Then I, Enoch, answered and said, The Lord will effect a new thing upon the earth. This have I explained, and seen in a vision. I have shown thee that *in* the generations of Jared my father, those who were from heaven disregarded the word of the Lord. Behold they committed crimes; laid aside their class, and intermingled with women. With them also they transgressed; married with them, and begot children.[144]

14 A great destruction therefore shall come upon all the earth; a deluge, a great destruction, shall take place in one year.

15 This child which is born to you shall survive on the earth, and his three sons shall be saved with him. When all mankind who are on earth shall die, he shall be safe.

16 And his posterity shall beget on the earth giants,

---

144. After this verse, one Greek papyrus adds, "who are not like spiritual beings, but creatures of flesh" (Milik, p. 210).

not spiritual, but carnal. Upon the earth shall a great punishment be inflicted, and it shall be washed from all corruption. Now therefore inform thy son Lamech, that he who is born is his child in truth; and he shall call his name *Noah,* for he shall be to you a survivor. He and his children shall be saved from the corruption which shall take place in the world; from all the sin and from all the iniquity which shall be consummated on earth in his days. Afterwards shall greater impiety take place than that which had been before consummated on the earth; for I am acquainted with holy mysteries, which the Lord himself has discovered and explained to me; and which I have read in the tablets of heaven.

17 In them I saw it written, that generation after generation shall transgress, until a righteous race shall arise; until transgression and crime perish from off the earth; until all goodness come upon it.

18 And now, my son, go tell thy son Lamech,

19 That the child which is born is his child in truth; and that there is no deception.

20 When Mathusala heard the word of his father Enoch, who had shown him every secret thing, he returned with understanding, and called the name of that child Noah; because he was to console the earth on account of all its destruction.

21 Another book, which Enoch wrote for his son Mathusala, and for those who should come after him, and preserve their purity of conduct in the latter days. You, who have laboured, shall wait in those days, until

the evil doers be consumed, and the power of the guilty be annihilated. Wait, until sin pass away; for their names shall be blotted out of the holy books; their seed shall be destroyed, and their spirits slain. They shall cry out and lament in the invisible waste, and in the bottomless fire shall they burn.[145] There I perceived, as it were, a cloud which could not be seen through; for from the depth of it I was unable to look upwards. I beheld also a flame of fire blazing brightly, and, as it were, glittering mountains whirled around, and agitated from side to side.

22 Then I inquired of one of the holy angels who was with me, and said, What is this splendid *object?* For it is not heaven, but a flame of fire alone which blazes; and *in it there is* the clamour of exclamation, of woe, and of great suffering.

23 He said, There, into that place which thou beholdest, shall be thrust the spirits of sinners and blasphemers; of those who shall do evil, and who shall pervert all which God has spoken by the mouth of the prophets; all which they ought to do.

For respecting these things there shall be writings and impressions above in heaven, that the angels may read them and know what shall happen both to sinners and to the spirits of the humble; to those who have suffered in their bodies, but have been rewarded by God; who have been injuriously treated by wicked

---

145. **In the bottomless fire shall they burn.** Literally, "in the fire shall they burn, where there is no earth" (Laurence, p. 178).

men; who have loved God; who have been attached neither to gold nor silver, nor to any good thing in the world, but have given their bodies to torment;

24 To those who from the period of their birth have not been covetous of earthly riches; but have regarded themselves as a breath passing away.

25 Such has been their conduct; and much has the Lord tried them; and their spirits have been found pure, that they might bless his name. All their blessings have I related in a book; and He has rewarded them; for they have been found to love heaven with an everlasting aspiration. *God has said,* While they have been trodden down by wicked men, they have heard from them revilings and blasphemies; and have been ignominiously treated, while they were blessing me. And now will I call the spirits of the good from the generation of light, and will change those who have been born in darkness; who have not in their bodies been recompensed with glory, as their faith may have merited.

26 I will bring them into the splendid light of those who love my holy name: and I will place each of them on a throne of glory, of glory *peculiarly* his own, and they shall be at rest during unnumbered periods. Righteous is the judgment of God;

27 For to the faithful shall he give faith in the habitations of uprightness. They shall see those, who having been born in darkness unto darkness shall be cast; while the righteous shall be at rest. Sinners shall cry out, beholding them, while they exist in splendour and

proceed forwards to the days and periods prescribed to them.

[Here ends the vision of Enoch the prophet. May the benediction of his prayer, and the gift of his appointed period, be with his beloved! Amen. *R. Laurence*]

BIBLICAL PARALLELS
TO THE
BOOK OF ENOCH

THE BATTLE OF THE ANGELS

BIBLICAL PARALLELS
TO THE BOOK OF ENOCH

ENOCH 1:6 ... Judgment shall come upon all, even upon all the righteous.

I PET. 4:17 For the time is come that judgment must begin at the house of God: and if it first begin at us, what shall the end be of them that obey not the gospel of God?

ENOCH 2 *Behold, he comes with ten thousands of his saints, to execute judgment upon them,* and destroy the wicked, and reprove all the carnal for everything which *the sinful and ungodly* have done, and committed against him.

26:2 Then Uriel, one of the holy angels who were with me, replied, This valley is the accursed of the accursed for ever. Here shall

JUDE 14 And Enoch also, the seventh from Adam, prophesied of these, saying, *Behold, the Lord cometh with ten thousands of his saints,*

15 *To execute judgment upon all,* and to convince all that are ungodly among them of all their ungodly deeds which they have ungodly committed, and of *all their hard speeches which ungodly sinners have*

be collected *all who utter with their mouths unbecoming language against God, and speak harsh things of His glory.*

spoken against him.*

ENOCH 6:9 The elect shall possess light, joy, and peace; *and they shall inherit the earth.*

MATT. 5:5 Blessed are the meek: *for they shall inherit the earth.*

ENOCH 9:3 ... Then they said to their Lord, the King, Thou art *Lord of lords, God of gods, King of kings.* The throne of thy glory is for ever and ever, and for ever and ever is thy name sanctified and glorified. *Thou art blessed and glorified.*

4 *Thou hast made all things; thou possessest power over all things; and all things are open and manifest before thee.* Thou beholdest all things, and nothing can be concealed from thee.

REV. 17:14 ... for he is *Lord of lords, and King of kings:* and they that are with him are called, and chosen, and faithful.

4:11 *Thou art worthy, O Lord, to receive glory and honour and power: for thou hast created all things,* and for thy pleasure they are and were created.

HEB. 4:13 Neither is there any creature that is not manifest in his sight: but *all things are naked and opened unto the eyes of him* with whom we have to do.

ENOCH 10:6 Again the Lord said to Raphael, Bind Azazyel hand and foot; cast him into darkness; and

JUDE 6 And the angels which kept not their first estate, but left their own habitation, *he hath re-*

opening the desert which is in Dudael, cast him in there.

7 Throw upon him hurled and pointed stones, covering him with darkness;

8 There shall he remain for ever; cover his face, that he may not see the light.

9 And in the great day of judgment let him be cast into the fire.

15 To Michael likewise the Lord said, Go and announce his crime to Samyaza, and to the others who are with him, who have been associated with women, that they might be polluted with all their impurity. And when all their sons shall be slain, when they shall see the perdition of their beloved, *bind them for seventy generations underneath the earth, even to the day of judgment,* and of consummation, until the judgment, the effect of which will last for ever, be completed.

served in everlasting chains under darkness unto the judgment of the great day.

II PET. 2:4 ...God spared not the angels that sinned, *but cast them down to hell, and delivered them into chains of darkness, to be reserved unto judgment.*

REV. 20:10 And the devil that deceived them was cast into the *lake of fire and brimstone,* where the beast and the false prophet are, and shall be tormented day and night for ever and ever.

16 *Then shall they be taken away into the lowest depths of the fire in torments; and in confinement shall they be shut up for ever.*

17 Immediately after this shall he, together with them, burn and perish; *they shall be bound until the consummation of many generations.*

ENOCH 14:23 No angel was capable of penetrating to view the face of Him, the Glorious and the Effulgent; *nor could any mortal behold Him. A fire was flaming around Him.*

24 ...*not one* of those who surrounded Him *was capable of approaching Him*...

I TIM. 6:16 Who only hath immortality, *dwelling in the light which no man can approach unto; whom no man hath seen, nor can see*...

ENOCH 14:24 ...among the *myriads of myriads* who were before Him.

REV. 5:11 ...and the number of them was *ten thousand times ten thousand,* and thousands of thousands.

ENOCH 18:16 *The stars which roll over fire* are

JUDE 13 ...*wandering stars,* to whom is reserved

those which transgressed the commandment of God before their time arrived...

the blackness of darkness for ever.

ENOCH 19:2 And being numerous in appearance made men profane, and caused them to err; so that *they sacrificed to devils as to gods.*

I COR. 10:20 But I say, that the things which the Gentiles sacrifice, *they sacrifice to devils, and not to God...*

ENOCH 21:5 Where I beheld the operation of a great fire blazing and glittering, in the midst of which there was a division. Columns of fire struggled together to the end of *the abyss,* and deep was their descent. But *neither its measurement nor magnitude was I able to discover; neither could I perceive its origin.* Then I exclaimed, How terrible is this place, and how difficult to explore!

6 Uriel, one of the holy angels who was with me, answered and said: Enoch, why art thou alarmed and amazed at this terrific place, at the sight of this place of suffering? *This,* he said, *is*

REV. 20:1 And I saw an angel come down from heaven, having the key of *the bottomless pit* and a great chain in his hand.

2 And he laid hold on the dragon, that old serpent, which is the Devil, and Satan, and bound him a thousand years,

3 And *cast him into the bottomless pit, and shut him up, and set a seal upon him...*

the prison of the angels; and here they are kept for ever.

ENOCH 22:9 ... Three separations have been made between the spirits of the dead...

10 Namely, by a chasm, by water, and by light above it.

12 Here their souls are separated.

LUKE 16:22 And it came to pass, that the beggar died, and was carried by the angels into Abraham's bosom: the rich man also died, and was buried;

23 And in hell he lift up his eyes, being in torments, and seeth Abraham afar off, and Lazarus in his bosom.

24 And he cried and said, Father Abraham, have mercy on me, and send Lazarus, that he may dip the tip of his finger in water, and cool my tongue; for I am tormented in this flame.

25 But Abraham said, Son, remember that thou in thy lifetime receivedst thy good things, and likewise Lazarus evil things: but now he is comforted, and thou art tormented.

26 And beside all this, *between us and you there is a great gulf fixed: so that they which would pass from hence to you cannot; neither* *can they pass to us, that would come from thence.*

ENOCH 24:9 And that tree of an agreeable smell, not one of carnal odour, there shall be no power to touch, until the period of the great judgment. When all shall be punished and consumed for ever, *this shall be bestowed on the righteous and humble. The fruit of this tree shall be given to the elect.* For towards the north life shall be planted in the holy place, towards the habitation of the everlasting King.

11 And I blessed the Lord of glory, the everlasting King, because *He has prepared this tree for the saints,* formed it, and declared that He would give it to them.

REV. 22:2 In the midst of the street of it, and on either side of the river, was there the tree of life, which bare twelve manner of fruits, and yielded her fruit every month: and the leaves of the tree were for the healing of the nations.

2:7 He that hath an ear, let him hear what the Spirit saith unto the churches; *To him that overcometh will I give to eat of the tree of life,* which is in the midst of the paradise of God.

22:14 Blessed are they that do his commandments, *that they may have right to the tree of life,* and may enter in through the gates into the city.

ENOCH 37:1 ...Hear from the beginning, and understand to the end, the holy things which I utter in the presence of the *Lord of spirits.*

2 ...Until the present

HEB. 12:9 ...shall we not much rather be in subjection unto the *Father of spirits,* and live?

period never has there been given before the *Lord of spirits* that which I have received... according to the pleasure of the *Lord of spirits*...

38:2 ... good works duly weighed by the *Lord of spirits*... those who have rejected the *Lord of spirits?*

4 ... the light of the countenances of the holy, the righteous, and the elect, has been seen by the *Lord of spirits.*

6 Nor thenceforwards shall any obtain commiseration from the *Lord of spirits*...

ENOCH 38:2 ... and where the place of rest for those who have rejected the Lord of spirits? *It would have been better for them, had they never been born.*

MATT. 26:24 ... Woe unto that man by whom the Son of man is betrayed! *it had been good for that man if he had not been born.*

ENOCH 39:1 In those days *shall the elect and holy race descend from the upper heavens,* and their seed shall then be with the sons of men.

I TIM. 5:21 I charge thee before God, and the Lord Jesus Christ, and *the elect angels*...

ENOCH 39:3 A cloud then snatched me up, and *the wind raised me above the surface of the earth, placing me at the extremity of the heavens.*

4 There I saw another vision; *I saw the habitations and couches of the saints.* There my eyes beheld their habitations with the angels, and their couches with the holy ones. They were entreating, supplicating, and praying for the sons of men; while righteousness like water flowed before them, and mercy like dew was scattered over the earth. And thus shall it be with them for ever and for ever.

7 Their residence I beheld under the wings of the Lord of spirits. All the holy and the elect sung before him, in appearance like a blaze of fire; *their mouths being full of blessings, and their lips glorifying the name of the Lord of spirits.* And righteousness incessantly dwelt before him.

II COR. 12:1 It is not expedient for me doubtless to glory. I will come to visions and revelations of the Lord.

2 I knew a man in Christ above fourteen years ago, *(whether in the body, I cannot tell; or whether out of the body, I cannot tell: God knoweth;) such an one caught up to the third heaven.*

3 And I knew such a man, (whether in the body, or out of the body, I cannot tell: God knoweth;)

4 How that he was caught up into paradise, and heard unspeakable words, which it is not lawful for a man to utter.

JOHN 14:2 *In my Father's house are many mansions:* if it were not so, I would have told you. I go to prepare a place for you.

REV. 19:1 And after these things I heard a great voice of much people in heaven, saying, *Alleluia; Salvation, and glory, and honour, and power, unto the Lord our God.*

ENOCH 40:2 On the four wings likewise of the Lord of spirits, on the four sides, I perceived others, besides those who were standing before him. Their names, too, I know; because the angel, who proceeded with me, declared them to me, discovering to me every secret thing.

3 Then I heard *the voices of those upon the four sides magnifying the Lord of glory.*

4 The first voice blessed the Lord of spirits for ever and for ever.

5 The second voice I heard blessing the elect One, and the elect who suffer on account of the Lords of spirits.

6 The third voice I heard petitioning and praying for those who dwell upon earth, and supplicate the name of the Lord of spirits.

7 The fourth voice I heard expelling *the impious angels,* and prohibiting them from entering into presence of the Lord of spirits, *to pre-*

REV. 4:6 And before the throne there was a sea of glass like unto crystal: and in the midst of the throne, and round about the throne, were *four beasts* full of eyes before and behind.

7 And the first beast was like a lion, and the second beast like a calf, and the third beast had a face as a man, and the fourth beast was like a flying eagle.

8 And the four beasts had each of them six wings about him; and they were full of eyes within: and *they rest not day and night, saying, Holy, holy, holy, Lord God Almighty, which was, and is, and is to come.*

REV. 12:10 ...for *the accuser of our brethren is* cast down, *which accused them* before our God day and night.

fer accusations against [*i.e.,* to accuse] *the inhabitants of the earth.*

8   After this I besought the angel of peace, who proceeded with me, to explain all that was concealed. I said to him, Who are those whom I have seen on the four sides, and whose words I have heard and written down?

ENOCH 40:9   ... And the fourth, who presides over repentance, and the hope of *those who will inherit eternal life...*

MATT. 19:29   And every one that hath forsaken houses, or brethren, or sisters, or father, or mother, or wife, or children, or lands, for my name's sake, shall receive an hundredfold, and *shall inherit everlasting life.*

ENOCH 45:3   *In that day shall the Elect One sit upon a throne of glory;* and *shall choose their conditions and countless habitations* (while their spirits within them shall be strengthened, when they behold my Elect One), shall choose them for those who

MATT. 25:31   When the Son of man shall come in his glory, and all the holy angels with him, *then shall he sit upon the throne of his glory:*

32   And before him shall be gathered all nations: *and he shall separate them one from another,* as a shepherd

have fled for protection to my holy and glorious name.

ENOCH 45:4 In that day I will cause *my Elect One* to dwell in the midst of them; *will change the face of heaven;* will bless it, and illuminate it for ever.

5 *I will also change the face of the earth;* will bless it; and cause those whom I have elected to dwell upon it...

ENOCH 46:2 ...This is the Son of man...who will reveal all the treasures of that which is concealed...

ENOCH 46:4 *He shall hurl kings from their thrones and their dominions;* because they will not exalt and praise him, nor humble themselves before him, by whom their kingdoms were granted to them. *The countenance likewise of the mighty shall He cast down,* filling them with confusion. Darkness shall be their habitation,

divideth his sheep from the goats.

LUKE 9:35 And there came a voice out of the cloud, saying, This is my Son, *the Elect One:* hear him.

II PET. 3:13 Nevertheless we, according to his promise, *look for new heavens and a new earth,* wherein dwelleth righteousness.

COL. 2:2 ...of Christ;

3 In whom are hid all the treasures of wisdom and knowledge.

LUKE 1:52 *He hath put down the mighty from their seats,* and exalted them of low degree.

and worms shall be their bed; nor from that their bed shall they hope to be again raised, because they exalted not the name of the Lord of spirits.

ENOCH 47:1 In that day the prayer of the holy and the righteous, and the blood of the righteous, shall ascend from the earth into the presence of the Lord of spirits.

2 In that day shall the holy ones assemble, who dwell above the heavens, and with united voice petition, supplicate, praise, laud, and bless the name of the Lord of spirits, on account of the blood of the righteous which has been shed; that the prayer of the righteous may not be intermitted before the Lord of spirits; *that for them he would execute judgment; and that his patience may not endure for ever.*

ENOCH 47:3 At that time I beheld *the Ancient of*

LUKE 18:7 And *shall not God avenge his own elect,* which cry day and night unto him, *though he bear long with them?*

II PET. 3:9 The Lord is not slack concerning his promise, as some men count slackness; but is longsuffering to us-ward, not willing that any should perish, but that all should come to repentance.

REV. 6:10 And they cried with a loud voice, *saying, How long, O Lord, holy and true, dost thou not judge and avenge our blood on them that dwell on the earth?*

DAN. 7:9 I beheld till the thrones were cast

days, while he sat upon the throne of his glory, while *the book of the living was opened in his presence,* and while all the powers which were above the heavens stood around and before him.

50:1 In those days *shall the earth deliver up from her womb, and hell deliver up from hers,* that which it has received; and destruction shall restore that which it owes.

2 He shall select the righteous and holy from among them; for the day of their salvation has approached.

54:12 *In those days shall the mouth of hell be opened, into which they shall be immerged;* hell shall destroy and swallow up sinners from the face of the elect.

down, and *the Ancient of days* did sit, whose garment was white as snow, and the hair of his head like the pure wool: his throne was like the fiery flame, and his wheels as burning fire.

10 A fiery stream issued and came forth from before him: thousand thousands ministered unto him, and ten thousand times ten thousand stood before him: *the judgment was set, and the books were opened.*

REV. 20:11 And I saw a great white throne, and him that sat on it, from whose face the earth and the heaven fled away...

12 And I saw the dead, small and great, stand before God; and the books were opened: and *another book was opened, which is the book of life:* and the dead were judged out of those things which were written in the books, according to their works.

13 *And the sea gave up*

the dead which were in it; and death and hell delivered up the dead which were in them: and they were judged every man according to their works.

14 And death and hell were *cast into the lake of fire.* This is the second death.

15 And whosoever was not found written in the book of life was *cast into the lake of fire.*

ENOCH 48:1 In that place I beheld *a fountain of righteousness, which never failed,* encircled by many springs of wisdom. Of these all the thirsty drank, and were filled with wisdom, having their habitation with the righteous, the elect, and the holy.

JOHN 4:14 But whosoever drinketh of the water that I shall give him shall never thirst; but the water that I shall give him shall be in him *a well of water springing up into everlasting life.*

REV. 7:17 For the Lamb which is in the midst of the throne shall feed them, and shall lead them unto *living fountains of waters:* and God shall wipe away all tears from their eyes.

REV. 21:6 And he said unto me, It is done. I am

Alpha and Omega, the beginning and the end. *I will give unto him that is athirst of the fountain of the water of life freely.*

ENOCH 48:6 ...They have hated and rejected *this world of iniquity, and have detested all its works and ways...*

GAL. 1:4 Who gave himself for our sins, that he might deliver us from *this present evil world...*

I JOHN 2:15 *Love not the world, neither the things that are in the world.* If any man love the world, the love of the Father is not in him.

ENOCH 48:8 For in the day of their anxiety and trouble their souls shall not be saved; and they shall be in subjection to those whom I have chosen.

9 I will cast them like hay into the fire, and like lead into the water. *Thus shall they burn in the presence of the righteous, and sink in the presence of the holy...*

REV. 14:9 And the third angel followed them, saying with a loud voice, If any man worship the beast and his image, and receive his mark in his forehead, or in his hand,

10 The same shall drink of the wine of the wrath of God, which is poured out without mixture into the cup of his indignation; and *he shall be tormented with fire and brimstone in the presence of the holy angels,* and in the presence of the Lamb.

ENOCH 48:11 ... *for they have denied the Lord of spirits, and his Messiah.*

15:2 *Wherefore have you forsaken the lofty and holy heaven,* ... and have lain with women; have *defiled yourselves with the daughters of men;* have taken to yourselves wives; have acted like the sons of the earth, and have begotten an impious offspring?

JUDE 4 For there are *certain men crept in unawares,* who were before of old ordained to this condemnation, ungodly men, *turning the grace of our God into lasciviousness, and denying the only Lord God, and our Lord Jesus Christ.*

ENOCH 48A:4 ... for the Elect One is in the presence of the Lord of spirits, *according to his own pleasure.*

EPH. 1:9 Having made known unto us the mystery of his will, *according to his good pleasure* which he hath purposed in himself.

ENOCH 50:2 ... the day of their salvation has approached.

LUKE 21:28 ... your redemption draweth nigh.

ENOCH 50:4 ... all the righteous shall become angels in heaven.

MATT. 22:30 For in the resurrection they ... are as the angels of God in heaven.

ENOCH 50:5 Their countenance shall be bright with joy; for in those days shall the Elect One be exalted.

MATT. 13:43 Then shall the righteous shine forth as the sun in the kingdom of their Father.

ENOCH 53:6 ...they became ministers of Satan, and *seduced those who dwell upon earth.*

REV. 13:14 And *deceiveth them that dwell on the earth* by the means of those miracles which he had power to do in the sight of the beast...

ENOCH 56:5 ...darkness has passed away. There shall be light interminable.

I JOHN 2:8 ...the darkness is past, and the true light now shineth.

ENOCH 60:13 He shall call to every power of the heavens, to all the holy above, and to the power of God. The Cherubim, the Seraphim, and the Ophanin, all the angels of power, and *all the angels of the Lords, namely, of the Elect One...*

II THESS. 1:7 And to you who are troubled rest with us, when *the Lord Jesus shall be revealed from heaven with his mighty angels.*

ENOCH 61:4 *The word of his mouth shall destroy all the sinners and all the ungodly,* who shall perish at his presence.

5 In that day shall all *the kings, the princes, the exalted, and those who possess the earth,* stand up, behold, and perceive, that he

II THESS. 2:8 And then shall that Wicked be revealed, *whom the Lord shall consume with the spirit of his mouth,* and shall destroy with the brightness of his coming.

II THESS. 1:8 In flaming fire taking vengeance on them that know not God...

is sitting on the throne of his glory; that before him the saints shall be judged in righteousness;

6 And that nothing, which shall be spoken before him, shall be spoken in vain.

7 *Trouble shall come upon them, as upon a woman in travail,* whose labour is severe, when her child comes to the mouth of the womb, and she finds it difficult to bring forth.

8 One portion of them shall look upon another. They shall be astonished, and shall humble their countenance;

9 *And trouble shall seize them, when they shall behold this Son of woman sitting upon the throne of his glory.*

9 Who shall be punished with everlasting destruction from the presence of the Lord, and from the glory of his power.

REV. 6:15 And *the kings of the earth, and the great men, and the rich men, and the chief captains, and the mighty men,* and every bondman, and every free man, hid themselves in the dens and in the rocks of the mountains;

16 And said to the mountains and rocks, *Fall on us, and hide us from the face of him that sitteth on the throne,* and from the wrath of the Lamb:

17 For the great day of his wrath is come; and who shall be able to stand?

I THESS. 5:3 For when they shall say, Peace and safety; *then sudden destruction cometh upon them, as travail upon a woman with child;* and they shall not escape.

MATT. 24:30 ...and *then shall all the tribes of*

the earth mourn, and they shall see the Son of man coming in the clouds of heaven with power and great glory.

ENOCH 61:10 Then shall the kings, the princes, and all who possess the earth, glorify him who has dominion over all things... *whom the Most High preserved in the presence of his power...*

MATT. 28:18 And Jesus came and spake unto them, saying, *All power is given unto me in heaven and in earth.*

ENOCH 61:17 And with this Son of man shall they dwell, eat, lie down, and rise up, for ever and ever.

REV. 3:20 Behold, I stand at the door, and knock: if any man hear my voice, and open the door, I will come in to him, and will sup with him, and he with me.

ENOCH 62:11 In his judgments he pays *no respect to persons...*

ACTS 10:34 Then Peter opened his mouth, and said, Of a truth I perceive that *God is no respecter of persons.*

ROM. 2:11 For *there is no respect of persons with God.*

EPH. 6:9 And, ye masters, do the same things

unto them, forbearing threatening: knowing that your Master also is in heaven; *neither is there respect of persons* with him.

COL. 3:25 But he that doeth wrong shall receive for the wrong which he hath done: and *there is no respect of persons*.

ENOCH 66:5 I beheld that valley in which there was great perturbation, and where the waters were troubled.

6 And when all this was effected, from the *fluid mass of fire*, and the perturbation which prevailed in that place, there arose a strong smell of sulphur, which became mixed with the waters; and *the valley of the angels*, who had been guilty of seduction, *burned underneath its soil*.

7 Through that valley also *rivers of fire were flowing, to which those angels shall be condemned*, who seduced the inhabitants of the earth.

MATT. 13:42 And shall cast them into *a furnace of fire:* there shall be wailing and gnashing of teeth.

25:41 Then shall he say also unto them on the left hand, *Depart from me, ye cursed, into everlasting fire, prepared for the devil and his angels.*

REV. 20:10 And the devil that deceived them was cast into the *lake of fire and brimstone,* where the beast and the false prophet are, and shall be tormented day and night for ever and ever.

ENOCH 68:39 He sat upon the throne of his glory; and the principal part of the judgment was assigned to him, the Son of man.

JOHN 5:22 For the Father judgeth no man, but hath committed all judgment unto the Son.

ENOCH 70:13 Then I fell upon my face, while all *my flesh was dissolved, and my spirit became changed.*

14 I cried out with a loud voice, with a powerful spirit, blessing, glorifying, and exalting.

15 And *those blessings,* which proceeded from my mouth, *became acceptable* in the presence of the Ancient of days.

HEB. 11:5 By faith *Enoch was translated* that he should not see death; and was not found, because God had translated him: for before his translation he had this testimony, that *he pleased God.*

ENOCH 76:2 ...frequently there descends he who is *blessed for ever.*

ROM. 9:5 ...of whom as concerning the flesh Christ came, who is over all, God *blessed for ever.*

II COR. 11:31 The God and Father of our Lord Jesus Christ, which is *blessed for evermore...*

ENOCH 79:1 In those days Uriel answered and said to me, Behold, I have

MATT. 24:7 For nation shall rise against nation, and kingdom against king-

showed thee all things, O Enoch;

2 And all things have I revealed to thee. Thou seest the sun, the moon, and those which conduct the stars of heaven, which cause all their operations, seasons, and arrivals to return.

3 *In the days of sinners the years shall be shortened.*

4 Their *seed shall be backward* in their prolific soil; and everything done on earth shall be subverted, and disappear in its season. *The rain shall be restrained,* and heaven shall stand still.

5 In those days *the fruits of the earth shall be late,* and not flourish in their season; and in their season the fruits of the trees shall be withholden.

6 *The moon shall change its laws,* and not be seen at its proper period. But in those days shall heaven be seen; and barrenness dom: and there shall be *famines, and pestilences, and earthquakes,* in divers places.

21 For then shall be *great tribulation,* such as was not since the beginning of the world to this time, no, nor ever shall be.

22 And except those days should be shortened, there should no flesh be saved: but for the elect's sake *those days shall be shortened.*

29 Immediately after the tribulation of those days *shall the sun be darkened, and the moon shall not give her light, and the stars shall fall from heaven,* and the powers of the heavens shall be shaken.

shall take place in the borders of the great chariots in the west. Heaven shall shine more than when illuminated by the orders of light; while *many chiefs among the stars of authority shall err,* perverting their ways and works.

7 Those shall not appear in their season, who command them, and all the classes of the stars shall be shut up against sinners.

ENOCH 85:1 Again I looked attentively, while sleeping, and surveyed heaven above.

2 And behold a single star fell from heaven.

ENOCH 88:92 I saw, too, that *he forsook the house of their fathers,* and their tower; giving them all into the power of lions to tear and devour them; into the power of every beast.

REV. 9:1 ... I saw a star fall from heaven unto the earth ...

LUKE 13:35 *Behold, your house is left unto you desolate:* and verily I say unto you, Ye shall not see me, until the time come when ye shall say, Blessed is he that cometh in the name of the Lord.

MATT. 23:38 *Behold, your house is left unto you desolate.*

ENOCH 89:29 And I saw a throne erected in a delectable land;

30 Upon this sat the Lord of the sheep, who received all *the sealed books;*

31 Which were *open before him.*

REV. 20:12 And I saw the dead, small and great, stand before God; *and the books were opened:* and another book was opened, which is the book of life: and the dead were judged out of those things which were written in the books, according to their works.

ENOCH 89:32 Then the Lord called *the first seven white ones,* and commanded them to bring before him the first of the first stars, which preceded the stars whose form partly resembled that of horses; the first star, which fell down first; and they brought them all before him.

REV. 1:4 ...Grace be unto you, and peace, from him which is, and which was, and which is to come; and from *the seven Spirits which are before his throne.*

4:5 And out of the throne proceeded lightnings and thunderings and voices: and there were seven lamps of fire burning before the throne, which are the seven Spirits of God.

ENOCH 89:33 ...Then the seventy shepherds were judged, and being found guilty, were *thrust into the flaming abyss.*

REV. 20:15 And whosoever was not found written in the book of life was *cast into the lake of fire.*

ENOCH 89:39 I also saw, that the Lord of the sheep produced *a new house,* great, and loftier than the former, which he bounded by the former circular spot. All its pillars were new, and its ivory new, as well as more abundant than the former ancient ivory, which he had brought out.

REV. 3:12 Him that overcometh will I make a pillar in the temple of my God, and he shall go no more out: and I will write upon him the name of my God, and the name of the city of my God, which is *new Jerusalem,* which cometh down out of heaven from my God: and I will write upon him my new name.

HEB. 11:10 For he looked for a city which hath foundations, whose builder and maker is God.

12:22 But ye are come unto mount Sion, and unto the *city of the living God,* the heavenly Jerusalem, and to an innumerable company of angels.

ENOCH 89:41 Then those three, who were *clothed in white,* and who, holding me by my hand, had before caused me to ascend...

REV. 3:5 He that overcometh, the same shall be *clothed in white raiment;* and I will not blot out his name out of the book of life, but I will confess his name before my Father, and before his angels.

ENOCH 90:5 Approach not integrity with a double heart; nor be associated with *double-minded men*...

JAMES 1:8 *A double-minded man* is unstable in all his ways.

ENOCH 91:3 ...In goodness and in righteousness shall he exist, and shall *walk in everlasting light*...

I JOHN 1:7 But if we *walk in the light,* as he is in the light, we have fellowship one with another...

ENOCH 92:17 The former heaven shall depart and pass away; a new heaven shall appear...

REV. 21:1 And I saw a new heaven and a new earth: for the first heaven and the first earth were passed away...

ENOCH 93:1 ...for the paths of righteousness are *worthy of acceptation*...

I TIM. 1:15 This is a faithful saying, and *worthy of all acceptation,* that Christ Jesus came into the world to save sinners...

ENOCH 93:7 ...*Woe to you who are rich,* for in your riches have you trusted; but from your riches you shall be removed; because you have not remembered the Most High in the days of your prosperity...

LUKE 6:24 But *woe unto you that are rich!* for ye have received your consolation.

JAMES 5:1 Go to now, ye rich men, weep and howl for your miseries that shall come upon you.

ENOCH 96:6 ...Woe to you who squander silver

LUKE 12:16 And he spake a parable unto them,

and gold, not obtained in righteousness, and say, We are rich, possess wealth, and have acquired everything which we can desire.

7 *Now then will we do whatsoever we are disposed to do;* for we have amassed silver; our barns are full, and the husbandmen of our families are like overflowing water.

25 To them there shall be no peace; *but they shall surely die suddenly.*

ENOCH 97:4 In those days you, O ye righteous, shall have been deemed worthy of having *your prayers rise up in remembrance;* and shall have deposited them in testimony

saying, The ground of a certain rich man brought forth plentifully:

17 And he thought within himself, saying, What shall I do, because I have no room where to bestow my fruits?

18 And he said, This will I do: I will pull down my barns, and build greater; and there will I bestow all my fruits and my goods.

19 *And I will say to my soul,* Soul, thou hast much goods laid up for many years; *take thine ease, eat, drink, and be merry.*

20 But God said unto him, *Thou fool, this night thy soul shall be required of thee:* then whose shall those things be, which thou hast provided?

ACTS 10:4 And when he looked on him, he was afraid, and said, What is it, Lord? And he said unto him, *Thy prayers and thine alms are come up for a memorial before God.*

before the angels, that they might record the sins of sinners in the presence of the Most High.

ENOCH 97:8 *They shall worship stones, and engrave golden, silver, and wooden images.* They shall worship impure spirits, demons, and every idol, in temples; but no help shall be obtained for them. Their hearts shall become impious through their folly, and their eyes be blinded with mental superstition. In their visionary dreams shall they be impious and superstitious, lying in all their actions, and worshipping a stone. Altogether shall they perish.

REV. 9:20 And the rest of the men which were not killed by these plagues yet repented not of the works of their hands, that *they should not worship devils, and idols of gold, and silver, and brass, and stone, and of wood:* which neither can see, nor hear, nor walk.

ENOCH 98:3 ...*The horse shall wade up to his breast,* and the chariot shall sink to its axle, *in the blood of sinners.*

REV. 14:20 And the winepress was trodden without the city, and *blood* came out of the winepress, *even unto the horse bridles*...

ENOCH 104:7 Now will I point out a mystery: *Many sinners shall turn and trans-*

I TIM. 4:1 Now the Spirit speaketh expressly, that in the latter times *some* gress against the word of uprightness.

8 *They shall speak evil things; they shall utter falsehood;* execute great undertakings; and compose books in their own words.

ENOCH 105:25 ... And now will I call the spirits of the good from *the generation of light,* and will change those who have been born in darkness...

shall depart from the faith, giving heed to seducing spirits, and doctrines of devils;

2 *Speaking lies in hypocrisy;* having their conscience seared with a hot iron.

EPH. 5:8 For ye were sometimes darkness, but now are ye light in the Lord: walk as *children of light.*

I THESS. 5:5 Ye are all the *children of light,* and the children of the day: we are not of the night, nor of darkness.

JOHN 12:36 While ye have light, believe in the light, that ye may be the *children of light.*

LUKE 16:8 ... the children of this world are in their generation wiser than the *children of light.*

ENOCH 105:26 I will bring them into the splendid light of those who love my holy name: and *I will place each of them on a*

REV. 3:21 To him that overcometh will *I grant to sit with me in my throne,* even as I also overcame, and am set down with my

throne of glory, of glory peculiarly his own...

Father in his throne.

MATT. 19:28 ...Verily I say unto you, That ye which have followed me, in the regeneration when the Son of man shall sit in the throne of his glory, *ye also shall sit upon twelve thrones, judging the twelve tribes of Israel.*

Concealed References
to the Watchers
(and Nephilim)
in Scripture

DAVID AND GOLIATH

CONCEALED REFERENCES TO THE WATCHERS (AND NEPHILIM) IN SCRIPTURE

Students of the Bible should take note that there are several different designations which apply to the seed of the Watchers in the Old Testament: the terms "the wicked," "the ungodly," "the enemy," "workers of iniquity," "wicked doers," "evildoers," "evil men," "wicked men," "mighty men," "the giant," "sons of the giant," "the unjust," "pagans," "heathen" and, on occasion, even "sinners" are some of the common ones. In the New Testament, the terms used include "serpents," "generation of vipers," "princes of this world," "rulers [originators] of the darkness of this world," and the singular "Wicked One" or "Evil One."

When they used these epithets, the heroes of the Bible were not talking about children of the Light gone astray. No, when you read these terms you can be certain that the prophets and patriarchs, the Lord's anointed, and Christ himself were specifically denouncing the inbred generation of the seed that was cast out and godless—the Watchers and their progeny, and the Nephilim, easily mistaken for the latter.

They knew them well—by hand-to-hand combat or the challenge of Light and Darkness heart-to-heart. These renegades were a law unto themselves, and *every imagination of the thoughts of their hearts,* as God and the council of his sons would determine, *was evil*—manufacturing a synthetic society of synthetic people—*continually.* In fact, it was God's judgment that the wickedness of their hearts and their works was so terrible that they must be utterly destroyed in the Flood:

"And God saw that the wickedness of man was great in the earth.... And it repented the Lord that he had made man on the earth, and it grieved him at his heart. And the Lord said, I will destroy man whom I have created from the face of the earth; both man and beast and the creeping thing and the fowls of the air; for it repenteth me that I have made them." (Gen. 6:5–7)

Although the Book of Genesis, recording the Noachian deluge which resulted in the sinking of Atlantis and the "great increase of the waters upon the earth," states that "every living substance was destroyed," it is evident from postdiluvian history that the "spirits of the giants"—*and* of the Watchers *and* of the Nephilim—returned to propagate their seed along with Shem, Ham, and Japheth, the saved of Noah.

Why and how this could have happened is the subject of a future work. One thing, however, is clear from both the Old and New Testaments: our antecedents who were the descendants of the Ancient of Days—and kindred souls of Light to the present hour—have known the Watchers. Their tracks have been traced backwards and forwards in the historical stream of earth's tumultuous events, as history repeats itself time and again because 'the wicked' are always there with their strategies in darkness.

Life after life our brothers and sisters have sacrificed their lives, writing in blood an indelible record of the murderous intent of the godless—those whom the masters of the Far East have called "the dying race"— one by one, "the extinguished self."

Silenced, but not forever, the cohorts of Light have risen from the battlefields of life to live in our hearts and souls as revolutionaries of the Spirit. And they will speak through us if our courage, our love, and our endurance be not overcome by the calumny, disinformation, and divide-and-conquer tactics of the enemy.

In the wisdom and peace of the Elders of the I AM Race, we remember the words of one of the most fearless foes of the Watchers (whom they also killed), that great defender of the Union: "that we here highly resolve that these dead shall not have died in vain." Let us here remember what their souls articulated in life and in death...and what President Abraham Lincoln decreed, "that this nation, under God, shall have a new birth of freedom; and that government of the people, by the people, for the people, shall not perish from the earth."

The ancient Teachers and Lawgivers sent to us from God knew that wickedness, evilness, and sinfulness were states of being, something you were by an original act of rebellion against the Most High and his sons—by a pact to work the works of the fallen Watchers—not something you turned into by human mistakes or errors of judgment or even transgressions of God's law, which the path of atonement through The Word could set aside for the children of God.

The Elders knew that the ungodly enemies of the Lord and his elect had cast themselves in the mold of the anti-Self from the moment of their betrayal of the Law of the One, and what's more, that by denying God, they had effectively extinguished the God flame within themselves and no longer had the fire of heart to break the curse of their self-imposed damnation.

In the following well-known biblical passages taken from the King James and Jerusalem translations, I have substituted the term "Watcher" for the generalities we find in Holy Writ that quite conceal the issue of 'the wicked, etc.' as well as the fact that they are not just some people who are feisty and hell-bent, who make life difficult for the more steady, reliable, unassuming gentle folk.

On the contrary, the insertion of the name "Watcher" at key points in these familiar phrases reveals a separate race of fallen angels that can be identified in and among all races by the mark of the beast—the number of his name. I propose that this 'number' is the spiritual, physical, and psychological 'genetic code' of the fallen ones.

Alike in their origin and in their end, they also operate the same in the middle: And once you've got their number, you can't miss them. They stand out like a sore thumb. See parading through the lives of our best biblical friends the same personalities with the same bad character traits, physical stature, and archetypal psychology—the proud, the heartless, the ambitious, the abominable. There they go, the spoilers with their unmistakable aura and vibration—a seething vortex of blackness and world condemnation.

With no light in the eye and no real love for anyone, including themselves, the Watchers (and the Nephilim) still seem to maneuver everyone else (almost) to do their bidding. But death and destruction follow in their wake. And one by one, we know them by these fruits.

To the revolutionaries of God who, with Joshua, go forth to confront the Adversary and to the sons of Jared, who mourned the descent of his offspring to the level of the Cain civilization, I offer this personal profile of the infamous, the superproud—the despisers of the people.

No longer the uncoded, their mark and number and name is taken straight from Scripture where their identity has been sealed for this hour of the coming of the Faithful and True. He, with his armies, shall smite those Watchers with a 'sharp sword'—the Sacred Word—and He shall rule them with a rod of iron. Let us join His ranks and in the words of Moses, Fear not, but stand still and see the salvation of the Lord.

Hannah's Prophecy
The Watcher Shall Not Prevail by His Strength

The bows of the *mighty men* [giants, Gibborim[1]] are broken, and they that stumbled are girded with strength.

He raiseth up the poor out of the dust and lifteth up the beggar from the dunghill to set them among *princes* and to make them inherit the throne of glory: for the pillars of the earth are the Lord's, and he hath set the world upon them.

He will keep the feet of his saints, and the Watchers shall be silent in darkness; for by strength shall no man prevail.

The adversaries of the Lord shall be broken to pieces; out of heaven shall he thunder upon the Watchers: the Lord shall judge the ends of the earth; and he shall give strength unto his king and exalt the horn of his anointed.   *I Sam.* 2:4, 8–10

N.B. The author's interpretations of these passages are based upon the King James and Jerusalem translations of the Bible. (See *The Scofield Reference Bible*, ed. C. I. Scofield [New York: Oxford University Press, 1945] and *The Jerusalem Bible*, ed. Alexander Jones [Garden City, N.Y.: Doubleday & Co., 1966].)

1. *Gibborim* are the "mighty men" mentioned in Gen. 6:4 as the progeny of the angels and the daughters of men. The Gibborim were equated with the "giants."

Wickedness Proceeds from the Watchers

As saith the proverb of the ancients, Wickedness proceedeth from the Watchers.   *I Sam. 24:13*

The Giants—Offspring of the Watchers and Nephilim

Caleb said, We must march in and conquer this land: we are well able to do it. But the men who had gone up with him answered, We are not able to march against this people; they are stronger than we are.

And they gave an evil report of the land which they had searched unto the children of Israel, saying, The country we went to reconnoitre is a country that devours its inhabitants. [In other words, it was known that the giants ate the people.] Every man we saw there was of enormous size. And there we saw the giants, the sons of Anak, descendants of the Nephilim: and we were in our own sight as grasshoppers, and so we were in their sight.   *Num. 13:30–33*

Moreover the Philistines had yet war again with Israel; and David went down with his guards and fought against the Philistines: and David waxed faint. And Ishbibenob, which was of the sons of the giant, the weight of whose spear weighed three hundred shekels of brass in weight, he being girded with a new sword, was confident he could kill David.

But Abishai the son of Zeruiah went to his rescue; he struck down the Philistine and killed him. Then the men of David sware unto him, saying, Thou shalt go no more out with us to battle, that thou quench not the light of Israel. [They saw David as the embodiment of the light of Israel and did not want him to engage in direct combat with the giants.]

And it came to pass after this that there was again a battle with the Philistines at Gob: then Sibbechai the Hushathite slew Saph, which was of the sons of the giant. And there was again a battle in Gob with the Philistines, where Elhanan, the son of Jaareoregim, a Bethlehemite, slew the brother of Goliath the Gittite, the staff of whose spear was like a weaver's beam.

And there was yet a battle in Gath, where was a man of great stature that had on every hand six fingers and on every foot six toes, four and twenty in number; and he also was born to the giant. And when he defied Israel, Jonathan, the son of Shimeah, the brother of David, slew him.

These four were born to the giant in Gath and fell by the hand of David and by the hand of his guards.

II Sam. 21:15–22

David's Song of Deliverance from the Watchers

And David spake unto the Lord the words of this song in the day that the Lord had delivered him out of the hand of all *his enemies* and out of the hand of Saul—the Nephilim king. And he said:

The Lord is my rock and my fortress and my deliverer; the God of my rock; in him will I trust: he is my shield and the horn of my salvation, my high tower and my refuge, my saviour; thou savest me from violence.

I will call on the Lord, who is worthy to be praised: so shall I be saved from *mine enemies*.

When the waves of death compassed me, the floods of *ungodly men* made me afraid. He delivered me from *my strong enemy* and from them that hated me: for they were too strong for me. The Watchers prevented me in the day of my calamity: but the Lord was my stay.

With the pure thou wilt shew thyself pure; and with *the froward* thou wilt shew thyself unsavoury. And the afflicted people thou wilt save: but thine eyes are upon *the haughty,* that thou mayest bring them down.

Thou hast girded me with strength to battle: the Watchers that rose up against me hast thou subdued under me. The Watchers looked, but there was none to save; even unto the Lord, but he answered the Watchers not.

It is God that avengeth me and that bringeth down the people under me and that bringeth me forth from *mine enemies;* thou also hast lifted me up on high above the Watchers that rose up against me; thou hast delivered me from *the violent man*.

II Sam. 22:1–5, 18–19, 27–28, 40, 42, 48–49

Solomon's Prayer
for the Lord's Justice upon the Watchers

Then hear thou from heaven, [O Lord,] and do, and judge thy servants by requiting the Watcher, by recompensing his way upon his own head, and by justifying the righteous, by giving him according to his righteousness.   *II Chron. 6:23*

The Candle of the Watcher Shall Be Put Out

Yea, the light of the Watcher shall be put out, and the spark of his fire (his brilliant flame) shall not shine. The light shall be dark in his tabernacle (tent), and his candle shall be put out with him, the lamp that shone on him is snuffed.

The steps of his strength shall be straitened, his vigorous stride grows cramped, and his own counsel (cunning) shall cast him down. For he is cast into a net by his own feet, and he walketh upon a snare. The gin (trap) shall take him by the heel, and the robber shall prevail against him.

Hidden in the earth is a noose to snare him, pitfalls lie across his path. Terrors (spirits of the giants) attack him on every side and shall drive him to his feet, step for step.

Hunger becomes his companion, by his side Disaster stands. Disease devours his flesh, Death's First-Born gnaws his limbs.

His confidence shall be rooted out of his tabernacle, and it shall bring him to the king of terrors. (He is torn from the shelter of his tent and dragged before the King of Terrors.)

The Lilith[2] makes her home under his roof, while people scatter brimstone[3] on his holding. His roots grow withered below, and his branches are blasted above.

His memory fades from the land, his name is forgotten in his homeland. He shall be driven from light into darkness and chased out of the world, without issue or posterity among his own people, none to live on where he has lived.

His tragic end appalls the West and fills the East with terror. A fate like his awaits every sinful house [dynasty of the Watchers], the home of *every man who knows not God* [whose consciousness is without the flame of God]. *Job 18:5–21*

Job Takes Note of the Watchers' Prosperity and the People's Sympathy toward Them to the End

Wherefore do the Watchers live, become old, yea, are mighty in power?

Their seed is established in their sight with them, and their offspring before their eyes. Their houses are

---

2. Lilith: in Semitic lore, a female evil spirit roaming in desolate places and attacking children; a demon (called a *succubus*) assuming female form to have sexual intercourse with men in their sleep. The succubus is the female counterpart of the male *incubus,* said to seduce women at night. In the plural form, these sex entities are called *succubi* or *succubae* and *incubi.*

3. Brimstone (sulphur) was the sign of a curse from God and of Sheol.

safe from fear, neither is the rod of God upon them. Their bull gendereth and faileth not; their cow calveth and casteth not her calf.

They send forth their little ones like a flock, and their children dance. They take the timbrel and harp and rejoice at the sound of the organ. They spend their days in wealth and in a moment go down to the grave.

Therefore the Watchers say unto God, Depart from us; for we desire not the knowledge of thy ways. What is the Almighty, that we should serve him? and what profit should we have, if we pray unto him?

Is it not true they held their fortune in their own two hands and in their counsels left no room for God? How often do we see the Watcher's candle put out, or disaster overtaking him, or all his goods destroyed by the wrath of God? How often do we see the Watcher harassed like a straw before the wind or swept off like chaff before a gale?

God, you say, reserves the Watcher's punishment for his children. No! Let him bear the penalty himself and suffer under it! Let him see his ruin with his own eyes and himself drink the anger of the Almighty.

When he has gone, how can the fortunes of his House affect him, when the number of his months is cut off? Shall any teach God knowledge? seeing he judgeth those that are high.

One dieth in his full strength, being wholly at ease and quiet. His breasts are full of milk, and his bones are moistened with marrow (the source of his strength is still with him). And another dieth in the bitterness of his soul and never eateth with pleasure. The Watchers shall lie down alike in the dust, and the worms shall cover them.

Behold, I know your thoughts and the devices (spiteful thoughts) which ye wrongfully imagine against me. For ye say, Where is the house of *the great lord?* and where are the dwelling places of *the wicked?*

Have you never asked those that have travelled, or have you misunderstood the tale they told, *The wicked man* is spared for the day of disaster and carried off in the day of wrath?

But who is there then to accuse him to his face for his deeds and pay him back for what he has done, and when he is on his way to his burial, when men are watching at his grave? The clods of the valley are laid gently on him, and a whole procession walks behind him.

Job 21:7–33

Walk Not in the Way of the Watchers

Blessed is the man that walketh not in the counsel of the Watchers, nor standeth in the way of *sinners*, nor sitteth in the seat of *the scornful*.

But his delight is in the law of the Lord; and in his law doth he meditate day and night. And he shall be like a tree planted by the rivers of water that bringeth forth his fruit in his season; his leaf also shall not wither; and whatsoever he doeth shall prosper.

The Watchers are not so: but are like *the chaff* which the wind driveth away. Therefore the Watchers shall not stand in the judgment, nor *sinners* in the congregation of the righteous. For the Lord knoweth the way of the righteous: but the way of the Watchers shall perish.   Ps. 1

The Watchers Take Counsel against the Lord's Anointed

Why do the Watchers rage and the people imagine a vain thing? (Why this impotent muttering of pagans?) *The kings of the earth* rise up in revolt and the Watchers take counsel together (the princes plot) against the Lord and against his anointed, saying, Let us break their bands asunder and cast away their cords from us.

He that sitteth in the heavens shall laugh: the Lord shall have the Watchers in derision. Then shall he speak unto the Watchers in his wrath and vex them in his sore displeasure, Yet have I set my King upon my holy hill of Zion.

I will declare the decree: the Lord hath said unto me, Thou art my Son; this day have I begotten thee. (I have become your Father.) Ask of me and I shall give thee the Watchers for thine inheritance and the uttermost parts of the earth for thy possession. Thou shalt break the Watchers with a rod of iron; thou shalt dash them in pieces like a potter's vessel.

Be wise now therefore, O ye kings: be instructed, ye judges of the earth. Serve the Lord with fear, and rejoice with trembling. Kiss the Son, lest he be angry, and ye perish from the way when his wrath is kindled but a little (for the Son's anger is very quick to blaze).

Blessed are all they that put their trust in him.

Ps. 2

God Judges the Watchers
and Saves His Oppressed People

I will be glad and rejoice in thee: I will sing praise to thy name, O thou most High.

When *mine enemies* are turned back, they shall fall and perish at thy Mighty I AM Presence. Thou hast rebuked *the heathen* [Nephilim], thou hast destroyed the Watchers, thou hast put out their name for ever and ever.

The Lord also will be a refuge for the oppressed, a refuge in times of trouble. And they that know thy name I AM THAT I AM will put their trust in thee: for thou, Lord, hast not forsaken them that seek thee.

The Watchers are sunk down in the pit that they made: in the net which they hid is their own foot taken. The Lord is known by the judgment which he executeth: the Watcher is snared in the work of his own hands.

The Watchers shall be turned into hell, and all the nations that forget God. For the needy shall not alway be forgotten: the expectation of the poor shall not perish for ever. *Ps. 9:2–3, 5, 9–10, 15–18*

The Watcher Spurns the I AM Presence, Murders the Innocent, and Says, "There Is No God!"

The Watcher in his pride doth persecute the poor: let them be taken in the devices that they have imagined. For the Watcher boasteth of his heart's desire and blesseth *the covetous,* whom the Lord abhorreth.

The Watcher, through the pride of his countenance, will not seek after God: God is not in all his thoughts. *The grasping man* blasphemes, the Watcher spurns the I AM Presence saying, His ways are always grievous; he will not make me pay! His judgments are far above out of sight: there is no God! This is the way the Watcher's mind works.

As for all his enemies, he puffeth at them. He sneers at all his rivals. The Watcher hath said in his heart, I shall not be moved: nothing can shake me, for I shall never be in adversity.

Himself untouched by disaster, he curses others. His mouth is full of cursing and deceit and fraud: under his tongue is mischief and vanity.

The Watcher sitteth in the lurking places of the villages; in the secret places doth he murder the innocent; his eyes are privily set against the poor. He lieth in wait secretly as a lion in his den; he lieth in wait to catch the poor. He doth catch the poor when he draweth him into his net. He croucheth and humbleth himself, that the poor may fall by his *strong ones*.

The Watcher hath said in his heart, God forgets, he hides his face, he does not see at all. Arise, O Lord; O God, lift up thine hand: forget not the humble. Wherefore doth the Watcher spurn God, assuring himself, He will not make me pay?

Break the power of the Watcher, of *the evil man*: seek out his wickedness till there is none to be found! The Mighty I AM Presence is King for ever and ever, *the pagans* are doomed to vanish from God's country.

Ps. 10:2–13, 15–16

David's Decree for the Watchers' Karma to Be upon the Watchers—Not upon the People

Unto thee will I cry, O Lord, my Mighty I AM Presence, my Rock: Draw me not away with the Watchers and with *the workers of iniquity,* which speak peace to their neighbours, but mischief is in their hearts.

Give them according to their deeds and according to the wickedness of their endeavours: give them after the work of their hands; render to them their desert.

Unto thee will I cry, O Lord, my Mighty I AM Presence, my Rock.

Ps. 28:1, 3–4

The I AM THAT I AM Turns the Karma of the Watchers upon Them to Their Death

The face of the Lord is against the Watchers to cut off the remembrance of them from the earth.

Evil shall slay the Watchers: and *they that hate the righteous* shall be desolate.

Ps. 34:16, 21

The Watcher Has No Fear of God but Flatters Himself to His Own Fall

The transgression of the Watcher saith within my heart that there is no fear of God before his eyes. For the Watcher flattereth himself in his own eyes, so much so that though his iniquity be found to be hateful, he will neither see nor repudiate his guilt.

The words of his mouth are iniquity and deceit: he

hath left off to be wise and to do good. The Watcher deviseth mischief upon his bed; he setteth himself in a way that is not good; he abhorreth not evil. Though he know the Truth, he persists in his evil course; he never rejects error.

How excellent is thy lovingkindness, O God! With thee is the fountain of life, the Mighty I AM Presence, my Source. The Watchers are fallen, they are cast down and shall not be able to rise again.   Ps. 36:1–4, 7, 9, 12

The Watchers Shall Be Cut Off—
The Lord's Servants Shall Inherit the Earth

Fret not thyself because of Watchers, neither be thou envious against *the workers of iniquity*. For they shall soon be cut down like the grass and wither as the green herb.

Trust in the Lord and do good; so shalt thou dwell in the land and verily thou shalt be fed. Delight thyself also in the Lord; and he shall give thee the desires of thine heart.

Commit thy way unto the Lord; trust also in him; and he shall bring it to pass. And he shall bring forth thy righteousness as the light, and thy judgment as the noonday.

Rest in the Lord, the Mighty I AM Presence, and wait patiently for him: fret not thyself because of him who prospereth in his way (making his fortune), because of the man who bringeth wicked devices to pass, scheming to bring down the poor and the needy.

Cease from anger and forsake wrath: fret not thyself in any wise to do evil. For *evildoers* shall be cut off: but those that wait upon the Lord, they shall inherit the earth.

For yet a little while and the Watcher shall not be: yea, thou shalt diligently consider his place, and it shall not be. But the meek shall inherit the earth and shall delight themselves in the abundance of peace. The humble shall have the land for their own use.

The Watcher plots against the just and grinds his teeth at him. The Lord shall laugh at him: for he seeth that his day is coming, his end is in sight.

The Watchers have drawn out the sword and have bent their bow to cast down the poor and needy and to slay such as be of upright conversation. Their sword shall enter into their own heart, and their bows shall be broken.

The little that a righteous man hath is better than the riches of many Watchers, since the arms of the Watchers shall be broken: but the Lord, the Mighty I AM Presence, upholdeth the righteous.

The Lord knoweth the days of the upright: and their inheritance shall be for ever. They shall not be ashamed in the evil time: and in the days of famine they shall be satisfied. But the Watchers shall perish, and *the enemies of the Lord* shall be as the fat of lambs: they shall consume; into smoke shall they consume away.

The wicked borroweth and payeth not again: but the righteous sheweth mercy and giveth. For such as be blessed of him shall inherit the earth; and *they that be cursed* (judged) of him shall be cut off.

The steps of a godly man—a man of God—are ordered by the Lord: and he delighteth in his way. Though he fall, he shall not be utterly cast down: for the Lord upholdeth him with his hand. I have been young and now am old; yet have I not seen the righteous forsaken, nor his seed begging bread. He is ever merciful and lendeth; and his seed is blessed.

Depart from evil and do good, and dwell for evermore. For the Lord loveth judgment and forsaketh not his saints; they are preserved for ever: but the seed of the Watchers shall be cut off. The righteous shall inherit the land and dwell therein for ever.

The mouth of the righteous—who attends THE LORD OUR RIGHTEOUSNESS—speaketh wisdom and his tongue talketh of judgment. The law of his God is in his heart; none of his steps shall slide.

The Watcher watcheth the righteous and seeketh to slay him. The Lord will not leave him in his hand, nor condemn him when he is judged. Wait on the Lord and keep his way, and he shall exalt thee to inherit the land: when the Watchers are cut off, thou shalt see it.

I have seen the Watcher in great power and spreading himself like a green bay tree. Yet the Watcher passed away, and, lo, he was not: yea, I sought him, but he could not be found.

Mark the perfect man—who is made in the image and likeness of God—and behold the upright: for the end of that man is peace. But *the transgressors* shall be destroyed together: the descendants of the Watchers shall be cut off (wiped out).

The salvation of the righteous is of the Lord: the Mighty I AM Presence is their strength in time of trouble. And the Lord shall help them and deliver them: he shall deliver them from the Watchers and save them because they trust in him.   Ps. 37

David's Decree When Saul, the Nephilim King, Sent His Henchmen to Kill Him

Deliver me from *mine enemies,* O my God: defend me from them that rise up against me. Deliver me from the *workers of iniquity,* the Watchers, and save me from *bloody men, murderers!*

For, lo, they lie in wait for my soul: *the mighty* [giants, Gibborim] are gathered against me; not for my transgression, nor for my sin, O Lord. They run and prepare themselves without my fault; awake to help me, and behold. Thou therefore, O Lord God of hosts, the God of Israel, awake to visit all the Nephilim: be not merciful to any *wicked transgressors.*

The Gibborim return at evening: they make a noise like a dog and go round about the city. Behold, they belch out with their mouth. Swords are in their lips; for who, say they, doth hear? But thou, O Lord, my Mighty I AM Presence, shalt laugh at them; thou shalt have all the Nephilim in derision.

Because of his strength will I wait upon thee: for

God is my defence. The God of my mercy shall prevent me: God shall let me see my desire upon *mine enemies*—the Watchers and their progeny. Slay them not, lest my people forget: scatter the fallen angels and the children of their fornication by thy power; and bring them down, O Lord our shield.

For the sin of their mouth and the words of their lips let them even be taken in their pride: and for cursing and lying which they speak. Consume them in wrath [the sacred fire], consume them, that they may not be: and let them know that God ruleth in Jacob unto the ends of the earth.

And at evening let the Gibborim return; and let them make a noise like a dog and go round about the city. Let them wander up and down for meat and grudge if they be not satisfied.

But I will sing of thy power; yea, I will sing aloud of thy mercy in the morning: for thou hast been my defence and refuge in the day of my trouble. Unto thee, O my strength, will I sing: for God is my defence and the God of my mercy.   Ps. 59

Retribution for the Watchers Who Slander the Upright in Heart

Hear my voice, O God, in my prayer: preserve my life from the fear of *the enemy*.

Hide me from the secret counsel of the Watchers, from the insurrection of the *workers of iniquity*, this mob of *evil men*, who whet their tongue like a sword and bend their bows to shoot their arrows, even bitter words, that they may shoot in secret at the perfect.

Suddenly do the Watchers shoot at him and fear not. They encourage themselves in an evil matter; urging each other on to their wicked purpose, they discuss where they will hide their traps. Who is going to see us? they say. Who can find out our wicked deeds?

The Watchers search out iniquities; they accomplish a diligent search, a plot they hatch: both the inward thought of every one of them and the heart is deep.

But God shall shoot at the Watchers with an arrow; suddenly shall they be wounded. [By the law of karma the arrow of God's law avenges the arrow of the wicked word.]

So shall they make their own tongue to fall upon themselves: all that see them will shake their heads and flee away. And all men shall fear and shall declare the work of God; for they shall wisely consider of his doing and understand why he has done it.

The righteous shall be glad in the Lord, the Mighty I AM Presence, and shall trust in him and his anointed; and all the upright in heart [those who have the divine spark] shall glory.   *Ps. 64*

The Watchers Perish at the Presence of God

As smoke is driven away, so drive them away: as wax melteth before the fire, so let the Watchers perish at the presence of God.   *Ps. 68:2*

God's Pronouncement in the Divine Assembly— The 'Gods' Have Lost Their Immortality: They Shall Die as Mortals

God stands in the divine assembly, among the gods he dispenses justice:

'No more mockery of justice, no more favoring the fallen Watchers! Let the weak and the orphan have justice, be fair to the wretched and destitute; rescue the weak and needy, save them from the clutches of the fallen Watchers!'

Ignorant and senseless, they carry on blindly, undermining the very basis of earthly society. I once said, 'You too are gods, sons of the Most High [you once had the divine spark], all of you,' but all the same, you shall die like other men; as one man, princes, you shall fall.

Rise, God, dispense justice throughout the world, since no nation is excluded from your ownership.[4]

Ps. 82 (See Jerusalem Bible)

---

4. Hebrew scholar Julian Morgenstern points out that in Psalm 82, those whom Yahweh is judging and condemning are "not at all the corrupt, human judges...[but] a certain, probably not overly large, group of the gods or angels themselves, who had committed some act of utmost sinful character, which aroused Yahweh's indignation to the highest pitch and justified a punishment which should be both logical and appropriate in character and extreme in degree. Quite certainly what followed immediately...in the original form of the [edited] Ps. was the arraignment by Yahweh of these sinning angels and the formal statement of the crime which they had committed.

"And what this may have been is now perfectly clear. They had been attracted by the physical beauty of the daughters of man and, in complete disregard of their divine, incorporeal, spiritual natures,

The Lord Will Destroy the Watchers

Lord, how long shall the Watchers, how long shall the Watchers triumph?   *Ps. 94:3*

I will early destroy all the Watchers of the land, that I may cut off all Watchers from the city of the Lord—the city of the Mighty I AM Presence and his elect.   *Ps. 101:8*

Horror hath taken hold upon me because of the Watchers that forsake thy law.

Salvation is far from the Watchers: for they seek not thy statutes.   *Ps. 119:53, 155*

had forsaken heaven, their natural abode, and descended to earth and consorted with these women in strictly human manner....

"Then, after the arraignment of these sinning angels and the formal declaration of their crime, vv. 6–7 continue with the final statement of Yahweh's denunciation and the formal announcement of punishment. 'I had thought that ye were gods, yea, sons of Elyon [the Most High] all of you.' The sentence voices most graphically the surprise and painful shock which Yahweh had experienced when the shameful conduct of these divine beings had become known to Him. How could gods, sons of Elyon, comport themselves in this unworthy manner, reject their divine natures completely and indulge themselves with human women in the most physical of human appetites?...

"It is readily seen that the revision of the original poem, in order to adapt it for incorporation into the official liturgy of the Jerusalem Temple was simple and systematic. The statement of the horrifying and almost inconceivable crime of the angels was removed in its entirety and in its stead was substituted, what must have seemed to these editors far more appropriate and far more in accord with their theological principles and ethical standards, the denunciation of corrupt, earthly judges which we now find in vv. 2–5a." (*Hebrew Union College Annual* 14[1939]: 114–16, 122–23).

Deliver me, O Lord, from the Watcher; preserve me from *the violent man*, which imagine mischiefs in their heart; continually are the Watchers gathered together for war.   *Ps. 140:1–2*

The Lord preserveth all them that love him: but all the Watchers will he destroy.   *Ps. 145:20*

The righteous shall never be removed: but the Watchers shall not inhabit the earth.   *Prov. 10:30*

The thoughts of the righteous are right: but the counsels of the Watchers are deceit.

The words of the Watchers are to lie in wait for blood: but the mouth of the upright shall deliver them.

The Watchers are overthrown and are not: but the house of the righteous shall stand.   *Prov. 12:5–7*

A wise king scattereth the Watchers and bringeth the wheel [of the Law] over them.   *Prov. 20:26*

When the Watchers rise, men hide themselves: but when they perish, the righteous increase.   *Prov. 28:28*

But it shall not be well with the Watcher, neither shall he prolong his days, which are as a shadow; because he feareth not before God.   *Eccles. 8:13*

But with righteousness shall he judge the poor and reprove with equity for the meek of the earth: and he shall smite the earth with the rod of his mouth, and with the breath of his lips shall he slay the Watchers. *Isa. 11:4*

But the Watchers are like the troubled sea when it cannot rest, whose waters cast up mire and dirt. There is no peace, saith my God, to the Watchers. *Isa. 57:20–21*

Many shall be purified and made white and tried; but the Watchers shall do wickedly: and none of the Watchers shall understand; but the wise shall understand. *Dan. 12:10*

And ye shall tread down the Watchers; for they shall be ashes under the soles of your feet in the day that I shall do this, saith the Lord of hosts. *Mal. 4:3*

Jesus Calls Forth the Karmic Woes upon the Watchers (Who Appear in the Guise of Scribes and Pharisees) for Their Betrayal of the People

Then spake Jesus to the multitude and to his disciples, saying:

The Watchers (who appear as the scribes and Pharisees) sit in Moses' seat. All therefore whatsoever the Watchers bid you observe, that observe and do; but do not ye after their works: for they say, and do not. For the Watchers bind heavy burdens and grievous to be borne and lay them on men's shoulders; but they themselves will not move them with one of their fingers.[5]

But all their works they do for to be seen of men:

5. The Watchers lay their karma on the backs of the people; they do not bear their own karmic burden: Taxation, usury, and the manipulation of money are means of making the people pay their way.

they make broad their phylacteries[6] and enlarge the borders of their garments, and the Watchers love the uppermost rooms at feasts and the chief seats in the synagogues and greetings in the markets, and to be called of men, Rabbi, Rabbi.

But be not ye called Rabbi: for one is your Master, even Christ; and all ye are brethren. And call no man your father upon the earth: for one is your Father, which is in heaven. Neither be ye called masters: for one is your Master, even Christ.

But he that is greatest among you shall be your servant. And whosoever shall exalt himself shall be abased; and he that shall humble himself shall be exalted.

But, *Woe!* unto you, scribes and Pharisees, Watchers! for ye shut up the kingdom of heaven against men: for ye neither go in yourselves, neither suffer ye them that are entering to go in.

Woe! unto you, scribes and Pharisees, hypocrites! for ye devour widows' houses, and for a pretence make long prayer: therefore ye shall receive the greater damnation.

Woe! unto you, scribes and Pharisees, Watchers! for ye compass sea and land to make one proselyte, and when he is made, ye make him twofold more the child of hell than yourselves.

---

6. A phylactery is a small, square leather box which contains strips of parchment inscribed with scriptural passages and is traditionally worn by Jewish men on the left arm and forehead during prayers. The Pharisees broadened the leather bands which held their phylacteries in place to attract attention to themselves.

Woe! unto you Watchers, ye blind guides, which say, Whosoever shall swear by the temple, it is nothing; but whosoever shall swear by the gold of the temple, he is a debtor! Ye fools and blind Watchers: for whether is greater, the gold or the temple that sanctifieth the gold?

And, Whosoever shall swear by the altar, it is nothing; but whosoever sweareth by the gift that is upon it, he is guilty. Ye fools and blind Watchers: for whether is greater, the gift or the altar that sanctifieth the gift?

Whoso therefore shall swear by the altar, sweareth by it and by all things thereon. And whoso shall swear by the temple, sweareth by it and by him that dwelleth therein. And he that shall swear by heaven, sweareth by the throne of God and by him that sitteth thereon.

Woe! unto you, scribes and Pharisees, Watchers! for ye pay tithe of mint and anise and cummin and have omitted the weightier matters of the law, judgment, mercy, and faith: these ought ye to have done and not to leave the other undone. Ye blind guides, which strain out a gnat and swallow a camel.

Woe! unto you, scribes and Pharisees, Watchers! for ye make clean the outside of the cup and of the platter, but within they are full of extortion and excess. Thou blind Pharisee, cleanse first that which is within the cup and platter, that the outside of them may be clean also.

Woe! unto you, scribes and Pharisees, Watchers! for ye are like unto whited sepulchres, which indeed appear beautiful outward but are within full of dead men's bones [discarnate entities] and of all uncleanness [astral substance and demons]. Even so ye also outwardly appear righteous unto men, but within ye are full of hypocrisy and iniquity.

Woe! unto you, scribes and Pharisees, Watchers! because ye build the tombs of the prophets and garnish the sepulchres of the righteous and say, If we had been in the days of our fathers, we would not have been partakers with them in the blood of the prophets. Wherefore ye be witnesses unto yourselves, that ye are the children of the Watchers which killed the prophets. Fill ye up then the measure of your fathers.

Ye *serpents,* ye *generation of vipers,* how can ye escape the damnation of hell? Wherefore, behold, I send unto you prophets and wise men and scribes: and some of them ye shall kill and crucify; and some of them shall ye scourge in your synagogues and persecute them from city to city, that upon you may come all the righteous blood shed upon the earth, from the blood of righteous Abel unto the blood of Zacharias, son of Barachias, whom ye slew between the temple and the altar.

Verily I say unto you Watchers, All these things shall come upon this *generation of the Wicked One*— the lineage and the dynasties of the Watchers.

O Jerusalem, Jerusalem, thou false hierarchy of Watchers that killest the prophets and stonest them which are sent unto thee, how often would I have gathered thy children, the children of Light in the Holy City, together, even as a hen gathereth her chickens under her wings, and ye would not allow it! Ye would not suffer them to come unto me. Ye stood in the doorway of the temple and prevented them from entering in to my heart.

Behold, your house is left unto you desolate. For I say unto you, Ye shall not see me henceforth, till ye shall say, Blessed is he that cometh in the name of the Lord. Blessed is the messenger of the I AM THAT I AM.   *Matt. 23*

The Watchers Do Not Comprehend the Mysteries of God

Howbeit we speak wisdom among them that are perfect; yet not the wisdom of this world, nor of the Watchers that come to nought.

But we speak the wisdom of God in a mystery, even the hidden wisdom, which God ordained before the world unto our glory, which none of the Watchers comprehended; for had they comprehended it, they would not have crucified the Lord of glory. *I Cor. 2:6–8*

The Enemy Is Not Flesh and Blood

Be strong in the Lord and in the power of his might. Put on the whole armour of God, that ye may be able to stand against the wiles of the devil.

For we wrestle not against flesh and blood, not against mere mortals, but against a wicked angelic evolution, against the Sovereignties and Powers of the Hierarchy of Fallen Angels, against the originators of the darkness of this world, the Watchers and their army of evildoers, against spiritual wickedness in high places.   *Eph. 6:10–12*

False Teachers Initiate Their Students in Bodily Corruption and in Challenging the Authority of the 'Glorious Ones'—the Sons of God and the Heavenly Hierarchy of Angels

As there have been *false prophets* in the history of our people who were Watchers, so you too will encounter *false teachers* in your midst who will be Watchers, who will secretly bring in damnable heresies, even denying the Master that bought them, and bring upon themselves swift destruction. And many shall follow their pernicious ways (shameful behaviour) and the Way of Truth will be brought into disrepute (shall be evil spoken of) on their account.

And through covetousness shall these Watchers with feigned words make merchandise of you; envying your light, they will eagerly try to buy you for themselves with insidious speeches; but for them the Condemnation of their words and their works, pronounced so long ago by the Ancient of Days, is at its work already, and Destruction is not asleep (their Damnation slumbereth not).

For if God spared not the angels, the Watchers, that sinned, but cast them down to the underworld (hell) and delivered them into chains of darkness (in dark underground caves) to be held there till the day of Judgment; and spared not the old world [the Atlantean world and the Cain civilization], but saved Noah the eighth person, a preacher of righteousness, bringing in the flood upon mankind and the creation of the disobedient Watchers;

And turning the cities of Sodom and Gomorrah into ashes, condemned the Watchers with an overthrow, making them an ensample unto those that after should live ungodly; and delivered just Lot, vexed with the filthy conversation of the Watchers (for that righteous man dwelling among them, in seeing and hearing, vexed his righteous soul from day to day with the Watchers' unlawful deeds),

The Lord knoweth how to deliver the godly out of temptations and to reserve the Watchers unto the day of judgment to be punished: but chiefly them that walk after the flesh, governed by their corrupt bodily desires, in the lust of uncleanness and despise government, having no respect for authority.

Presumptuous are these sons of the Watchers, self-willed, they are not afraid to speak evil of dignities—that is, of the glorious ones who are in the hierarchy of angels. Whereas angels, which are greater in power and might, bring not railing accusation against them before the Lord.

But these sons of the Watchers, as natural brute beasts [Homo sapiens without the Christ mind], made to be taken and destroyed, they speak evil of the things that they understand not; and shall utterly perish in their own corruption; and shall receive the reward of unrighteousness, the reward of evil for the evil that they do, as they count it pleasure to riot in the day time.

Spots they are, these sons of the Watchers, and blemishes, sporting themselves with their own deceivings while they feast with you; having eyes full of adultery and that cannot cease from sin; beguiling unstable souls; an heart they have exercised with covetous practices (greed is the one lesson their minds have learnt);

Cursed children which have forsaken the right way and are gone astray, following the way of Balaam, the son of Beor the Watcher, who loved the wages of unrighteousness, who thought he could profit best by sinning until he was called to order for his faults; but was rebuked for his iniquity: the dumb ass speaking with man's voice forbad the madness of the prophet.

These Watchers are wells without water, clouds that are carried with a tempest: to whom the mist of darkness (the dark underworld) is reserved for ever. For when the Watchers speak great swelling words of vanity (which is all hollow), they allure through the lusts of the flesh, through much wantonness, those who were clean escaped from the paganism of those who live in error—playing on their bodily desires with debaucheries.

While the Watchers promise them liberty, they themselves are the *servants of corruption:* for of whom a man is overcome, of the same is he brought in bondage. For if after they have escaped the pollutions of the world-system of the Watchers through the knowledge of the Lord and Saviour Jesus Christ, they are again entangled therein and over-come, the latter end is worse with them than the beginning.

For it had been better for them not to have known the way of righteousness than, after they have known it, to turn from the holy commandment delivered unto them. But it is happened unto them according to the true proverb, The dog is turned to his own vomit again; and the sow that was washed to her wallowing in the mire.   *II Pet. 2*

Fathers and Sons Overcome the Wicked One

I write unto you, fathers, because ye have known him that is from the beginning. I write unto you, young men, because ye have overcome the Watcher, *the Wicked One*. I write unto you, little children, because ye have known the Father.

I have written unto you, fathers, because ye have known him that is from the beginning. I have written unto you, young men, because ye are strong, and the word of God abideth in you, and ye have overcome the Watcher, *the Wicked One*.   *I John 2:13–14*

Fight Hard for the Faith Entrusted to the Saints

Jude, the servant of Jesus Christ and brother of James, to them that are sanctified by God the Father and preserved in Jesus Christ and called: Mercy unto you, and peace and love, be multiplied.

Beloved, when I gave all diligence to write unto you of the salvation in which we all share, I have been forced by the dangers these heretic Watchers represent to write to you now and appeal to you to fight hard for the faith which has been once and for all entrusted to the saints.

Certain people have infiltrated among you (creeping in unawares). They are the ones about whom you were warned in the ancient texts, whom God ordained to this Condemnation. These *ungodly men* denied all religion, turning the grace of our God into lasciviousness (immorality), denying the only Lord God and rejecting the Master Jesus Christ.

I will therefore put you in remembrance, though ye once knew this, how that the Lord, having saved the people out of the land of Egypt, afterward destroyed them that believed not (did not trust him) [or his divine direction through his messenger Moses]. And the angels, the Watchers, which kept not their first estate but left their own habitation (sphere), he hath reserved in everlasting chains under darkness unto the judgment of the Great Day.[7]

Even as Sodom and Gomorrah and the cities about them in like manner, giving themselves over to fornication [with the fallen angels] and going after alien

---

7. Scofield interprets this to mean the judgment by Jehovah ['the Mighty I AM Presence'] of Satan and other fallen angels with him (Scofield, *Scofield Reference Bible*, p. 1328, n. 2).

flesh, are set forth for an example, suffering the vengeance of eternal fire.

Likewise also these *filthy dreamers* defile the flesh, despise the authority of the angels, and speak evil of dignities, verbally abusing the glorious angels as well. Yet Michael the archangel, when contending with the devil he disputed about the body of Moses, durst not bring against him a railing accusation, but said, The Lord rebuke thee.

But these sons of the Watchers, using violent language, speak evil of those things which they know not; but what they know naturally, as brute beasts [Homo sapiens without the Christ mind], in those things they corrupt themselves.

Woe! unto the sons of the Watchers (may they get what they deserve) [i.e., may their karma be upon them!], for they have gone in the way of Cain,[8] and ran greedily after the error of Balaam[9] for reward, and perished in the gainsaying of Core.[10]

These are spots in your feasts of charity when they

8. Type of religious natural man, who believes in a God and in "religion," but after his own will, and who rejects redemption by the blood of Christ, the incarnate Word (Scofield, pp. 1328–29, n. 3).

9. The error of Balaam was his supposing that a righteous God *must* curse the evil Israel, which Balaam deduced from the reasoning of natural morality rather than the higher morality of the Cross (Scofield, p. 1329, n. 1).

10. The sin of Korah (Core) was denial of the authority of Moses as God's chosen spokesman and intrusion into the priest's office (Scofield, p. 1329, n. 2). See Num. 16.

feast with you, feeding themselves without fear: clouds they are without water, these Watchers, carried about of winds; trees whose fruit withereth, without fruit, twice dead, plucked up by the roots; raging waves of the sea, foaming out their own shame; *wandering stars* [fallen angels], to whom is reserved the blackness of darkness for ever!

And Enoch also, the seventh from Adam, prophesied of these, saying, Behold, the Lord cometh with ten thousands of his saints to execute judgment upon all and to convince all that are the ungodly Watchers among them of all their ungodly deeds which they have ungodly committed and of all their hard speeches which *ungodly sinners* have spoken against him.

These are *murmurers, complainers,* walking after their own lusts; and their mouth speaketh great swelling words, having men's persons in admiration because of advantage.

But, beloved, remember ye the words which were spoken before of the apostles of our Lord Jesus Christ; how that they told you there should be *mockers in the last time* who should walk after their own ungodly lusts. These be they who separate themselves, sensual, having not the Spirit. These unspiritual and selfish people are nothing but mischief-makers.

But ye, beloved, building up yourselves on your most holy faith, praying in the Holy Ghost, keep yourselves in the love of God, looking for the mercy of our Lord Jesus Christ unto eternal life.

When there are some who have doubts, reassure them; have compassion making a difference; when there are some to be saved from the fire, pull them out; but there are others to whom you must be kind with great caution, keeping your distance even from outside clothing which is contaminated by vice.

Now unto him that is able to keep you from falling and to present you faultless before the presence of his glory with exceeding joy, to the only wise God our Saviour, be glory and majesty, dominion and power, which he had before time began, both now and forever. Amen.[11]

The Epistle of Jude

---

11. For further insights, see the *Jerusalem Bible* translation of the Epistle of Jude in its entirety.

ADDITIONAL CONCEALED REFERENCES TO THE WATCHERS (AND NEPHILIM) IN SCRIPTURE

Adversaries (of the Lord)
Deut. 32:41–43
Isa. 1:24
Isa. 59:18
Nah. 1:2

Bloody man (murderer)
Ps. 5:6

Bloody men (murderers)
Ps. 26:9–10
Ps. 139:19–20

Children of this world
Luke 16:8

Covetous
Luke 16:14

Deceitful workers
II Cor. 11:13–15

Enemies
Ps. 21:8–12

Ps. 35
Phil. 3:18–19

Enemy
Deut. 33:27
I Sam. 24:3–4
I Sam. 26:7–8
II Sam. 22:18
Job 16:9–11
Ps. 8:2
Ps. 18:17
Ps. 41:11
Ps. 74:3–4, 10, 18
Ps. 143:3
Matt. 13:24–30, 36–43

Evil man
Prov. 2:11–15
Prov. 17:11
Prov. 29:6

Jer. 6:26–30
Jer. 12:1
Nah. 1:3, 15
Hab. 1:13–17
Mal. 3:18
Matt. 13:49–50
II Thess. 2:8–9

Wicked one
Matt. 13:19, 38
I John 5:18

Workers of iniquity
Job 31:3
Job 34:22
Ps. 5:5
Ps. 14:1–5
Ps. 53:1–5
Ps. 92:7, 9
Ps. 94:2–7, 16, 23
Ps. 125:5
Ps. 141:9–10
Prov. 10:29
Prov. 21:15
Luke 13:25–27

Iniquity
Matt. 7:21–23
Matt. 13:41

SPIRITUAL SOLUTIONS

For judgment I AM come into this world.

Jesus

SPIRITUAL SOLUTIONS

Two thousand years ago Jesus told Peter, "I will give unto thee the keys of the kingdom of heaven: and whatsoever thou shalt bind on earth shall be bound in heaven: and whatsoever thou shalt loose on earth shall be loosed in heaven."[1] Today Jesus gives us these keys for the binding of the fallen angels.

The apostle Paul affirmed this empowerment when he told the Christians at Corinth: "Do ye not know that the saints shall judge the world? And if the world shall be judged by you, are ye unworthy to judge the smallest matters? Know ye not that we shall judge [the fallen] angels?"[2]

Jesus has given us a specific prayer for the binding of the fallen angels and foul spirits who prey upon the children of God. It is called "They Shall Not Pass! A Call for the Judgment of the Fallen Angels Who Have Sworn Enmity against the Children of God."

"They Shall Not Pass!" is an empowerment to

1. Matt. 16:19. 2. I Cor. 6:2, 3.

check the proliferation of evil, to halt injustices. We do not give this prayer to get even with individuals. We give it because without our intense supplications for divine intercession, many innocent souls could become the victims of the greed, lust or hatred of evildoers, from child abusers to international terrorists. We always submit our prayers to the will of God, for God is the ultimate judge.

"They Shall Not Pass!" is an accelerated form of spoken prayer known as "decrees." Decrees, like prayers, are spoken petitions to God. But more than that, they are commands for the will of God to be manifest. When we decree, we are scientifically commanding God's light to enter our world for alchemical change. We are directing God to send his light and his angels into action for personal and world transformation.

Many have wondered why it is really necessary to *ask* God to help us. Isn't he omniscient? Doesn't he already know our problems and how to take care of them?

According to God's laws, he and his heavenly representatives may not intervene in human affairs unless we specifically ask them to. When God created us he gave us free will, and he respects that free will. You can think of earth as a laboratory where God has given us the freedom to experiment and to evolve. If he hadn't given us free will and let us experience the good and bad results of our actions, we wouldn't be able to learn from—and grow from—the lessons of life.

THE TUBE OF LIGHT

Before giving "They Shall Not Pass!" it is best to establish a forcefield of protection around yourself with the "Tube of Light" decree. The tube of light, shown in the Chart of Your Divine Self (page 358), is a shield of protective white light about nine feet in diameter that descends from God and extends beneath your feet.

The tube of light can guard against malicious energies that may be directed at you through someone's anger, condemnation, hatred or jealousy. When you are unprotected, these negative energies can make you irritable or depressed and can even cause you to have accidents. The tube of light helps you stay centered and at peace.

It's a good idea to give your "Tube of Light" decree each morning before the hustle and bustle of the day begins. If throughout the day you feel de-energized, depleted or vulnerable, you can repeat this decree as needed.

Visualization and meditation:

As you recite the "Tube of Light" decree, see the dazzling white light from your I AM Presence,* brighter than the sun shining on new-fallen snow, coalescing to form an impenetrable wall of light around you. Inside this scintillating tube of light, see yourself enfolded with the violet flame, the spiritual fire of the Holy Spirit.

---

*The personal presence of God with you, depicted as the upper figure in the Chart of Your Divine Self (see page 358).

From time to time throughout the day, you can reinforce this spiritual protection by visualizing the tube of
light around you and repeating this decree.

> Beloved I AM Presence bright,
> Round me seal your tube of light
> From ascended master flame
> Called forth now in God's own name.
> Let it keep my temple free
> From all discord sent to me.
>
> I AM calling forth violet fire
> To blaze and transmute all desire,
> Keeping on in freedom's name
> Till I AM one with the violet flame.
>
> *(give decree 3 times)*

ARCHANGEL MICHAEL, GUARDIAN OF OUR SPIRITUAL PRACTICE

The next step in creating a forcefield of protection
is to invoke the intercession of Archangel Michael.
Archangel Michael is the most revered of angels in
Jewish, Christian and Islamic scriptures and tradition.
In the Old Testament, Archangel Michael figures as
the guardian of Israel. He appeared to Joshua as he
prepared to lead the Israelites into battle at Jericho and
revealed himself as "captain of the hosts of the LORD."

In one of the Dead Sea Scrolls, Michael is the
"mighty, ministering angel" through whom God promises to send perpetual help to the sons of light. In

ARCHANGEL MICHAEL

But the prince of the kingdom of Persia withstood me one and twenty days: but, lo, Michael, one of the chief princes [archangels], came to help me; and I remained there with the kings of Persia....

But I will shew thee that which is noted in the scripture of truth: and there is none that holdeth with me in these things, but Michael your prince....

And at that time shall Michael stand up, the great prince which standeth for the children of thy people: and there shall be a time of trouble, such as never was since there was a nation even to that same time: and at that time thy people shall be delivered, every one that shall be found written in the book.

And many of them that sleep in the dust of the earth shall awake, some to everlasting life, and some to shame and everlasting contempt.

And they that be wise shall shine as the brightness of the firmament; and they that turn many to righteousness as the stars for ever and ever.

Daniel

Catholic tradition, he is the patron and protector of the Church. In Muslim lore, he is Mika'il, the angel of nature who provides both food and knowledge to man.

Archangel Michael has numberless angels at his command whose job is to protect the children of God from physical and spiritual dangers. He is the guardian angel who oversees our spiritual practice.

You can give decrees to Archangel Michael every morning for the protection of yourself and loved ones, and you can give them at night to protect you while your soul travels out of your body during sleep. Throughout the day whenever you feel the need to reinforce God's protection around yourself or around those who may be suffering, you can stop and summon this powerful archangel.

Visualization and meditation:

Start by saying a prayer to Archangel Michael and his legions of angels to place their protective energy around you as you go through the day.

Visualize Archangel Michael as a majestic angel, arrayed in shining armour and wearing a brilliant sapphire-blue cape. See him standing before you, then behind you, then to your left, to your right, beneath, above and in the center of your form. See him accompanied by untold numbers of angels who will protect and escort you wherever you go.

Imagine Archangel Michael wielding a sword of blue flame to deliver you from all negative conditions that work against your soul's progress on the spiritual path. You can also imagine yourself wearing a helmet and armour of blue steel that will prevent any physical or spiritual danger from reaching your body or mind.

TRAVELING PROTECTION

Lord* Michael before,
Lord Michael behind,
Lord Michael to the right,
Lord Michael to the left,
Lord Michael above,
Lord Michael below,
Lord Michael, Lord Michael wherever I go!

I AM his love protecting here!
I AM his love protecting here!
I AM his love protecting here!

(give decree 3 or 9 times)

LORD MICHAEL

In the name of the beloved mighty victorious Presence of God, I AM in me, in the name of Jesus Christ, I call to my very own beloved Holy Christ Self, Holy Christ Selves of all children of the Light, beloved Archangel Michael and hosts of the LORD, legions of angels from the Great Central Sun, Mighty Elohim, seraphim and cherubim of God, for the protection of my life and family and all children of the Light:

---

*Lord is used here as a term of honor and does not connote equivalence to the Godhead.

Give entire decree 3 or 9 times:

1. Lord Michael, Lord Michael,
    I call unto thee—
    Wield thy sword of blue flame
    And now cut me free!

Refrain: Blaze God-power, protection
    Now into my world,
    Thy banner of faith
    Above me unfurl!
    Transcendent blue lightning
    Now flash through my soul,
    I AM by God's mercy
    Made radiant and whole!

2. Lord Michael, Lord Michael,
    I love thee, I do—
    With all thy great faith
    My being imbue!

(Repeat refrain)

3. Lord Michael, Lord Michael
    And legions of blue—
    Come seal me, now keep me
    Faithful and true!

(Repeat refrain)

Coda: I AM with thy blue flame
    Now full-charged and blest,
    I AM now in Michael's
    Blue-flame armor dressed!

(give coda 3 times)

"THEY SHALL NOT PASS!"
A Call for the Judgment of the Fallen Angels
Who Have Sworn Enmity against the Children of God
by Jesus Christ

Instruction:

When you have given the "Tube of Light" decree and decrees to Archangel Michael to establish a strong forcefield of protection, you are ready to give "They Shall Not Pass!"

Make a prayer specifically naming the conditions you want halted, such as:

> **In the name of the beloved mighty victorious Presence of God, I AM in me, and my very own beloved Holy Christ Self, I call to the seven archangels and all the hosts of the LORD to take command over** [give your personal prayer here to turn around conditions like child abuse, crime, drug trafficking, terrorism, etc.]**.**
>
> **I ask that my prayers be multiplied to assist all souls in distress. I thank you and I accept it done this hour in full power, according to the will of God.**

You can repeat "They Shall Not Pass!" a number of times for the binding of fallen angels and the liberation of all people. When you have finished, give the "And in full faith..." closing.

The most effective posture for giving this decree is to stand and raise your right hand to shoulder height using the *abhaya* mudra (gesture of fearlessness). The palm is turned outward and the fingers pointed upward. Place your left hand at the center of your chest, where your heart chakra is located, with the thumb and first two fingers pointing inward.

> In the Name of the I AM THAT I AM,
> I invoke the Electronic Presence of Jesus Christ:
> They shall not pass!
> They shall not pass!
> They shall not pass!
> By the authority of the cosmic cross of white fire
>   it shall be:
> That all that is directed against the Christ
>   within me, within the holy innocents,
>   within our beloved Messengers,
>   within every son and daughter of God
> Is now turned back
>   by the authority of Alpha and Omega,
>   by the authority of
>   my Lord and Saviour Jesus Christ,
>   by the authority of Saint Germain!
> I AM THAT I AM
>   within the center of this temple
>   and I declare in the fullness of the entire
>   Spirit of the Great White Brotherhood:
> That those who, then, practice the black arts
>   against the children of the Light
> Are now bound by the hosts of the LORD,

Do now receive the judgment of the Lord Christ
 within me, within Jesus
 and within every ascended master,
Do now receive, then,
 the full return—multiplied
 by the energy of the Cosmic Christ—
 of their nefarious deeds
 which they have practiced
 since the very incarnation of the Word!
Lo, I AM a Son of God!
Lo, I AM a Flame of God!
Lo, I stand upon the Rock of the living Word
And I declare with Jesus, the living Son of God:
They shall not pass!
They shall not pass!
They shall not pass!
Elohim. Elohim. Elohim. (*chant the last line*)

To be given once after you have concluded your decrees:

And in full faith I consciously accept this manifest, manifest, manifest! *(give 3 times)* right here and now with full power, eternally sustained, all-powerfully active, ever expanding and world enfolding until all are wholly ascended in the light and free!

Beloved I AM! Beloved I AM! Beloved I AM!

CHART OF YOUR DIVINE SELF

THE CHART OF
YOUR DIVINE SELF

The reason we can call to God and he will answer is because we are connected to him. We are his sons and daughters. We have a direct relationship to God and he has placed a portion of himself in us. In order to better understand this relationship, the ascended masters have designed the Chart of Your Divine Self.

The Chart of Your Divine Self is a portrait of you and of the God within you. It is a diagram of yourself and your potential to become who you really are. It is an outline of your spiritual anatomy.

The upper figure is your "I AM Presence," the Presence of God that is individualized in each one of us. Your I AM Presence is surrounded by seven concentric spheres of spiritual energy that make up what is called your "causal body." The spheres of pulsating energy contain the record of the good works you have performed since your very first incarnation on earth. They are like your cosmic bank account.

THE HIGHER SELF

The middle figure in the chart represents the "Holy Christ Self," who is also called the Higher Self. You can think of your Holy Christ Self as your chief guardian angel and dearest friend, your inner teacher and voice of conscience.

Just as the I AM Presence is the presence of God that is individualized for each of us, so the Holy Christ Self is the presence of the universal Christ that is individualized for each of us. "The Christ" is actually a title given to those who have attained oneness with their Higher Self, or Christ Self. That's why Jesus was called "Jesus, the Christ." *Christ* comes from the Greek word *christos,* meaning "anointed"—anointed with the light of God.

What the Chart shows is that each of us has a Higher Self, or "inner Christ," and that each of us is destined to become one with that Higher Self— whether we call it the Christ, the Buddha, the Tao or the Atman. This "inner Christ" is what the Christian mystics sometimes refer to as the "inner man of the heart," and what the Upanishads mysteriously describe as a being the "size of a thumb" who "dwells deep within the heart."

We all have moments when we feel that connection with our Higher Self—when we are creative, loving, joyful. But there are other moments when we feel out of sync with our Higher Self—moments when we become angry, depressed, lost. What the spiritual path is all about is learning to sustain the connection to the higher part of ourselves so that we can make our greatest contribution to humanity.

THE DIVINE SPARK

The shaft of white light descending from the I AM Presence through the Holy Christ Self to the lower figure in the Chart is the crystal cord (sometimes called the silver cord). It is the "umbilical cord," the lifeline, that ties you to Spirit.

Your crystal cord also nourishes that special, radiant flame of God that is ensconced in the secret chamber of your heart. It is called the threefold flame, or divine spark, because it is literally a spark of sacred fire that God has transmitted from his heart to yours. This flame is called "threefold" because it engenders the primary attributes of Spirit —power, wisdom and love.

The mystics of the world's religions have contacted the divine spark, describing it as the seed of divinity within. Buddhists, for instance, speak of the "germ of Buddhahood" that exists in every living being. In the Hindu tradition, the Katha Upanishad speaks of the "light of the Spirit" that is concealed in the "secret high place of the heart" of all beings.

Likewise, the fourteenth-century Christian theologian and mystic Meister Eckhart teaches of the divine spark when he says, "God's seed is within us." There is a part of us, says Eckhart, that "remains eternally in the Spirit and is divine.... Here God glows and flames without ceasing."

When we decree, we meditate on the flame in the secret chamber of our heart. This secret chamber is your own private meditation room, your interior castle, as Teresa of Avila called it. In Hindu tradition, the devotee visualizes a jeweled island in his heart. There he sees himself before a beautiful altar, where he worships his teacher in deep meditation.

Jesus spoke of entering the secret chamber of the heart when he said: "When thou prayest, enter into thy closet, and when thou hast shut thy door, pray to thy Father which is in secret; and thy Father which seeth in secret shall reward thee openly." Going into your closet to pray is going into another dimension of consciousness. It's entering into the heart and closing the door on the outside world.

YOUR SOUL'S POTENTIAL

The lower figure in the Chart of Your Divine Self represents you on the spiritual path, surrounded by the violet flame, the spiritual fire of the Holy Spirit, and the protective white light of God. The soul is the living potential of God—the part of you that is mortal but that can become immortal.

The purpose of your soul's evolution on earth is to grow in self-mastery, balance your karma and fulfill your mission on earth so that you can return to the spiritual dimensions that are your real home.

On Embodied Angels—
Then and Now

SATAN APPROACHING THE CONFINES
OF THE EARTH

THE ORIGEN CONSPIRACY

If Origen of Alexandria (186–255) was the most influential theologian of the early Greek Church —and he was—why have you never heard of "Saint Origen"?

In the early sixth century, when some of Origen's brilliant theological deductions about the nature of men and angels were gaining renewed popularity in Palestinian monasteries, anti-Origenist monks from Jerusalem took action. They conspired with a Roman deacon named Pelagius, a papal legate who exercised ungodly influence over the weak-willed Pope Vigilius.

Pelagius convinced the powerful Byzantine emperor Justinian to promulgate an imperial edict anathematizing certain of Origen's teachings in 543. Pope Vigilius endorsed the move.

Justinian's despotic control over the Church was such that priests, bishops, and even the pope were essentially powerless to resist his imperial doctrinal decrees. Justinian believed he and his wife, the power-mad ex-prostitute Theodora, were the elect of God to whom He had entrusted the entire Christian empire, including Rome. Together they made dogma and translated it into law—adding clerical approvals as a mere formality.[1]

In 553, Justinian arranged the Fifth Ecumenical Council (the Second Council of Constantinople). This time the pope refused to attend. Justinian responded by arresting him and appointing Pelagius as the new pontiff.

Because there exists today no manuscript documenting any papal approval whatsoever of the council's fifteen anathemas against Origen, some scholars deny that Origen's condemnation at this council was ever formalized through ratification by the Holy See.

But experts agree that in essence and in practice, Justinian and the bishops of Rome, Alexandria, Antioch, and Jerusalem condemned Origen's teaching on *certain points* and proclaimed it heretical—even if it did lack the signature of the Vicar of Christ.[2]

And apparently all Christian churches in the Byzantine empire under the yoke of Justinian (Rome included) forbade Origen's controversial teachings—most especially his premises concerning the preexistence of souls, which undergird the doctrine of reincarnation. In the centuries that followed, that doctrine was actively taught mostly among the heretical Cathars, Hermetic philosophers, alchemists, Rosicrucians, Christian Kabalists, and the like. For Catholic Christians it became a nonsubject, more than forgotten—dead by neglect.

So what *else* was controversial about Origen's works? Origen seems to have thought that whenever angels fall (which they could do at any time, depending on their own free will), they then walk the earth as men. If they persist in their evil ways, they ultimately become demons, which have, according to Origen, "cold and obscure bodies."[3]

For Origen, there were no hard-and-fast boundaries between angels and men. One fragment quotes him as teaching that "angels may become men or demons, and again from the latter they may rise to be men or angels."[4] Origen further explains the transition of angels' bodies to men's bodies in the following way:

When intended for the more imperfect spirits, it [the material substance] becomes solidified, thickens, and forms the bodies of this visible world. If it is serving higher intelligences, it shines with the brightness of the celestial bodies and serves as a garb for the angels of God, and the children of the Resurrection.[5]

Elsewhere he elaborates on this theme, describing how an incorporeal spirit gradually assumes a physical body:

If any rational, incorporeal, invisible creature is negligent, it will gradually fall to lower levels and there assume a body. The sort of body it assumes will depend on the place it falls into. Thus, it will first take on an ethereal body, then an aerial one; as it draws near the earth it will put on a coarser one still, and in the end it will be harnessed to human flesh.[6]

Origen also speaks of

> those souls which, on account of their excessive mental defects, stood in need of bodies of a grosser and more solid nature.[7]

One more comment of Origen explains further that there are

> those who, either owing to mental deficiencies, deserved to enter into bodies, or those who were carried away by their desire for visible things, and those also who, either willingly or unwillingly, were compelled...to perform certain services to such as had fallen into that condition.[8]

Later Church sources quote Origen's idea that some of the spirits originally created by God (which were, in his view, even higher than the angels) fell in the following manner: "No longer desiring the sight of God," Origen says that the spirits eventually "gave themselves over to worse things, each one following his own inclinations, and...they have taken bodies more or less subtile," according to the degree of their crime.[9]

Origen is also quoted as believing that these spirits who fell were those "in whom the divine love had grown cold" and states that these could have been "hidden in gross bodies such as ours, and have been called men."[10]

In that statement, Origen evinces the belief that certain men are actually the embodiments of wicked angels.

Fragments of his other teachings elaborate on this idea. Origen pursues at one point a lengthy analysis of Ezekiel's description of the prince of Tyre (Ezek. 28:12–19), showing that the prince described was actually "a certain angel who received the office of governing the nation of the Tyrians"—an angel who had fallen from his former holy place and was cast forth upon the earth. Origen's point is that the passage obviously describes no ordinary human prince, but "some superior power which had fallen away from a higher position, and had been reduced to a lower and worse condition."[11]

In his own words, he attempts to prove that "those opposing and malignant powers were not formed or created so by nature, but fell from a better to a worse position, and were converted into wicked beings."[12] Origen does not discount the possibility that this fallen angel had incarnated and literally governed the Tyrians. Indeed, that idea fits in well with Origen's teaching that fallen angels can become men.

But Origen also believed that *good* angels could incarnate in human bodies for divine purposes. In his *Commentary on the Gospel of John,* Origen concludes that John the Baptist was an angel who deliberately chose to become incarnate in order to minister to Christ. Origen says,

> From the beginning, those who have occupied the most eminent positions among men and been

markedly superior to others have been angels in human form. This explains the passage in Scripture which says that John was one of God's messengers, or angels, who came in the body to bear witness to the light.[13]

In Greek, the word for *messenger* is *angelos,* from which we get the English word *angel.* Our word *evangelist* has the literal meaning "one who brings a good message"—i.e., the gospel. The linguistic connection between *messenger* and *angel* is probably what prompted Origen's comment that the message-bearer John the Baptist must have been an angel.

One can only wonder whether Origen did not state in some now-destroyed writing the converse of that statement: namely, that the worst among men have been fallen angels or demons in human form. Here the lost pieces of Origen's angelology are sorely missed, for Origen is saying that both wicked angels and good angels incarnate among men—but whatever else he said on the subject vanished long ago.

The Second Council of Constantinople in 553 A.D. pronounced the following anathema against Origen's teaching:

If anyone shall say that the creation of all reasonable things includes only intelligences without bodies and altogether immaterial, having neither number nor name, so that there is unity between them all by identity of substance, force and energy, and by their union with and knowledge of God the Word; but that *no longer desiring the sight of God, they gave themselves over to worse things, each one following his own inclinations, and that they have taken bodies more or less subtile,* and have received names, for among the heavenly Powers there is a difference of names as there is also a difference of bodies; and thence some became and are called Cherubims, others Seraphims, and Principalities, and Powers, and Dominations, and Thrones, and Angels, and as many other heavenly orders as there may be: let him be anathema.[14] (emphasis added)

The council also directed two other anathemas against Origen:

If anyone shall say that *the reasonable creatures in whom the divine love had grown cold have been hidden in gross bodies such as ours, and have been called men,* while those who have attained the lowest degree of wickedness have shared cold and obscure bodies and are become and called demons and evil spirits: let him be anathema.

If anyone shall say that a psychic condition has come from an angelic or archangelic state, and moreover that a demoniac and a human condition has come from a psychic condition, and that from a human state they may become again angels and demons, and that each order of heavenly virtues is either all from those below or from those above, or from those above and below: let him be anathema.[15] (emphasis added)

Thus three of the fifteen anathemas against Origen curse his teaching on the incarnation of fallen spirits and angels becoming men. The long proclamation condemning each of Origen's ideas, "If anyone shall say [this]: let him be anathema"—let him be cursed— must have weighed heavily upon the conscience of the believer. Would anyone thereafter dare to believe that fallen angels could incarnate?

So despised—or perhaps, so *feared*—were the writings of Origen that only tattered fragments remain of the 6,000 works he wrote. Even in his own lifetime, Origen had to contend with falsifications of his works and forgeries under his name. Later Church Fathers, like Vincent of Lerins, quote Origen as the example of a prominent teacher who became a misleading light.

Origen endured the tortures instigated against Christians by the Roman emperor Decius—chains, an iron collar, and the rack. Upon the death of the Tormentor, he was released from the innermost dungeons of the imperial prison at Tyre in 251. Weak in body, mighty in spirit, Origen died in 254.

"If orthodoxy were a matter of intention," comments Oxford's Dean of Christ Church Henry Chadwick, "no theologian could be more orthodox than Origen."[16] In truth, he stood in steadfast support of the Church and the Faith. Yet in his own lifetime bishops and priests alike spurned him. For what? For purity of heart?

It was a dead-robed orthodoxy that crucified Origen, the Best exponent of Christ's doctrine, the Best of teachers, the Best of priests, and the Best of the embodied angels. Those who should have loved and defended him as brother feared him as heretic—and treated him worse. They put him on a cross inscribed "anathema."

Who will take him down?

We will—we will lay him in a tomb lined with white lilies and inscribe thereon "Origen—Bodhisattva of the Western Church."

NOTES

1. See Milton V. Anastos, *Justinian's Despotic Control over the Church...and his Letter to Pope John II in 533,* Recueil des travaux de l'Institut d'Etudes byzantines, no. 8 (Belgrade, 1964).

2. See *Dictionary of Christian Biography,* s.v. "Origenistic Controversies," pp. 152–56.

3. The Fifth Ecumenical Council, "The Anathemas against Origen," no. 4, in *The Seven Ecumenical Councils of the Undivided Church,* ed. Henry R. Percival, A Select Library of Nicene and Post-Nicene Fathers of the Christian Church, ed. Philip Schaff and Henry Wace, 2d ser., 14 vols. to date (1890–1899; reprint ed., Grand Rapids, Mich.: Wm. B. Eerdmans, 1979–), 14(1899):318.

4. Origen, *De Principiis* [On First Principles], trans. Frederick Crombie, in *Fathers of the Third Century,* ed. A. Cleveland Coxe, The Ante-Nicene Fathers, ed. Alexander Roberts and James Donaldson, 10 vols. to date (1867–1895; reprint ed., Grand Rapids, Mich.: Wm. B. Eerdmans, 1978–), 4(1885):267.

5. *The Catholic Encyclopedia,* s.v. "Origen."

6. Jean Daniélou, *Origen,* trans. Walter Mitchell (New York: Sheed and Ward, 1955), p. 218.

7. Origen, p. 342.

8. Ibid., p. 343.

9. Fifth Ecumenical Council, "The Anathemas against Origen," no. 2, 14:318.

10. Ibid., no. 4.

11. Origen, pp. 258–59. The *New Catholic Encyclopedia* (s.v. "Demon, Theology of"), commenting on Origen's teaching, states that this fallen angel "could be none other than Satan." This is a doctrinal interpretation that has no basis in the original text of Origen (which discusses the multiplicity of the fallen ones), or in Ezekiel for that matter.

12. Origen, p. 258.

13. Daniélou, p. 249.

14. Fifth Ecumenical Council, "The Anathemas against Origen," no. 2, 14:318.

15. Ibid., nos. 4, 5.

16. *Encyclopaedia Britannica,* 15th ed., s.v. "Origen."

RAMIFICATIONS OF
MEN AND ANGELS

It seems that ever since the fall of the angels (not Adam and Eve), pride and lust have been the cause of iniquity on planet Earth.

If people understood that conscious minds, embodied as fallen ones in their midst, use every advantage in the media to turn their attention to the lusts of the flesh and the eye, and the pride of life, might they not all the more resist temptation—knowing it is part of a conspiracy against their souls, the very revenge of the archdeceivers against their innocence and against the mutual love and promised presence of the Father and Son who take up their abode within the obedient and loving heart?

This promise is given to the servant-sons of God—not to the Watchers and the Nephilim. And they have never ceased their campaign to 'get even'.

After *Man, know thyself* the most important injunction in the battle of life is *Know thy enemy.* What the fallen angels who invaded the early Church—

at what level we know not—conspired to take from God's people was an accurate and scientific knowledge of the enemy and his modus operandi.

Could these "rulers of the darkness of this world" who purvey their "spiritual wickedness in high places" be the wolves in sheep's clothing—the false Christs and false prophets against whom Jesus warned?

Making the victim believe that the seed of the lie is born in his *own* mind and therefore conditioning him to accept the immediate guilt of self-incrimination for sin, rather than rise up to overthrow the *real* enemy, both within and without—this is the brainwashing of the principalities and powers of the fallen angels.

Their technique ought to be kept in mind wherever mass manipulation becomes a factor in deciding the issues of life—where definitions are redefined and the Truth is seen as the lie, and the Liar is heralded as the saviour of men and nations.

What many Catholics today sense as "something wrong" with the Church—something they cannot quite put their finger on—may very well be the infiltration of their ranks by fallen angels who have clouded the issues of Truth and error to their own devices.

There is nothing intrinsically wrong with the institution of the Church or with religious organization. There is nothing wrong with Jesus Christ or the office of his Vicar. There is nothing wrong with God and his true angels.

People may fail—but God never fails. And the

Rock of Christ upon which the Church is built remains the witness for Truth in the heart of every son of God. When the individual dedicates his temple to be the dwelling place of the Holy Spirit, when through his loving obedience Father and Son dwell with him and in him (John 14:23), he becomes a 'member' of the Mystical Body of God—a white stone in the temple made without hands, eternal in the heavens. And the gates of hell shall not prevail against this the living Church, which by definition is, must be, *universal and triumphant.*

The revelations of Enoch and the exposé of the fallen angels' conspiracy against Truth within both church and state need not bring a message of despair. For did not our Lord, the great World Teacher, and his messenger John the Baptist expose and denounce the seed of the wicked as a generation of vipers and the violent who storm heaven and take it by force, prying the secrets of creation as impostors of the Word?

If we then take heart and courageously lay the ax at the root of the trees of doctrinal error to make way for the tall tree of Truth noted for its good fruit, then hope, blest hope, is born.

And we will learn much about ourselves from this exposure of the seed of the wicked: Is our faith in man or in God? Have we made gods of the Church Fathers and the saints, believing them incapable of human error during their lifetimes? Do we stand straight as pillars of Truth or do we yet grovel in the idolatry of mortals *and embodied angels?*

Certainly we do not imply that the Church Fathers were themselves fallen angels, but that the "convoluted logic" (to borrow a term) in which they managed to get themselves entangled had its origin in sources they were ill-equipped to deal with. One might say, "fools rush in where angels fear to tread."

One can forgive them for being duped (even for duping others), but to prolong the error once Truth has dawned places a dark cloud in the sky of our heavenly aspiration. No doubt the bigoted defense of the personages and principles of Error while in the presence of the towering figures of Christ and his true apostles in every age will ultimately disclose on which bank of the river our leaders are encamped.

Therefore we 'condemn' not, lest we be 'condemned'. For with what judgment we judge, we shall be judged: and with what measure we mete, it shall be measured to us again. For even "Michael the archangel, when contending with the devil...durst not bring against him a railing accusation, but said, The Lord rebuke thee."

The fact that someone has erred—"to err is human, to forgive, divine"—does not mean he is evil. The frailty of the mortal state is such in saints and sinners alike. Sainthood is not won by intellectual prowess, but by a humble heart and true love for the brethren in Christ—by receptivity to the chastening hand of the Spirit, no matter who or what the instrument, and by a willingness to be God-taught and to surrender one's most cherished concepts when they are proven erroneous by the enlightenment of the Holy Spirit.

The spirit of scientific inquiry and investigation, the setting aside of former theories outlived and outworn, ought to permeate the world of religion as it does science. For only when we go forward on both fronts with an objective, empirical, as well as spiritual approach can these two pillars of our civilization bear witness to each other's lasting strength to uphold the temple of self-discovery in ever-succeeding ages—ages in which we push back the barriers to our cosmic self-awareness.

Now let us put the past with its limited and self-limiting conclusions in the flame of Truth. By transmutation and love, not condemnation, let us walk together on the pathway to the Sun.

We can, by our God-given conscience and free will, reject the premises of the fallen ones and demand that our representatives in church and in state give us the whole Truth and nothing but the Truth. And if they do not, we will give the Truth to them. And the Truth shall awaken many, as the Lord told Daniel: some to everlasting life, and some to shame and everlasting contempt of that Christ Truth and his messengers.

Thus shall the betrayers of the people be exposed by their actions and their consciousness, and the facts and the alternatives be made clear. And all people bond and free shall be able to choose Life and not death—

and to accept the consequences of their choices.

But we are not on a witch-hunt. No, never! Let God deal with the proud and the unruly. Has he not said, "Vengeance is mine; I will repay"? Our Armageddon is in the arena of the heart and the soul—and the seat of the conscious mind. When we know the Truth and preach the way of righteousness, the true followers of God as his dear children will believe and will be set free from the philosophical snares, both political and religious, of these archdeceivers.

It is not the latter whom we would convince or convert. Their judgment is already set in the Book of Enoch. It never was in our hands. But the matter of salvation unto the sons of God is. With our Lord Jesus Christ we must go after the lost sheep and return them to the true Shepherd and his fold.

The legacy of Truth vouchsafed to us by our Father Enoch, by John the Baptist and Jesus Christ, and by Origen of Alexandria—all of whom taught us an essential lesson of fallen angels incarnate among men— is our birthright. They recorded knowledge we were supposed to have had all along.

We have endured mist-covered centuries of lies and half-truths because, left to their ignorance, men lacked the tools of self-knowledge to fully disclose the nature of the Liar and his lie.

But as Enoch foresaw, the time would come when, sword of Truth in hand, we would take to ourselves the shield of the Lord's wisdom and his counsel and go forth to fight for that soul liberation which only the living Truth can deliver.

The time is now. See the Faithful and True, with his armies and his saints, marching across the continents of the world, delivering the innocent-of-heart in every nation from the long night of self-ignorance, artificially (i.e., *with artifice*) prolonged by the Watchers and the Nephilim.

"And none can stay his hand, or say unto him, What doest Thou?"

C. S. Lewis on Bad Angels

Cambridge scholar and author C. S. Lewis wrote about the modus operandi of "bad angels" in his renowned Screwtape Letters. *His psychological analysis of these bad angels is keenly descriptive of embodied Watchers.*

The commonest question is whether I really "believe in the Devil."

Now, if by "the Devil" you mean a power opposite to God and, like God, self-existent from all eternity, the answer is certainly No. There is no uncreated being except God. God has no opposite. No being could attain a "perfect badness" opposite to the perfect goodness of God; for when you have taken away every kind of good thing (intelligence, will, memory, energy, and existence itself) there would be none of him left.

The proper question is whether I believe in devils. I do. That is to say, I believe in angels, and I believe that some of these, by the abuse of their free will, have become enemies to God and, as a corollary, to us. These we may call devils. They do not differ in nature from good angels, but their nature is depraved. *Devil* is the opposite of *angel* only as Bad Man is the opposite of Good Man. Satan, the leader or dictator of devils, is the opposite, not of God, but of Michael.

I believe this not in the sense that it is part of my creed, but in the sense that it is one of my opinions. My religion would not be in ruins if this opinion were shown to be false. Till that happens—and proofs of a negative are hard to come by—I shall retain it. It seems to me to explain a good many facts. It agrees with the plain sense of Scripture, the tradition of Christendom, and the beliefs of most men at most times. And it conflicts with nothing that any of the sciences has shown to be true.

It should be (but it is not) unnecessary to add that a belief in angels, whether good or evil, does not mean a belief in either as they are represented in art and literature. Devils are depicted with bats' wings and good angels with birds' wings, not because anyone holds that moral deterioration would be likely to turn feathers into membrane, but because most men like birds better than bats. They are given wings at all in order to suggest the swiftness of unimpeded intellectual energy. They are given human form because man is the only rational creature we know....

In the plastic arts these symbols have steadily degenerated. Fra Angelico's angels carry in their face and gesture the peace and authority of Heaven. Later come the chubby infantile nudes of Raphael; finally the soft, slim, girlish, and consolatory angels of nineteenth century art, shapes so feminine that they avoid being voluptuous only by their total insipidity—the frigid houris of a teatable paradise. They are a pernicious symbol. In Scripture the visitation of an angel is always alarming; it has to begin by saying "Fear not." The Victorian angel looks as if it were going to say, "There, there."...

I like bats much better than bureaucrats. I live in the Managerial Age, in a world of "Admin." The greatest evil is not now done in those sordid "dens of crime" that Dickens loved to paint. It is not done even in concentration camps and labour camps. In those we see its final result. But it is conceived and ordered (moved, seconded, carried, and minuted) in clean, carpeted, warmed, and well-lighted offices, by quiet men with white collars and cut fingernails and smooth-shaven cheeks who do not need to raise their voice. Hence, naturally enough, my symbol for Hell is something like the bureaucracy of a police state or the offices of a thoroughly nasty business concern....

On the surface, manners are normally suave. Rudeness to one's superiors would obviously be suicidal; rudeness to one's equals might put them on their guard before you were ready to spring your mine. For of course "Dog eat dog" is the principle of the whole organisation. Everyone wishes everyone else's discrediting, demotion, and ruin; everyone is an expert in the confidential report, the pretended alliance, the stab in the back. Over all this their good manners, their expressions of grave respect, their "tributes" to one another's invaluable services form a thin crust. Every now and then it gets punctured, and the scalding lava of their hatred spurts out....

Bad angels, like bad men, are entirely practical. They have two motives. The first is fear of punishment: for as totalitarian countries have their camps for torture, so my Hell contains deeper Hells, its "houses of correction." Their second motive is a kind of hunger. I feign that devils can, in a spiritual sense, eat one another; and us. Even in human life we have seen the passion to dominate, almost to digest, one's fellow; to make his whole intellectual and emotional life merely an extension of one's own—to hate one's hatreds and resent one's grievances and indulge one's egoism through him as well as through oneself. His own little store of passion must of course be suppressed to make room for ours. If he resists this suppression he is being very selfish.

On Earth this desire is often called "love." In Hell I feign that they recognise it as hunger. But there the hunger is more ravenous, and a fuller satisfaction is possible. There, I suggest, the stronger spirit—there are perhaps no bodies to impede the operation—can really and irrevocably suck the weaker into itself and permanently gorge its own being on the weaker's outraged individuality. It is (I feign) for this that devils desire human souls and the souls of one another. It is for this that Satan desires all his own followers and all the sons of Eve and all the host of Heaven. His dream is of the day when all shall be inside him and all that says "I" can say it only through him. This, I surmise, is the bloated-spider parody, the only imitation he can understand, of that unfathomed bounty whereby God turns tools into servants and servants into sons, so that they may be at last reunited to Him in the perfect freedom of a love offered from the height of the utter individualities which he has liberated them to be....

"My heart"—I need no other's—"showeth me the wickedness of the ungodly."

The Screwtape Letters

Then was Jesus led up of the Spirit into the wilderness to be tempted of the devil.

And when he had fasted forty days and forty nights, he was afterward an hungred.

And when the tempter came to him, he said, If thou be the Son of God, command that these stones be made bread.

But he answered and said, It is written, Man shall not live by bread alone, but by every word that proceedeth out of the mouth of God.

Then the devil taketh him up into the holy city, and setteth him on a pinnacle of the temple,

And saith unto him, If thou be the Son of God, cast thyself down: for it is written, He shall give his angels charge concerning thee: and in their hands they shall bear thee up, lest at any time thou dash thy foot against a stone.

Jesus said unto him, It is written again, Thou shalt not tempt the Lord thy God.

Again, the devil taketh him up into an exceeding high mountain, and sheweth him all the kingdoms of the world, and the glory of them;

And saith unto him, All these things will I give thee, if thou wilt fall down and worship me.

Then saith Jesus unto him, Get thee hence, Satan: for it is written, Thou shalt worship the Lord thy God, and him only shalt thou serve.

Then the devil leaveth him, and, behold, angels came and ministered unto him.

Matthew 4:1–11

THE TEMPTATION OF JESUS

The Book of the
Secrets of Enoch

TRANSLATED BY

W. R. MORFILL, M.A.

*In the day that God created man, in the likeness
of God made he him;*

*Male and female created he them; and blessed them,
and called their name* Adam, *in the day when they were
created.*

*And Adam lived an hundred and thirty years,
and begat a son in his own likeness, after his image;
and called his name* Seth:

*And Seth lived an hundred and five years,
and begat* Enos:

And Enos lived ninety years, and begat Cainan:

And Cainan lived seventy years, and begat
Mahalaleel:

*And Mahalaleel lived sixty and five years,
and begat* Jared:

*And Jared lived an hundred sixty and two years,
and he begat* Enoch:

*And Enoch lived sixty and five years,
and begat* Methuselah:

*And Enoch walked with God after he begat Methu-
selah three hundred years, and begat sons and daughters:*

*And all the days of Enoch were three hundred sixty
and five years:*

*And Enoch walked with God: and he was not;
for God took him.*

*And Methuselah lived an hundred eighty and
seven years, and begat* Lamech:

*And Lamech lived an hundred eighty and two years,
and begat a son:*

And he called his name Noah, *saying, This same shall
comfort us concerning our work and toil of our hands,
because of the ground which the Lord hath cursed.*

*And Noah was five hundred years old: and Noah
begat* Shem, Ham, *and* Japheth.

Genesis

TO THE SONS OF JARED

And now, my children, mark well all the words of your father, that I tell you, lest you regret, saying: 'Why did our father not tell us?'

Enoch, son of Jared, to his children
The Book of the Secrets of Enoch

Prologue on the Sons of Jared

Taken from the Second Book of Adam and Eve

CHAPTER 19

The children of Jared are led astray.

1 Then God revealed to him [Jared] again the promise He had made to Adam; He explained to him the 5,500 years, and revealed unto him the mystery of His coming upon the earth.

2 And God said to Jared, "As to that fire which thou hast taken from the altar to light the lamp withal, let it abide with you to give light to the bodies;[1] and let it not come out of the cave, until the body of Adam comes out of it.

3 "But, O Jared, take care of the fire, that it burn bright in the lamp; neither go thou again out of the cave, until thou receivest an order through a vision, and not in an apparition, when seen by thee.

4 "Then command again thy people not to hold intercourse with the children of Cain, and not to learn

---

1. The bodies of Adam, Seth, Enos, Cainan, Mahalaleel were buried in the Cave of Treasures.

their ways; for I am God who loves not hatred and works of iniquity."

5 God gave also many other commandments to Jared, and blessed him. And then withdrew His Word from him.

6 Then Jared drew near with his children, took some fire, and came down to the cave, and lighted the lamp before the body of Adam; and he gave his people commandments as God had told him to do.

7 This sign happened to Jared at the end of his four hundred and fiftieth year; as did also many other wonders, we do not record. But we record only this one for shortness sake, and in order not to lengthen our narrative.

8 And Jared continued to teach his children eighty years; but after that they began to transgress the commandments he had given them, and to do many things without his counsel. They began to go down from the Holy Mountain one after another, and to mix with the children of Cain, in foul fellowships.

9 Now the reason for which the children of Jared went down the Holy Mountain, is this, that we will now reveal unto you.

CHAPTER 20

Ravishing music; strong drink loosed among the sons of Cain. They don colorful clothing. The children of Seth look on with longing eyes. They revolt from wise counsel; they descend the mountain

*into the valley of iniquity. They can not ascend
the mountain again.*

1 After Cain had gone down to the land of dark
soil, and his children had multiplied therein, there was
one of them, whose name was Genun, son of Lamech
the blind who slew Cain.

2 But as to this Genun, Satan came into him in his
childhood; and he made sundry trumpets and horns,
and string instruments, cymbals and psalteries, and
lyres and harps, and flutes; and he played on them at
all times and at every hour.

3 And when he played on them, Satan came into
them, so that from among them were heard beautiful
and sweet sounds, that ravished the heart.

4 Then he gathered companies upon companies
to play on them; and when they played, it pleased well
the children of Cain, who inflamed themselves with
sin among themselves, and burnt as with fire; while
Satan inflamed their hearts, one with another, and increased lust among them.

5 Satan also taught Genun to bring strong drink
out of corn; and this Genun used to bring together
companies upon companies in drink-houses; and
brought into their hands all manner of fruits and
flowers; and they drank together.

6 Thus did this Genun multiply sin exceedingly;
he also acted with pride, and taught the children of
Cain to commit all manner of the grossest wickedness,
which they knew not; and put them up to manifold

doings which they knew not before.

7 Then Satan, when he saw that they yielded to Genun and hearkened to him in every thing he told them, rejoiced greatly, increased Genun's understanding, until he took iron and with it made weapons of war.

8 Then when they were drunk, hatred and murder increased among them; one man used violence against another to teach him evil, taking his children and defiling them before him.

9 And when men saw they were overcome, and saw others that were not overpowered, those who were beaten came to Genun, took refuge with him, and he made them his confederates.

10 Then sin increased among them greatly; until a man married his own sister, or daughter, or mother, and others; or the daughter of his father's sister, so that there was no more distinction of relationship, and they no longer knew what is iniquity; but did wickedly, and the earth was defiled with sin; and they angered God the Judge, who had created them.

11 But Genun gathered together companies upon companies, that played on horns and on all the other instruments we have already mentioned, at the foot of the Holy Mountain; and they did so in order that the children of Seth who were on the Holy Mountain should hear it.

12 But when the children of Seth heard the noise, they wondered, and came by companies, and stood on

the top of the mountain to look at those below; and they did thus a whole year.

13 When, at the end of that year, Genun saw that they were being won over to him little by little, Satan entered into him, and taught him to make dyeingstuffs for garments of divers patterns, and made him understand how to dye crimson and purple and what not.

14 And the sons of Cain who wrought all this, and shone in beauty and gorgeous apparel, gathered together at the foot of the mountain in splendour, with horns and gorgeous dresses, and horse races, committing all manner of abominations.

15 Meanwhile the children of Seth, who were on the Holy Mountain, prayed and praised God, in the place of the hosts of angels who had fallen; wherefore God had called them "angels," because He rejoiced over them greatly.

16 But after this, they no longer kept His commandment, nor held by the promise He had made to their fathers; but they relaxed from their fasting and praying, and from the counsel of Jared their father. And they kept on gathering together on the top of the mountain, to look upon the children of Cain, from morning until evening, and upon what they did, upon their beautiful dresses and ornaments.

17 Then the children of Cain looked up from below, and saw the children of Seth, standing in troops on the top of the mountain; and they called to them to come down to them.

18 But the children of Seth said to them from above, "We don't know the way." Then Genun, the son of Lamech, heard them say they did not know the way, and he bethought himself how he might bring them down.

19 Then Satan appeared to him by night, saying, "There is no way for them to come down from the mountain on which they dwell; but when they come to-morrow, say to them, 'Come ye to the western side of the mountain; there you will find the way of a stream of water, that comes down to the foot of the mountain, between two hills; come down that way to us.'"

20 Then when it was day, Genun blew the horns and beat the drums below the mountain, as he was wont. The children of Seth heard it, and came as they used to do.

21 Then Genun said to them from down below, "Go to the western side of the mountain, there you will find the way to come down."

22 But when the children of Seth heard these words from him, they went back into the cave to Jared, to tell him all they had heard.

23 Then when Jared heard it, he was grieved; for he knew that they would transgress his counsel.

24 After this a hundred men of the children of Seth gathered together, and said among themselves, "Come, let us go down to the children of Cain, and see what they do, and enjoy ourselves with them."

25 But when Jared heard this of the hundred men, his very soul was moved, and his heart was grieved. He then arose with great fervour, and stood in the midst of them, and adjured them by the blood of Abel the just, "Let not one of you go down from this holy and pure mountain, in which our fathers have ordered us to dwell."

26 But when Jared saw that they did not receive his words, he said unto them, "O my good and innocent and holy children, know that when once you go down from this holy mountain, God will not allow you to return again to it."

27 He again adjured them, saying, "I adjure by the death of our father Adam, and by the blood of Abel, of Seth, of Enos, of Cainan, and of Mahalaleel, to hearken to me, and not to go down from this holy mountain; for the moment you leave it, you will be reft of life and of mercy; and you shall no longer be called 'children of God,' but 'children of the devil.'"

28 But they would not hearken to his words.

29 Enoch at that time was already grown up, and in his zeal for God, he arose and said, "Hear me, O ye sons of Seth, small and great—when ye transgress the commandment of our fathers, and go down from this holy mountain—ye shall not come up hither again for ever."

30 But they rose up against Enoch, and would not hearken to his words, but went down from the Holy Mountain.

31 And when they looked at the daughters of Cain, at their beautiful figures, and at their hands and feet dyed with colour, and tattooed in ornaments on their faces, the fire of sin was kindled in them.

32 Then Satan made them look most beautiful before the sons of Seth, as he also made the sons of Seth appear of the fairest in the eyes of the daughters of Cain, so that the daughters of Cain lusted after the sons of Seth like ravenous beasts, and the sons of Seth after the daughters of Cain, until they committed abomination with them.

33 But after they had thus fallen into this defilement, they returned by the way they had come, and tried to ascend the Holy Mountain. But they could not, because the stones of that holy mountain were of fire flashing before them, by reason of which they could not go up again.

34 And God was angry with them, and repented of them because they had come down from glory, and had thereby lost or forsaken their own purity or innocence, and were fallen into the defilement of sin.

35 Then God sent His Word to Jared, saying, "These thy children, whom thou didst call 'My children,'—behold they have transgressed My commandment, and have gone down to the abode of perdition, and of sin. Send a messenger to those that are left, that they may not go down, and be lost."

36 Then Jared wept before the Lord, and asked of Him mercy and forgiveness. But he wished that his

soul might depart from his body, rather than hear these words from God about the going down of his children from the Holy Mountain.

37 But he followed God's order, and preached unto them not to go down from that holy mountain, and not to hold intercourse with the children of Cain.

38 But they heeded not his message, and would not obey his counsel.

CHAPTER 21

Jared dies in sorrow for his sons who had gone astray. A prediction of the Flood.

1 After this another company gathered together, and they went to look after their brethren; but they perished as well as they. And so it was, company after company, until only a few of them were left.

2 Then Jared sickened from grief, and his sickness was such that the day of his death drew near.

3 Then he called Enoch his eldest son, and Methuselah Enoch's son, and Lamech the son of Methuselah, and Noah the son of Lamech.

4 And when they were come to him he prayed over them and blessed them, and said to them, "Ye are righteous, innocent sons; go ye not down from this holy mountain; for behold, your children and your children's children have gone down from this holy mountain, and have estranged themselves from this holy mountain, through their abominable lust and transgression of God's commandment.

5 "But I know, through the power of God, that He will not leave you on this holy mountain, because your children have transgressed His commandment and that of our fathers, which we had received from them.

6 "But, O my sons, God will take you to a strange land, and ye never shall again return to behold with your eyes this garden and this holy mountain.

7 "Therefore, O my sons, set your hearts on your own selves, and keep the commandment of God which is with you. And when you go from this holy mountain, into a strange land which ye know not, take with you the body of our father Adam, and with it these three precious gifts and offerings, namely, the gold, the incense, and the myrrh; and let them be in the place where the body of our father Adam shall lay.

8 "And unto him of you who shall be left, O my sons, shall the Word of God come, and when he goes out of this land he shall take with him the body of our father Adam, and shall lay it in the middle of the earth, the place in which salvation shall be wrought."

9 Then Noah said unto him, "Who is he of us that shall be left?"

10 And Jared answered, "Thou art he that shall be left. And thou shalt take the body of our father Adam from the cave, and place it with thee in the ark when the flood comes.

11 "And thy son Shem, who shall come out of thy loins, he it is who shall lay the body of our father

Adam in the middle of the earth, in the place whence salvation shall come."

12 Then Jared turned to his son Enoch, and said unto him, "Thou, my son, abide in this cave, and minister diligently before the body of our father Adam all the days of thy life; and feed thy people in righteousness and innocence."

13 And Jared said no more. His hands were loosened, his eyes closed, and he entered into rest like his fathers. His death took place in the three hundred and sixtieth year of Noah, and in the nine hundred and eighty-ninth year of his own life; on the twelfth of Takhsas on a Friday.

14 But as Jared died, tears streamed down his face by reason of his great sorrow, for the children of Seth, who had fallen in his days.

15 Then Enoch, Methuselah, Lamech and Noah, these four, wept over him; embalmed him carefully, and then laid him in the Cave of Treasures. Then they rose and mourned for him forty days.

16 And when these days of mourning were ended, Enoch, Methuselah, Lamech and Noah remained in sorrow of heart, because their father had departed from them, and they saw him no more.

CHAPTER 22

Only three righteous men left in the world. The evil conditions of men prior to the Flood.

1 But Enoch kept the commandment of Jared his

father, and continued to minister in the cave.

2 It is this Enoch to whom many wonders happened, and who also wrote a celebrated book; but those wonders may not be told in this place.

3 Then after this, the children of Seth went astray and fell, they, their children and their wives. And when Enoch, Methuselah, Lamech and Noah saw them, their hearts suffered by reason of their fall into doubt full of unbelief; and they wept and sought of God mercy, to preserve them, and to bring them out of that wicked generation.

4 Enoch continued in his ministry before the Lord three hundred and eighty-five years, and at the end of that time he became aware through the grace of God, that God intended to remove him from the earth.

5 He then said to his son, "O my son, I know that God intends to bring the waters of the Flood upon the earth, and to destroy our creation.

6 "And ye are the last rulers over this people on this mountain; for I know that not one will be left you to beget children on this holy mountain; neither shall any one of you rule over the children of his people; neither shall any great company be left of you, on this mountain."

7 Enoch said also to them, "Watch over your souls, and hold fast by your fear of God and by your service of Him, and worship Him in upright faith, and serve Him in righteousness, innocence and judgment, in repentance and also in purity."

8 When Enoch had ended his commandments to them, God transported him from that mountain to the land of life, to the mansions of the righteous and of the chosen, the abode of Paradise of joy, in light that reaches up to heaven; light that is outside the light of this world; for it is the light of God, that fills the whole world, but which no place can contain.

9 Thus, because Enoch was in the light of God, he found himself out of the reach of death; until God would have him die.

10 Altogether, not one of our fathers or of their children, remained on that holy mountain, except those three, Methuselah, Lamech, and Noah. For all the rest went down from the mountain and fell into sin with the children of Cain. Therefore were they forbidden that mountain, and none remained on it but those three men.

INTRODUCTION

An entirely different Enoch manuscript has survived in the Slavonic language. This text, dubbed "2 Enoch" and commonly called "the Slavonic Enoch," was discovered in 1886 by a Professor Sokolov in the archives of the Belgrade Public Library. It appears that just as the Ethiopic Enoch ("1 Enoch") had escaped the sixth-century Church suppression of Enoch texts in the Mediterranean area, so a Slavonic Enoch had survived far away, long after the originals from which it was copied were destroyed or hidden away.

Specialists in the Enoch texts surmise that the missing original from which the Slavonic was copied was probably a Greek manuscript. This may have been, in turn, based upon a Hebrew or Aramaic manuscript.

Many Aramaic fragments of 1 Enoch have been recovered in the past few decades from the Qumran caves which preserved the scriptures of the Essenes, showing the importance of Enoch to the Essene community. It is also possible that the core of the Slavonic

Enoch, the Book of the Secrets of Enoch, was known to the Essene brotherhood, although none of its records have been found in the few scattered remnants of that community.

The Slavonic text bears evidence of many later additions to the original manuscript. Such editorializing is common in religious texts, and it can include, unfortunately, the deletion of teachings considered "erroneous."

Because of certain calendrical data in the Slavonic Enoch, some claim the text cannot be earlier than the seventh century A.D. Most scholars see Christian influences in the Slavonic Enoch and therefore assign it, at the earliest, to the first century A.D.

But some see these troublesome passages not as evidence of Christian authorship, but as later Christian interpolations into an earlier manuscript. Enochian specialist R. H. Charles, for instance, believes that even the better of the two Slavonic manuscripts contains interpolations and is, in textual terms, "corrupt."

Most scholars agree that the Slavonic Enoch is an eclectic and syncretistic text, perhaps compiled by Christian writers but probably having origins in an earlier tradition. It may be dependent upon 1 Enoch, although it is recognized as a separate part of the literary tradition concerning the patriarch Enoch.

The Slavonic Enoch thus could preserve another part of a profound teaching on the fallen angels known to the early Judaic peoples but mainly lost to us. For this reason, the Slavonic Enoch is valuable, despite its editorial shortcomings.

So although the fingerprints of many centuries of later editors are left upon this manuscript, they do not necessarily invalidate the authenticity and antiquity of this book and its teaching. The ring of truth echoes from many of its pages.

As with the Ethiopic text of 1 Enoch, the chapters of this book may be spartan editions of several separate and larger books. Many scholars have seen in 1 Enoch separate books titled: the Ancient Book, the First and Second Books of the Watchers, the First Book of Secrets or the Vision of Wisdom, the Vision of Noah and History, and the Book of Astronomy. There could be a similar set of resources, differently compiled, behind the Slavonic Enoch.

Enoch tells us here that he wrote 366 books. Why, then, should we not postulate some one or two or ten of his "lost" books behind this Slavonic Enoch?

[Our inclusion of the Book of the Secrets of Enoch and the apocryphal works that follow in "Enoch in the Forgotten Books" does not indicate that they are necessarily of the same spiritual caliber as the Book of Enoch, which is the longest and most important document in the Enochian literature. But these lesser works do underscore the authenticity of the Book of Enoch, both by thematic borrowing (as in the Book of the Secrets of Enoch) and in direct citation (as in the Book of Jubilees and the Testaments of the Twelve Patriarchs).]

"AND THE LORD SUMMONED ME..."

THE BOOK OF THE
SECRETS OF ENOCH

CHAPTER 1

*An account of the mechanism of the world showing
the machinery of the sun and moon in operation.
Astronomy and an interesting ancient calendar.
See Chapter 15–17 also 21. What the world was
like before Creation, see Chapter 24. Chapter 26
is especially picturesque. A unique account of
how Satan was created (Chapter 29.)*

1 There was a wise man, a great artificer, and the
Lord conceived love for him and received him, that he
should behold the uppermost dwellings and be an eye-
witness of the wise and great and inconceivable and
immutable realm of God Almighty, of the very wonderful and glorious and bright and many-eyed station
of the Lord's servants, and of the inaccessible throne of
the Lord, and of the degrees and manifestations of the
incorporeal hosts, and of the ineffable ministration of
the multitude of the elements, and of the various

apparition and inexpressible singing of the host of Cherubim, and of the boundless light.

2 At that time, he said, when my 165th year was completed, I begat my son Mathusal.

3 After this too I lived two hundred years and completed of all the years of my life three hundred and sixty-five years.

4 On the first day of the first month I was in my house alone and was resting on my couch and slept.

5 And when I was asleep, great distress came up into my heart, and I was weeping with my eyes in sleep, and I could not understand what this distress was, or what would happen to me.

6 And there appeared to me two men, exceeding big, so that I never saw such on earth; their faces were shining like the sun, their eyes too *were* like a burning light, and from their lips was fire coming forth with clothing and singing of various kinds in appearance purple, their wings *were* brighter than gold, their hands whiter than snow.

7 They were standing at the head of my couch and began to call me by my name.

8 And I arose from my sleep and saw clearly those two men standing in front of me.

9 And I saluted them and was seized with fear and the appearance of my face was changed from terror, and those men said to me:

10 'Have courage, Enoch, do not fear; the eternal God sent us to thee, and lo! thou shalt to-day ascend

with us into heaven, and thou shalt tell thy sons and all thy household all that they shall do without thee on earth in thy house, and let no one seek thee till the Lord return thee to them.'

11 And I made haste to obey them and went out from my house, and made to the doors, as it was ordered me, and summoned my sons Mathusal and Regim and Gaidad and made known to them all the marvels those *men* had told me.

CHAPTER 2

The Instruction. How Enoch instructed his sons.

Listen to me, my children, I know not whither I go, or what will befall me; now therefore, my children, I tell you: turn not from God before the face of the vain, who made not Heaven and earth, for these shall perish and those who worship them, and may the Lord make confident your hearts in the fear of him. And now, my children, let no one think to seek me, until the Lord return me to you.

CHAPTER 3

Of Enoch's assumption; how the angels took him into the first heaven.

It came to pass, when Enoch had told his sons, that the angels took him on to their wings and bore him up on to the first heaven and placed him on the clouds. And there I looked, and again I looked higher, and saw the ether, and they placed me on the first heaven and showed me a very great Sea, greater than the earthly sea.

CHAPTER 4

Of the angels ruling the stars.

They brought before my face the elders and rulers of the stellar orders, and showed me two hundred angels, who rule the stars and *their* services to the heavens, and fly with their wings and come round all those who sail.

CHAPTER 5

Of how the angels keep the store-houses of the snow.

And here I looked down and saw the treasure-houses of the snow, and the angels who keep their terrible store-houses, and the clouds whence they come out and into which they go.

CHAPTER 6

Of the dew and of the olive-oil, and various flowers.

They showed me the treasure-house of the dew, like oil of the olive, and the appearance of its form, as of all the flowers of the earth; further many angels guarding the treasure-houses of these *things, and* how they are made to shut and open.

CHAPTER 7

Of how Enoch was taken on to the second heaven.

1 And those men took me and led me up on to the second heaven, and showed me darkness, greater than

earthly darkness, and there I saw prisoners hanging, watched, awaiting the great and boundless judgement, and these angels were dark-looking, more than earthly darkness, and incessantly making weeping through all hours.

2 And I said to the men who were with me: 'Wherefore are these incessantly tortured?' they answered me: 'These are God's apostates, who obeyed not God's commands, but took counsel with their own will, and turned away with their prince, who also *is* fastened on the fifth heaven.'

3 And I felt great pity for them, and they saluted me, and said to me: 'Man of God, pray for us to the Lord'; and I answered to them: 'Who am I, a mortal man, that I should pray for angels? who knoweth whither I go, or what will befall me? or who will pray for me?'

CHAPTER 8

Of the assumption of Enoch to the third heaven.

1 And those men took me thence, and led me up on to the third heaven, and placed me there; and I looked downwards, and saw the produce of these places, such as has never been known for goodness.

2 And I saw all the sweet-flowering trees and beheld their fruits, which were sweet-smelling, and all the foods borne *by them* bubbling with fragrant exhalation.

3 And in the midst of the trees that of life, in that place whereon the Lord rests, when he goes up into par-

adise; and this tree is of ineffable goodness and fragrance, and adorned more than every existing thing; and on all sides *it is* in form gold-looking and vermilion and fire-like and covers all, and it has produce from all fruits.

4 Its root is in the garden at the earth's end.

5 And paradise is between corruptibility and incorruptibility.

6 And two springs come out which send forth honey and milk, and their springs send forth oil and wine, and they separate into four parts, and go round with quiet course, and go down into the PARADISE OF EDEN, between corruptibility and incorruptibility.

7 And thence they go forth along the earth, and have a revolution to their circle even as other elements.

8 And here there is no unfruitful tree, and every place is blessed.

9 And *there are* three hundred angels very bright, who keep the garden, and with incessant sweet singing and never-silent voices serve the Lord throughout all days and hours.

10 And I said: 'How very sweet is this place,' and those men said to me:

CHAPTER 9

The showing to Enoch of the place of the righteous and compassionate.

This place, O Enoch, is prepared for the righteous, who endure all manner of offence from those that exasperate their souls, who avert their eyes from iniquity, and make righteous judgement, and give bread to the hungering, and cover the naked with clothing, and raise up the fallen, and help injured orphans, and who walk without fault before the face of the Lord, and serve him alone, and for them is prepared this place for eternal inheritance.

CHAPTER 10

Here they showed Enoch the terrible place and
various tortures.

1 And those two men led me up on to the Northern side, and showed me there a very terrible place, and *there were* all manner of tortures in that place: cruel darkness and unillumined gloom, and there is no light there, but murky fire constantly flameth aloft, and *there is* a fiery river coming forth, and that whole place is everywhere fire, and everywhere *there is* frost and ice, thirst and shivering, while the bonds are very cruel, and the angels fearful and merciless, bearing angry weapons, merciless torture, and I said:

2 'Woe, woe, how very terrible is this place.'

3 And those men said to me: This place, O Enoch, is prepared for those who dishonour God, who on earth practise sin against nature, which is child-corruption after the sodomitic fashion, magic-making, enchantments and devilish witchcrafts, and who boast of their wicked deeds, stealing, lies, calumnies, envy, rancour, fornication, murder, and who, accursed, steal the souls of men, who, seeing the poor take away their

goods and themselves wax rich, injuring them for other men's goods; who being able to satisfy the empty, made the hungering to die; being able to clothe, stripped the naked; and who knew not their creator, and bowed down to soulless (*sc.* lifeless) gods, who cannot see nor hear, vain gods, *who also* built hewn images and bow down to unclean handiwork, for all these is prepared this place amongst these, for eternal inheritance.

CHAPTER 11

Here they took Enoch up on to the fourth heaven
where is the course of sun and moon.

1 Those men took me, and led me up on to the fourth heaven, and showed me all the successive goings, and all the rays of the light of sun and moon.

2 And I measured their goings, and compared their light, and saw that the sun's light is greater than the moon's.

3 Its circle and the wheels on which it goes always, like a wind going past with very marvellous speed, and day and night it has no rest.

4 Its passage and return *are accompanied by* four great stars, *and* each star has under it a thousand stars, to the right of the sun's wheel, *and by* four to the left, each having under it a thousand stars, altogether eight thousand, issuing with the sun continually.

5 And by day fifteen myriads of angels attend it, and by night a thousand.

6 And six-winged ones issue with the angels

before the sun's wheel into the fiery flames, and a hundred angels kindle the sun and set it alight.

CHAPTER 12

Of the very marvellous elements of the sun.

1   And I looked and saw other flying elements of the sun, whose names *are* Phoenixes and Chalkydri, marvellous and wonderful, with feet and tails in the form of a lion, and a crocodile's head, their appearance *is* empurpled, like the rainbow; their size *is* nine hundred measures, their wings *are like* those of angels, each *has* twelve, and they attend and accompany the sun, bearing heat and dew, as it is ordered them from God.

2   Thus *the sun* revolves and goes, and rises under the heaven, and its course goes under the earth with the light of its rays incessantly.

CHAPTER 13

The angels took Enoch and placed him in the east
at the sun's gates.

1   Those men bore me away to the east, and placed me at the sun's gates, where the sun goes forth according to the regulation of the seasons and the circuit of the months of the whole year, and the number of the hours day and night.

2   And I saw six gates open, each gate having sixty-one stadia and a quarter of one stadium, and I measured *them* truly, and understood their size to *be* so much, through which the sun goes forth, and goes to

the west, and is made even, and rises throughout all the months, and turns back again from the six gates according to the succession of the seasons; thus *the period* of the whole year is finished after the returns of the four seasons.

CHAPTER 14

They took Enoch to the west.

1 And again those men led me away to the western parts, and showed me six great gates open corresponding to the eastern gates, opposite to where the sun sets, according to the number of the days three hundred and sixty-five and a quarter.

2 Thus again it goes down to the western gates, *and* draws away its light, the greatness of its brightness, under the earth; for since the crown of its shining is in heaven with the Lord, and guarded by four hundred angels, while the sun goes round on wheel under the earth, and stands seven great hours in night, and spends half *its course* under the earth, when it comes to the eastern approach in the eighth hour of the night, it brings its lights, and the crown of shining, and the sun flames forth more than fire.

CHAPTER 15

*The elements of the sun, the Phoenixes and
        Chalkydri broke into song.*

1 Then the elements of the sun, called Phoenixes and Chalkydri break into song, therefore every bird flutters with its wings, rejoicing at the giver of light,

and they broke into song at the command of the Lord.

2 The giver of light comes to give brightness to the whole world, and the morning guard takes shape, which is the rays of the sun, and the sun of the earth goes out, and receives its brightness to light up the whole face of the earth, and they showed me this calculation of the sun's going.

3 And the gates which it enters, these are the great gates of the computation of the hours of the year; for this reason the sun is a great creation, whose circuit *lasts* twenty-eight years, and begins again from the beginning.

CHAPTER 16

They took Enoch and again placed him in the east at the course of the moon.

1 Those men showed me the other course, that of the moon, twelve great gates, crowned from west to east, by which the moon goes in and out of the customary times.

2 It goes in at the first gate to the western places of the sun, by the first gates with *thirty*-one *days* exactly, by the second gates with thirty-one days exactly, by the third with thirty days exactly, by the fourth with thirty days exactly, by the fifth with thirty-one days exactly, by the sixth with thirty-one days exactly, by the seventh with thirty days exactly, by the eighth with thirty-one days perfectly, by the ninth with thirty-one days exactly, by the tenth with thirty days perfectly, by the eleventh with thirty-one days exactly, by the twelfth

with twenty-eight days exactly.

3 And it goes through the western gates in the order and number of the eastern, and accomplishes the three hundred and sixty-five and a quarter days of the solar year, while the lunar year has three hundred and fifty-four, and there are wanting *to it* twelve days of the solar circle, which are the lunar epacts of the whole year.

4 [Thus, too, the great circle contains five hundred and thirty-two years.]

5 The quarter *of a day* is omitted for three years, the fourth fulfils *it* exactly.

6 Therefore they are taken outside of heaven for three years and are not added to the number of days, because they change the time of the years to two new months towards completion, to two others towards diminution.

7 And when the western gates are finished, it returns and goes to the eastern to the lights, and goes thus day and night about the heavenly circles, lower than all circles, swifter than the heavenly winds, and spirits and elements and angels flying; each angel has six wings.

8 It has a sevenfold course in nineteen years.

CHAPTER 17

Of the singings of the angels, which it is impossible to describe.

In the midst of the heavens I saw armed soldiers, serving the Lord, with tympana and organs, with incessant voice, with sweet voice, with sweet and incessant *voice* and various singing, which it is impossible to describe, and *which* astonishes every mind, so wonderful and marvellous is the singing of those angels, and I was delighted listening to it.

CHAPTER 18

Of the taking of Enoch on to the fifth heaven.

1 The men took me on to the fifth heaven and placed me, and there I saw many and countless soldiers, called Grigori, of human appearance, and their size *was* greater than that of great giants and their faces withered, and the silence of their mouths perpetual, and there was no service on the fifth heaven, and I said to the men who were with me:

2 'Wherefore are these very withered and their faces melancholy, and their mouths silent, and *wherefore* is there no service on this heaven?'

3 And they said to me: These are the Grigori, who with their prince Satanail rejected the Lord of light, and after them are those who are held in great darkness on the second heaven, and three of them went down on to earth from the Lord's throne, to the place Ermon, and broke through their vows on the shoulder of the hill Ermon and saw the daughters of men how good they are, and took to themselves wives, and befouled the earth with their deeds, who in all times of their age made lawlessness and mixing, and giants are born and marvellous big men and great enmity.

4 And therefore God judged them with great judgement, and they weep for their brethren and they will be punished on the Lord's great day.

5 And I said to the Grigori: 'I saw your brethren and their works, and their great torments, and I prayed for them, but the Lord has condemned them *to be* under earth till heaven and earth shall end for ever.'

6 And I said: 'Wherefore do you wait, brethren, and do not serve before the Lord's face, and have not put your services before the Lord's face, lest you anger your Lord utterly?'

7 And they listened to my admonition, and spoke to the four ranks in heaven, and lo! as I stood with those two men four trumpets trumpeted together with great voice, and the Grigori broke into song with one voice, and their voice went up before the Lord pitifully and affectingly.

CHAPTER 19

Of the taking of Enoch on to the sixth heaven.

1 And thence those men took me and bore me up on to the sixth heaven, and there I saw seven bands of angels, very bright and very glorious, and their faces shining more than the sun's shining, glistening, and there is no difference in their faces, or behaviour, or manner of dress; and these make the orders, and learn the goings of the stars, and the alteration of the moon, or revolution of the sun, and the good government of the world.

2 And when they see evildoing they make com-

mandments and instruction, and sweet and loud singing, and all *songs* of praise.

3 These are the archangels who are above angels, measure all life in heaven and on earth, and the angels who are *appointed* over seasons and years, the angels who are over rivers and sea, and who are over the fruits of the earth, and the angels who are over every grass, giving food to all, to every living thing, and the angels who write all the souls of men, and all their deeds, and their lives before the Lord's face; in their midst are six Phoenixes and six Cherubim and six six-winged ones continually with one voice singing one voice, and it is not possible to describe their singing, and they rejoice before the Lord at his footstool.

CHAPTER 20

Hence they took Enoch into the seventh heaven.

1 And those two men lifted me up thence on to the seventh heaven, and I saw there a very great light, and fiery troops of great archangels, incorporeal forces, and dominions, orders and governments, cherubim and seraphim, thrones and many-eyed ones, nine regiments, the Ioanit stations of light, and I became afraid, and began to tremble with great terror, and those men took me, and led me after them, and said to me:

2 'Have courage, Enoch, do not fear,' and showed me the Lord from afar, sitting on His very high throne. For what is there on the tenth heaven, since the Lord dwells here?

3 On the tenth heaven is God, in the Hebrew tongue he is called Aravat.

4 And all the heavenly troops would come and stand on the ten steps according to their rank, and would bow down to the Lord, and would again go to their places in joy and felicity, singing songs in the boundless light with small and tender voices, gloriously serving him.

CHAPTER 21

Of how the angels here left Enoch, at the end of the
seventh heaven, and went away from him unseen.

1 And the cherubim and seraphim standing about the throne, the six-winged and many-eyed ones do not depart, standing before the Lord's face doing his will, and cover his whole throne, singing with gentle voice before the Lord's face: 'Holy, holy, holy, Lord Ruler of Sabaoth, heavens and earth are full of Thy glory.'

2 When I saw all these things, those men said to me: 'Enoch, thus far is it commanded us to journey with thee,' and those men went away from me and thereupon I saw them not.

3 And I remained alone at the end of the seventh heaven and became afraid, and fell on my face and said to myself: 'Woe is me, what has befallen me?'

4 And the Lord sent one of his glorious ones, the archangel Gabriel, and *he* said to me: 'Have courage, Enoch, do not fear, arise before the Lord's face into eternity, arise, come with me.'

5 And I answered him, and said in myself: 'My Lord, my soul is departed from me, from terror and trembling,' and I called to the men who led me up to this place, on them I relied, and *it is* with them I go before the Lord's face.

6 And Gabriel caught me up, as a leaf caught up by the wind, and placed me before the Lord's face.

7 And I saw the eighth heaven, which is called in the Hebrew tongue Muzaloth, changer of the seasons, of drought, and of wet, and of the twelve signs of the zodiac, which are above the seventh heaven.

8 And I saw the ninth heaven, which is called in Hebrew Kuchavim, where are the heavenly homes of the twelve signs of the zodiac.

CHAPTER 22

In the tenth heaven the archangel Michael led Enoch
to before the Lord's face.

1 On the tenth heaven, Aravoth, I saw the appearance of the Lord's face, like iron made to glow in fire, and brought out, emitting sparks, and it burns.

2 Thus I saw the Lord's face, but the Lord's face is ineffable, marvellous and very awful, and very, very terrible.

3 And who am I to tell of the Lord's unspeakable being, and of his very wonderful face? And I cannot tell the quantity of his many instructions, and various voices, the Lord's throne very great and not made with hands, nor the quantity of those standing round him,

troops of cherubim and seraphim, nor their incessant singing, nor his immutable beauty, and who shall tell of the ineffable greatness of his glory?

4 And I fell prone and bowed down to the Lord, and the Lord with his lips said to me:

5 'Have courage, Enoch, do not fear, arise and stand before my face into eternity.'

6 And the archistratege Michael lifted me up, and led me to before the Lord's face.

7 And the Lord said to his servants tempting them: 'Let Enoch stand before my face into eternity,' and the glorious ones bowed down to the Lord, and said: 'Let Enoch go according to Thy word.'

8 And the Lord said to Michael: 'Go and take Enoch from out his earthly garments, and anoint him with my sweet ointment, and put him into the garments of My glory.'

9 And Michael did thus, as the Lord told him. He anointed me, and dressed me, and the appearance of that ointment is more than the great light, and his ointment is like sweet dew, and its smell mild, shining like the sun's ray, and I looked at myself, and was like one of his glorious ones.

10 And the Lord summoned one of his archangels by name Pravuil, whose knowledge was quicker in wisdom than the other archangels, who wrote all the deeds of the Lord; and the Lord said to Pravuil:

11 'Bring out the books from my store-houses, and a reed of quick-writing, and give *it* to Enoch, and

deliver to him the choice and comforting books out of thy hand.'

CHAPTER 23

Of Enoch's writing, how he wrote his wonderful journeyings and the heavenly apparitions and himself wrote three hundred and sixty-six books.

1 And he was telling me all the works of heaven, earth and sea, and all the elements, their passages and goings, and the thunderings of the thunders, the sun and moon, the goings and changes of the stars, the seasons, years, days, and hours, the risings of the wind, the numbers of the angels, and the formation of their songs, and all human things, the tongue of every human song and life, the commandments, instructions, and sweet-voiced singings, and all things that it is fitting to learn.

2 And Pravuil told me: 'All the things that I have told thee, we have written. Sit and write all the souls of mankind, however many of them are born, and the places prepared for them to eternity; for all souls are prepared to eternity, before the formation of the world.'

3 And all double thirty days and thirty nights, and I wrote out all things exactly, and wrote three hundred and sixty-six books.

CHAPTER 24

Of the great secrets of God, which God revealed and
told to Enoch, and spoke with him face to face.

1 And the Lord summoned me, and said to me:
'Enoch, sit down on my left with Gabriel.'

2 And I bowed down to the Lord, and the Lord
spoke to me: Enoch, beloved, all thou seest, all things
that are standing finished I tell to thee even before the
very beginning, all that I created from non-being, and
visible things from invisible.

3 Hear, Enoch, and take in these my words, for
not to My angels have I told my secret, and I have not
told them their rise, nor my endless realm, nor have
they understood my creating, which I tell thee to-day.

4 For before all things were visible, I alone used to
go about in the invisible things, like the sun from east
to west, and from west to east.

5 But even the sun has peace in itself, while I
found no peace, because I was creating all things, and
I conceived the thought of placing foundations, and of
creating visible creation.

CHAPTER 25

God relates to Enoch, how out of the very lowest
darkness comes down the visible and invisible.

1 I commanded in the very lowest *parts,* that
visible things should come down from invisible, and
Adoil came down very great, and I beheld him, and lo!

he had a belly of great light.

2 And I said to him: 'Become undone, Adoil, and let the visible *come* out of thee.'

3 And he came undone, and a great light came out. And I *was* in the midst of the great light, and as there is born light from light, there came forth a great age, and showed all creation, which I had thought to create.

4 And I saw that *it was* good.

5 And I placed for myself a throne, and took my seat on it, and said to the light: 'Go thou up higher and fix thyself high above the throne, and be a foundation to the highest things.'

6 And above the light there is nothing else, and then I bent up and looked up from my throne.

CHAPTER 26

God summons from the very lowest a second time that Archas, heavy and very red should come forth.

1 And I summoned the very lowest a second time, and said: 'Let Archas come forth hard,' and he came forth hard from the invisible.

2 And Archas came forth, hard, heavy, and very red.

3 And I said: 'Be opened, Archas, and let there be born from thee,' and he came undone, an age came forth, very great and very dark, bearing the creation of all lower things, and I saw that *it was* good and said to him:

4 'Go thou down below, and make thyself firm, and be for a foundation for the lower things,' and it happened and he went down and fixed himself, and became the foundation for the lower things, and below the darkness there is nothing else.

CHAPTER 27

Of how God founded the water, and surrounded it
with light, and established on it seven islands.

1 And I commanded that there should be taken from light and darkness, and I said: 'Be thick,' and it became thus, and I spread it out with the light, and it became water, and I spread it out over the darkness, below the light, and then I made firm the waters, that is to say the bottomless, and I made foundation of light around the water, and created seven circles from inside, and imaged it (*sc.* the water) like crystal wet and dry, that is to say like glass, *and* the circumcession of the waters and the other elements, and I showed each one of them its road, and the seven stars each one of them in its heaven, that they go thus, and I saw that it was good.

2 And I separated between light and between darkness, that is to say in the midst of the water hither and thither, and I said to the light, that it should be the day, and to the darkness, that it should be the night, and there was evening and there was morning the first day.

CHAPTER 28

The week in which God showed Enoch all his
wisdom and power, throughout all the seven
days, how he created all the heavenly and earthly
forces and all moving things even down to man.

1 And then I made firm the heavenly circle, and *made* that the lower water which is under heaven collect itself together, into one whole, and that the chaos become dry, and it became so.

2 Out of the waves I created rock hard and big, and from the rock I piled up the dry, and the dry I called earth, and the midst of the earth I called abyss, that is to say the bottomless, I collected the sea in one place and bound it together with a yoke.

3 And I said to the sea: 'Behold I give thee *thy* eternal limits, and thou shalt not break loose from thy component parts.'

4 Thus I made fast the firmament. This day I called me the first-created [Sunday].

CHAPTER 29

Then it became evening, and then again morning,
and it was the second day [Monday]. The fiery
Essence.

1 And for all the heavenly troops I imaged the image and essence of fire, and my eye looked at the very hard, firm rock, and from the gleam of my eye the lightning received its wonderful nature, *which* is both

fire in water and water in fire, and one does not put out the other, nor does the one dry up the other, therefore the lightning is brighter than the sun, softer than water and firmer than hard rock.

2 And from the rock I cut off a great fire, and from the fire I created the orders of the incorporeal ten troops of angels, and their weapons are fiery and their raiment a burning flame, and I commanded that each one should stand in his order.

Here Satanail with his angels was thrown down from the height.

3 And one from out the order of angels, having turned away with the order that was under him, conceived an impossible thought, to place his throne higher than the clouds above the earth, that he might become equal in rank to my power.

4 And I threw him out from the height with his angels, and he was flying in the air continuously above the bottomless.

CHAPTER 30

And then I created all the heavens, and the third day was, [Tuesday.]

1 On the third day I commanded the earth to make grow great and fruitful trees, and hills, and seed to sow, and I planted Paradise, and enclosed it, and placed as armed *guardians* flaming angels, and thus I created renewal.

2 Then came evening, and came morning the fourth day.

3 [Wednesday]. On the fourth day I commanded that there should be great lights on the heavenly circles.

4 On the first uppermost circle I placed the stars, Kruno, and on the second Aphrodit, on the third Aris, on the fifth Zeus, on the sixth Ermis, on the seventh lesser the moon, and adorned it with the lesser stars.

5 And on the lower I placed the sun for the illumination of day, and the moon and stars for the illumination of night.

6 The sun that it should go according to each animal (*sc.* signs of the zodiac), twelve, and I appointed the succession of the months and their names and lives, their thunderings, and their hour-markings, how they should succeed.

7 Then evening came and morning came the fifth day.

8 [Thursday]. On the fifth day I commanded the sea, that it should bring forth fishes, and feathered birds of many varieties, and all animals creeping over the earth, going forth over the earth on four legs, and soaring in the air, male sex and female, and every soul breathing the spirit of life.

9 And there came evening, and there came morning the sixth day.

10 [Friday]. On the sixth day I commanded my wisdom to create man from seven consistencies: one, his flesh from the earth; two, his blood from the dew; three, his eyes from the sun; four, his bones from stone; five, his intelligence from the swiftness of the angels

and from cloud; six, his veins and his hair from the grass of the earth; seven, his soul from my breath and from the wind.

11 And I gave him seven natures: to the flesh hearing, the eyes for sight, to the soul smell, the veins for touch, the blood for taste, the bones for endurance, to the intelligence sweetness (*sc.* enjoyment).

12 I conceived a cunning saying to say, I created man from invisible and from visible nature, of both are his death and life and image, he knows speech like some created thing, small in greatness and again great in smallness, and I placed him on earth, a second angel, honourable, great and glorious, and I appointed him as ruler to rule on earth and to have my wisdom, and there was none like him of earth of all my existing creatures.

13 And I appointed him a name, from the four component parts, from east, from west, from south, from north, and I appointed for him four special stars, and I called his name Adam, and showed him the two ways, the light and the darkness, and I told him:

14 'This is good, and that bad,' that I should learn whether he has love towards me, or hatred, that it be clear which in his race love me.

15 For I have seen his nature, but he has not seen his own nature, therefore *through* not seeing he will sin worse, and I said 'After sin *what is there* but death?'

16 And I put sleep into him and he fell asleep. And I took from him a rib, and created him a wife, that

death should come to him by his wife, and I took his last word and called her name mother, that is to say, Eva.

CHAPTER 31

God gives over paradise to Adam, and gives him a
command to see the heavens opened, and that he
should see the angels singing the song of victory.

1 Adam has life on earth, and I created a garden in Eden in the east, that he should observe the testament and keep the command.

2 I made the heavens open to him, that he should see the angels singing the song of victory, and the gloomless light.

3 And he was continuously in paradise, and the devil understood that I wanted to create another world, because Adam was lord on earth, to rule and control it.

4 The devil is the evil spirit of the lower places, as a fugitive he made Sotona from the heavens as his name was Satanail, thus he became different from the angels, *but his nature* did not change *his* intelligence as far as *his* understanding of righteous and sinful *things*.

5 And he understood his condemnation and the sin which he had sinned before, therefore he conceived thought against Adam, in such form he entered and seduced Eva, but did not touch Adam.

6 But I cursed ignorance, but what I had blessed previously, those I did not curse, I cursed not man, nor

the earth, nor other creatures, but man's evil fruit, and his works.

CHAPTER 32

After Adam's sin God sends him away into the earth
'whence I took thee,' but does not wish to ruin
him for all years to come.

1 I said to him: 'Earth thou art, and into the earth whence I took thee thou shalt go, and I will not ruin thee, but send thee whence I took thee.

2 'Then I can again take thee at My second coming.'

3 And I blessed all my creatures visible and invisible. And Adam was five and half hours in paradise.

4 And I blessed the seventh day, which is the Sabbath, on which he rested from all his works.

CHAPTER 33

God shows Enoch the age of this world, its existence
of seven thousand years, and the eighth thousand
is the end, neither years, nor months, nor weeks,
nor days.

1 And I appointed the eighth day also, that the eighth day should be the first-created after my work, and that *the first seven* revolve in the form of the seventh thousand, and that at the beginning of the eighth thousand there should be a time of not-counting, endless, with neither years nor months nor weeks nor days nor hours.

2 And now, Enoch, all that I have told thee, all

that thou hast understood, all that thou hast seen of heavenly things, all that thou hast seen on earth, and all that I have written in books by my great wisdom, all these things I have devised and created from the uppermost foundation to the lower and to the end, and there is no counsellor nor inheritor to my creations.

3 I am self-eternal, not made with hands, and without change.

4 My thought is my counsellor, my wisdom and my word are made, and my eyes observe all things how they stand here and tremble with terror.

5 If I turn away my face, then all things will be destroyed.

6 And apply thy mind, Enoch, and know him who is speaking to thee, and take thou the books which thou thyself hast written.

7 And I give thee Samuil and Raguil, who led thee up, and the books, and go down to earth, and tell thy sons all that I have told thee, and all that thou hast seen, from the lower heaven up to my throne, and all the troops.

8 For I created all forces, and there is none that resisteth me or that does not subject himself to me. For all subject themselves to my monarchy, and labour for my sole rule.

9 Give them the books of the handwriting, and they will read *them* and will know me for the creator of all things, and will understand how there is no other God but me.

10 And let them distribute the books of thy hand-writing—children to children, generation to generation, nations to nations.

11 And I will give thee, Enoch, my intercessor, the archistratege Michael, for the handwritings of thy fathers Adam, Seth, Enos, Cainan, Mahaleleel, and Jared thy father.

CHAPTER 34

God convicts the idolaters and sodomitic fornicators, and therefore brings down a deluge upon them.

1 They have rejected my commandments and my yoke, worthless seed has come up, not fearing God, and they would not bow down to me, but have begun to bow down to vain gods, and denied my unity, and have laden the whole earth with untruths, offences, abominable lecheries, namely one with another, and all manner of other unclean wickednesses, which are disgusting to relate.

2 And therefore I will bring down a deluge upon the earth and will destroy all men, and the whole earth will crumble together into great darkness.

CHAPTER 35

God leaves one righteous man of Enoch's tribe with his whole house, who did God's pleasure according to his will.

1 Behold from their seed shall arise another generation, much afterwards, but of them many will be very insatiate.

2 He who raises that generation, *shall* reveal to them the books of thy handwriting, of thy fathers, *to them* to whom he must point out the guardianship of the world, to the faithful men and workers of my pleasure, who do not acknowledge my name in vain.

3 And they shall tell another generation, and those *others* having read shall be glorified thereafter, more than the first.

CHAPTER 36

God commanded Enoch to live on earth thirty days,
*   to give instruction to his sons and to his*
*   children's children. After thirty days he was*
*   again taken on to heaven.*

1 Now, Enoch, I give thee the term of thirty days to spend in thy house, and tell thy sons and all thy household, that all may hear from my face what is told them by thee, that they may read and understand, how there is no other God but me.

2 And that they may always keep my commandments, and begin to read and take in the books of thy handwriting.

3 And after thirty days I shall send my angel for thee, and he will take thee from earth and from thy sons to me.

CHAPTER 37

Here God summons an angel.

1 And the Lord called up one of the older angels, terrible and menacing, and placed him by me, in

appearance white as snow, and his hands like ice, having the appearance of great frost, and he froze my face, because I could not endure the terror of the Lord, just as it is not possible to endure a stove's fire and the sun's heat, and the frost of the air.

2 And the Lord said to me: 'Enoch, if thy face be not frozen here, no man will be able to behold thy face.'

CHAPTER 38

Mathusal continued to have hope and to await his
father Enoch at his couch day and night.

1 And the Lord said to those men who first led me up: 'Let Enoch go down on to earth with you, and await him till the determined day.'

2 And they placed me by night on my couch.

3 And Mathusal expecting my coming, keeping watch by day and by night at my couch, was filled with awe when he heard my coming, and I told him, 'Let all my household come together, that I tell them everything.'

CHAPTER 39

Enoch's pitiful admonition to his sons with weeping
and great lamentation, as he spoke to them.

1 Oh my children, my beloved ones, hear the admonition of your father, as much as is according to the Lord's will.

2 I have been let come to you to-day, and announce to you, not from my lips, but from the Lord's lips, all that is and was and all that is now, and all

that will be till judgement-day.

3 For the Lord has let me come to you, you hear therefore the words of my lips, of a man made big for you, but I am one who has seen the Lord's face, like iron made to glow from fire it sends forth sparks and burns.

4 You look now upon my eyes, *the eyes* of a man big with meaning for you, but I have seen the Lord's eyes, shining like the sun's rays and filling the eyes of man with awe.

5 You see now, my children, the right hand of a man that helps you, but I have seen the Lord's right hand filling heaven as he helped me.

6 You see the compass of my work like your own, but I have seen the Lord's limitless and perfect compass, which has no end.

7 You hear the words of my lips, as I heard the words of the Lord, like great thunder incessantly with hurling of clouds.

8 And now, my children, hear the discourses of the father of the earth, how fearful and awful it is to come before the face of the ruler of the earth, how much more terrible and awful it is to come before the face of the ruler of heaven, the controller of quick and dead, and of the heavenly troops. Who can endure that endless pain?

CHAPTER 40

Enoch admonishes his children truly of all things
from the Lord's lips, how he saw and heard and
wrote down.

1 And now, my children, I know all things, for this *is* from the Lord's lips, and this my eyes have seen, from beginning to end.

2 I know all things, and have written all things into books, the heavens and their end, and their plenitude, and all the armies and their marchings.

3 I have measured and described the stars, the great countless multitude *of them.*

4 What man has seen their revolutions, and their entrances? For not even the angels see their number, while I have written all their names.

5 And I measured the sun's circle, and measured its rays, counted the hours, I wrote down too all things that go over the earth, I have written the things that are nourished, and all seed sown and unsown, which the earth produces and all plants, and every grass and every flower, and their sweet smells, and their names, and the dwelling-places of the clouds, and their composition, and their wings, and how they bear rain and raindrops.

6 And I investigated all things, and wrote the road of the thunder and of the lightning, and they showed me the keys and their guardians, their rise, the way they go; it is let out in measure (*sc.* gently) by a chain, lest by a heavy chain and violence it hurl down the angry clouds and destroy all things on earth.

7 I wrote the treasure-houses of the snow, and the store-houses of the cold and the frosty airs, and I observed their season's key-holder, he fills the clouds

with them, and does not exhaust the treasure-houses.

8 And I wrote the resting-places of the winds and observed and saw how their key-holders bear weighing-scales and measures; first, they put them in *one* weighing-scale, then in the other the weights and let them out according to measure cunningly over the whole earth, lest by heavy breathing they make the earth to rock.

9 And I measured out the whole earth, its mountains, and all hills, fields, trees, stones, rivers, all existing things I wrote down, the height from earth to the seventh heaven, and downwards to the very lowest hell, and the judgement-place, and the very great, open and weeping hell.

10 And I saw how the prisoners are in pain, expecting the limitless judgement.

11 And I wrote down all those being judged by the judge, and all their judgements (*sc.* sentences) and all their works.

CHAPTER 41

Of how Enoch lamented Adam's sin.

1 And I saw all forefathers from *all* time with Adam and Eva, and I sighed and broke into tears and said of the ruin of their dishonour:

2 'Woe is me for my infirmity and *for that* of my forefathers,' and thought in my heart and said:

3 'Blessed *is* the man who has not been born or who has been born and shall not sin before the Lord's face, that he come not into this place, nor bring the yoke of this place.'

CHAPTER 42

Of how Enoch saw the key-holders and guards
of the gates of hell standing.

I saw the key-holders and guards of the gates of hell standing, like great serpents, and their faces like extinguished lamps, and their eyes of fire, their sharp teeth, and I saw all the Lord's works, how they are right, while the works of man are some *good*, and others bad, and in their works are known those who lie evilly.

CHAPTER 43

Enoch shows his children how he measured and
wrote out God's judgements.

1 I, my children, measured and wrote out every work and every measure and every righteous judgement.

2 As *one* year is more honourable than another, so is *one* man more honourable than another, some for great possessions, some for wisdom of heart, some for particular intellect, some for cunning, one for silence of lip, another for cleanliness, one for strength, another for comeliness, one for youth, another for sharp wit, one for shape of body, another for sensibility, let it be heard everywhere, but there is none better than he who fears God, he shall be more glorious in time to come.

CHAPTER 44

Enoch instructs his sons, that they revile not
the face of man, small or great.

1 The Lord with his hands having created man,

in the likeness of his own face, the Lord made him small and great.

2 Whoever reviles the ruler's face, and abhors the Lord's face, has despised the Lord's face, and he who vents anger on any man without injury, the Lord's great anger will cut him down, he who spits on the face of man reproachfully, will be cut down at the Lord's great judgement.

3 Blessed is the man who does not direct his heart with malice against any man, and helps the injured and condemned, and raises the broken down, and shall do charity to the needy, because on the day of the great judgement every weight, every measure and every makeweight *will be* as in the market, that is to say *they are* hung on scales and stand in the market, *and every one* shall learn his own measure, and according to his measure shall take his reward.

CHAPTER 45

God shows how he does not want from men sacrifices,
nor burnt-offerings, but pure and contrite hearts.

1 Whoever hastens to make offering before the Lord's face, the Lord for his part will hasten that offering by granting of his work.

2 But whoever increases his lamp before the Lord's face and make not true judgement, the Lord will *not* increase his treasure in the realm of the highest.

3 When the Lord demands bread, or candles, or flesh (*sc.* cattle), or any other sacrifice, then that is

nothing; but God demands pure hearts, and with all
that *only* tests the heart of man.

CHAPTER 46

Of how an earthly ruler does not accept from man
abominable and unclean gifts, then how much
more does God abominate unclean gifts, but
sends them away with wrath and does not
accept his gifts.

1 Hear, my people, and take in the words of my lips.

2 If any one bring any gifts to an earthly ruler, and
have disloyal thoughts in his heart, and the ruler know
this, will he not be angry with him, and not refuse his
gifts, and not give him over to judgement?

3 Or *if* one man make himself appear good to another by deceit of tongue, but *have* evil in his heart,
then will not *the other* understand the treachery of his
heart, and himself be condemned, since his untruth
was plain to all?

4 And when the Lord shall send a great light, then
there will be judgement for the just and the unjust, and
there no one shall escape notice.

CHAPTER 47

Enoch instructs his sons from God's lips, and hands
them the handwriting of this book.

1 And now, my children, lay thought on your
hearts, mark well the words of your father, which are
all *come* to you from the Lord's lips.

2 Take these books of your father's handwriting and read them.

3 For the books are many, and in them you will learn all the Lord's works, all that has been from the beginning of creation, and will be till the end of time.

4 And if you will observe my handwriting, you will not sin against the Lord; because there is no other except the Lord, neither in heaven, nor in earth, nor in the very lowest *places,* nor in the *one* foundation.

5 The Lord has placed the foundations in the unknown, and has spread forth heavens visible and invisible; he fixed the earth on the waters, and created countless creatures, and who has counted the water and the foundation of the unfixed, or the dust of the earth, or the sand of the sea, or the drops of the rain, or the morning dew, or the wind's breathings? Who has filled earth and sea, and the indissoluble winter?

6 I cut the stars out of fire, and decorated heaven, and put it in their midst.

CHAPTER 48

Of the sun's passage along the seven circles.

1 That the sun go along the seven heavenly circles, which are the appointment of one hundred and eighty-two thrones, that it go down on a short day, and again one hundred and eighty-two, that it go down on a big day, and he has two thrones on which he rests, revolving hither and thither above the thrones of the months, from the seventeenth day of the month Tsivan it goes

down to the month Thevan, from the seventeenth of Thevan it goes up.

2 And thus it goes close to the earth, then the earth is glad and makes grow its fruit, and when it goes away, then the earth is sad, and trees and all fruits have no florescence.

3 All this he measured, with good measurement of hours, and fixed a measure by his wisdom, of the visible and the invisible.

4 From the invisible he made all things visible, himself being invisible.

5 Thus I make known to you, my children, and distribute the books to your children, into all your generations, and amongst the nations who shall have the sense to fear God, let them receive them, and may they come to love them more than any food or earthly sweets, and read them and apply themselves to them.

6 And those who understand not the Lord, who fear not God, who accept not, but reject, who do not receive them (*sc.* the books), a terrible judgement awaits these.

7 Blessed is the man who shall bear their yoke and shall drag them along, for he shall be released on the day of the great judgement.

CHAPTER 49

Enoch instructs his sons not to swear either by heaven or earth, and shows God's promise, even in the mother's womb.

1 I swear to you, my children, but I swear not by any oath, neither by heaven nor by earth, nor by any other creature which God created.

2 The Lord said: 'There is no oath in me, nor injustice, but truth.'

3 If there is no truth in men, let them swear by the words 'yea, yea,' or else, 'nay, nay.'

4 And I swear to you, yea, yea, that there has been no man in his mother's womb, *but that* already before, even to each one there is a place prepared for the repose of that soul, and a measure fixed how much it is intended that a man be tried in this world.

5 Yea, children, deceive not yourselves, for there has been previously prepared a place for every soul of man.

CHAPTER 50

Of how none born on earth can remain hidden nor
his work remain concealed, but he (sc. God) bids
us be meek, to endure attack and insult, and not
to offend widows and orphans.

1 I have put every man's work in writing and none born on earth can remain hidden nor his works remain concealed.

2 I see all things.

3 Now therefore, my children, in patience and meekness spend the number of your days, that you inherit endless life.

4 Endure for the sake of the Lord every wound, every injury, every evil word and attack.

5 If ill-requitals befall you, return *them* not either to neighbour or enemy, because the Lord will return *them* for you and be your avenger on the day of great judgement, that there be no avenging here among men.

6 Whoever of you spends gold or silver for his brother's sake, he will receive ample treasure in the world to come.

7 Injure not widows nor orphans nor strangers, lest God's wrath come upon you.

CHAPTER 51

Enoch instructs his sons, that they hide not treasures
in the earth, but bids them give alms to the poor.

1 Stretch out your hands to the poor according to your strength.

2 Hide not your silver in the earth.

3 Help the faithful man in affliction, and affliction will not find you in the time of your trouble.

4 And every grievous and cruel yoke that come upon you bear all for the sake of the Lord, and thus you will find your reward in the day of judgement.

5 It is good to go morning, midday, and evening into the Lord's dwelling, for the glory of your creator.

6 Because every breathing *thing* glorifies him, and every creature visible and invisible returns him praise.

CHAPTER 52

God instructs his faithful, how they are to praise
his name.

1 Blessed is the man who opens his lips in praise of God of Sabaoth and praises the Lord with his heart.

2 Cursed every man who opens his lips for the bringing into contempt and calumny of his neighbour, because he brings God into contempt.

3 Blessed is he who opens his lips blessing and praising God.

4 Cursed is he before the Lord all the days of his life, who opens his lips to curse and abuse.

5 Blessed is he who blesses all the Lord's works.

6 Cursed is he who brings the Lord's creation into contempt.

7 Blessed is he who looks down and raises the fallen.

8 Cursed is he who looks to and is eager for the destruction of what is not his.

9 Blessed is he who keeps the foundations of his fathers made firm from the beginning.

10 Cursed is he who perverts the decrees of his forefathers.

11 Blessed is he who implants peace and love.

12 Cursed is he who disturbs those that love their neighbours.

13 Blessed is he who speaks with humble tongue and heart to all.

14 Cursed is he who speaks peace with his tongue, while in his heart there is no peace but a sword.

15 For all these things will be laid bare in the

weighing-scales and in the books, on the day of the great judgement.

CHAPTER 53

*[Let us not say: 'Our father is before God, he will
     stand forward for us on the day of judgement,' for
     there father cannot help son, nor yet son father.]*

1 And now, my children, do not say: 'Our father is standing before God, and is praying for our sins,' for there is there no helper of any man who has sinned.

2 You see how I wrote all works of every man, before his creation, *all* that is done amongst all men for all time, and none can tell or relate my handwriting, because the Lord sees all the imaginings of man, how they are vain, where they lie in the treasure-houses of the heart.

3 And now, my children, mark well all the words of your father, that I tell you, lest you regret, saying: 'Why did our father not tell us?'

CHAPTER 54

*Enoch instructs his sons, that they should hand
     the books to others also.*

1 At that time, not understanding this let these books which I have given you be for an inheritance of your peace.

2 Hand them to all who want them, and instruct them, that they may see the Lord's very great and marvellous works.

CHAPTER 55

Here Enoch shows his sons, telling them with tears:
   'My children, the hour has approached for me to
   go up on to heaven; behold, the angels are stand-
   ing before me.'

1 My children, behold, the day of my term and the time have approached.

2 For the angels who shall go with me are standing before me and urge me to my departure from you; they are standing here on earth, awaiting what has been told them.

3 For to-morrow I shall go up on to heaven, to the uppermost Jerusalem to my eternal inheritance.

4 Therefore I bid you do before the Lord's face all *his* good pleasure.

CHAPTER 56

Methosalam asks of his father blessing, that he
   (sc. Methosalam) may make him (sc. Enoch)
   food to eat.

1 Methosalam having answered his father Enoch, said: 'What is agreeable to thy eyes, father, that I may make before thy face, that thou mayst bless our dwellings, and thy sons, and that thy people may be made glorious through thee, and then *that* thou mayst depart thus, as the Lord said?'

2 Enoch answered to his son Methosalam *and* said: 'Hear, child, from the time when the Lord anointed me with the ointment of his glory, *there has*

been no food in me, and my soul remembers not
earthly enjoyment, neither do I want anything earthly.'

CHAPTER 57

Enoch bade his son Methosalam to summon all
his brethren.

1 'My child Methosalam, summon all thy brethren
and all your household and the elders of the people,
that I may talk to them and depart, as is planned for
me.'

2 And Methosalam made haste, and summoned
his brethren, Regim, Riman, Uchan, Chermion, Gaidad,
and all the elders of the people before the face of his
father Enoch; and he blessed them, *and* said to them:

CHAPTER 58

Enoch's instruction to his sons.

1 Listen to me, my children, to-day.

2 In those days when the Lord came down on to
earth for Adam's sake, and visited all his creatures,
which he created himself, after all these he created
Adam, and the Lord called all the beasts of the earth,
all the reptiles, and all the birds that soar in the air, and
brought them all before the face of our father Adam.

3 And Adam gave the names to all things living on
earth.

4 And the Lord appointed him ruler over all,
and subjected to him all things under his hands, and
made them dumb and made them dull that they be

commanded of man, and be in subjection and obedience to him.

5 Thus also the Lord created every man lord over all his possessions.

6 The Lord will not judge a single soul of beast for man's sake, but adjudges the souls of men to their beasts in this world; for men have a special place.

7 And as every soul of man is according to number, similarly beasts will not perish, nor all souls of beasts which the Lord created, till the great judgement, and they will accuse man, if he feed them ill.

CHAPTER 59

Enoch instructs his sons wherefore they may not
touch beef because of what comes from it.

1 Whoever defiles the soul of beasts, defiles his own soul.

2 For man brings clean animals to make sacrifice for sin, that he may have cure of his soul.

3 And if they bring for sacrifice clean animals, and birds, man has cure, he cures his soul.

4 All is given you for food, bind it by the four feet, that is to make good the cure, he cures his soul.

5 But whoever kills beast without wounds, kills his own soul and defiles his own flesh.

6 And he who does any beast any injury whatsoever, in secret, it is evil practice, and he defiles his own soul.

CHAPTER 60

He who does injury to soul of man, does injury
*   to his own soul, and there is no cure for his flesh,*
*   nor pardon for all time. How it is not fitting to*
*   kill man neither by weapon nor by tongue.*

1 He who works the killing of a man's soul, kills his own soul, and kills his own body, and there is no cure for him for all time.

2 He who puts a man in any snare, shall stick in it himself, and there is no cure for him for all time.

3 He who puts a man in any vessel, his retribution will not be wanting at the great judgement for all time.

4 He who works crookedly or speaks evil against any soul, will not make justice for himself for all time.

CHAPTER 61

Enoch instructs his sons to keep themselves from
*   injustice and often to stretch forth hands to the*
*   poor, to give a share of their labours.*

1 And now, my children, keep your hearts from every injustice, which the Lord hates. Just as a man asks (*sc.* something) for his own soul from God, so let him do to every living soul, because I know all things, how in the great time (*sc.* to come) are many mansions prepared for men, good for the good, and bad for the bad, without number many.

2 Blessed are those who enter the good houses, for in the bad (*sc.* houses) there is no peace nor return (*sc.* from them).

3 Hear, my children, small and great! When man puts a good thought in his heart, brings gifts from his labours before the Lord's face and his hands made them not, then the Lord will turn away his face from the labour of his hand, and he (*sc.* man) cannot find the labour of his hands.

4 And if his hands made it, but his heart murmur, and his heart cease not making murmur incessantly, he has not any advantage.

CHAPTER 62

*Of how it is fitting to bring one's gift with faith,
    because there is no repentance after death.*

1 Blessed is the man who in his patience brings his gifts with faith before the Lord's face, because he will find forgiveness of sins.

2 But if he take back his words before the time, there is no repentance for him; and if the time pass and he do not of his own will what is promised, there is no repentance after death.

3 Because every work which man does before the time, is all deceit before men, and sin before God.

CHAPTER 63

*Of how not to despise the poor, but to share with
    them equally, lest thou be murmured against
    before God.*

1 When man clothes the naked and fills the hungry, he will find reward from God.

2 But if his heart murmur, he commits a double evil: ruin of himself and of that which he gives; and for him there will be no finding of reward on account of that.

3 And if his own heart is filled with his food and his own flesh (*sc.* clothed) with his clothing, he commits contempt, and will forfeit all his endurance of poverty, and will not find reward of his good deeds.

4 Every proud and magniloquent man is hateful to the Lord, and every false speech, clothed in untruth; it will be cut with the blade of the sword of death, and thrown into the fire, and shall burn for all time.

CHAPTER 64

Of how the Lord calls up Enoch, and people took counsel to go and kiss him at the place called Achuzan.

1 When Enoch had spoken these words to his sons, all people far and near heard how the Lord was calling Enoch. They took counsel together:

2 'Let us go and kiss Enoch,' and two thousand men came together and came to the place Achuzan where Enoch was, and his sons.

3 And the elders of the people, the whole assembly, came and bowed down and began to kiss Enoch and said to him:

4 'Our father Enoch, be thou blessed of the Lord, the eternal ruler, and now bless thy sons and all the people, that we may be glorified to-day before thy face.

5 'For thou shalt be glorified before the Lord's face for all time, since the Lord chose thee, rather than all men on earth, and designated thee writer of all his creation, visible and invisible, and redeemer of the sins of man, and helper of thy household.'

CHAPTER 65

Of Enoch's instruction of his sons.

1 And Enoch answered all his people saying: 'Hear, my children, before that all creatures were created, the Lord created the visible and invisible things.

2 And as much time as there was and went past, understand that after all that he created man in the likeness of his own form, and put into him eyes to see, and ears to hear, and heart to reflect, and intellect wherewith to deliberate.

3 And the Lord saw all man's works, and created all his creatures, and divided time, from time he fixed the years, and from the years he appointed the months, and from the months he appointed the days, and of days he appointed seven.

4 And in those he appointed the hours, measured them out exactly, that man might reflect on time and count years, months, and hours, *their* alternation, beginning, and end, and that he might count his own life, from the beginning until death, and reflect on his sin and write his work bad and good; because no work is hidden before the Lord, that every man might know his works and never transgress all his commandments, and

keep my handwriting from generation to generation.

5 When all creation visible and invisible, as the Lord created it, shall end, then every man goes to the great judgement, and then all time shall perish, and the years, and thenceforward there will be neither months nor days nor hours, they will be stuck together and will not be counted.

6 There will be one aeon, and all the righteous who shall escape the Lord's great judgement, shall be collected in the great aeon, for the righteous the great aeon will begin, and they will live eternally, and then too there will be amongst them neither labour, nor sickness, nor humiliation, nor anxiety, nor need, nor violence, nor night, nor darkness, but great light.

7 And they shall have a great indestructible wall, and a paradise bright and incorruptible, for all corruptible things shall pass away, and there will be eternal life.

CHAPTER 66

Enoch instructs his sons and all the elders of the
people, how they are to walk with terror and
trembling before the Lord, and serve him alone
and not bow down to idols, but to God, who
created heaven and earth and every creature,
and to his image.

1 And now, my children, keep your souls from all injustice, such as the Lord hates.

2 Walk before his face with terror and trembling and serve him alone.

3 Bow down to the true God, not to dumb idols, but bow down to his picture, and bring all just offerings before the Lord's face. The Lord hates what is unjust.

4 For the Lord sees all things; when man takes thought in his heart, then he counsels the intellects, and every thought is always before the Lord, who made firm the earth and put all creatures on it.

5 If you look to heaven, the Lord is there; if you take thought of the sea's deep and all the under-earth, the Lord is there.

6 For the Lord created all things. Bow not down to things made by man, leaving the Lord of all creation, because no work can remain hidden before the Lord's face.

7 Walk, my children, in long-suffering, in meekness, honesty, in provocation, in grief, in faith and in truth, in *reliance on* promises, in illness, in abuse, in wounds, in temptation, in nakedness, in privation, loving one another, till you go out from this age of ills, that you become inheritors of endless time.

8 Blessed are the just who shall escape the great judgement, for they shall shine forth more than the sun sevenfold, for in this world the seventh part is taken off from all, light, darkness, food, enjoyment, sorrow, paradise, torture, fire, frost, and other things; he put all down in writing, that you might read and understand.'

CHAPTER 67

The Lord let out darkness on to earth and covered
the people and Enoch, and he was taken up on
high, and light came again in the heaven.

1 When Enoch had talked to the people, the Lord sent out darkness on to the earth, and there was darkness, and it covered those men standing with Enoch, and they took Enoch up on to the highest heaven, where the Lord *is;* and he received him and placed him before his face, and the darkness went off from the earth, and light came again.

2 And the people saw and understood not how Enoch had been taken, and glorified God, and found a roll in which was traced 'the invisible God'; and all went to their homes.

CHAPTER 68

1 Enoch was born on the sixth day of the month Tsivan, and lived three hundred and sixty-five years.

2 He was taken up to heaven on the first day of the month Tsivan and remained in heaven sixty days.

3 He wrote all these signs of all creation, which the Lord created, and wrote three hundred and sixty-six books, and handed them over to his sons and remained on earth thirty days, and was again taken up to heaven on the sixth day of the month Tsivan, on the very day and hour when he was born.

4 As every man's nature in this life is dark, so are

also his conception, birth, and departure from this life.

5 At what hour he was conceived, at that hour he was born, and at that hour too he died.

6 Methosalam and his brethren, all the sons of Enoch, made haste, and erected an altar at the place called Achuzan, whence and where Enoch had been taken up to heaven.

7 And they took sacrificial oxen and summoned all people and sacrificed the sacrifice before the Lord's face.

8 All people, the elders of the people and the whole assembly came to the feast and brought gifts to the sons of Enoch.

9 And they made a great feast, rejoicing and making merry three days, praising God, who had given them such a sign through Enoch, who had found favour with him, and that they should hand it on to their sons from generation to generation, from age to age.

10 Amen.

ENOCH IN THE
FORGOTTEN BOOKS

THE DOVE SENT FORTH FROM THE ARK

THE BOOK OF JUBILEES
OR
THE LITTLE GENESIS
(EXCERPTS)

The Patriarchs from Adam to Noah; Life of Enoch;
Death of Adam and Cain.

IV, 13 And in the seventh jubilee[1] in the third week
Enos took Nôâm his sister to be his wife, and she bare
him a son in the third year of the fifth week, and he
called his name Kenan.

14 And at the close of the eighth jubilee Kenan
took Mûalêlêth his sister to be his wife, and she bare
him a son in the ninth jubilee, in the first week in the
third year of this week, and he called his name Maha-
lalel.

15 And in the second week of the tenth jubilee Ma-
halalel took unto him to wife Dînâh, the daughter of
Barâkî'êl the daughter of his father's brother, and she
bare him a son in the third week in the sixth year, and
he called his name Jared, for in his days the angels of
the Lord descended on the earth, those who are named

---

1. A jubilee is a period of 49 years. A week is a "year-week," a period
of 7 years.

the Watchers, that they should instruct the children of men, and that they should do judgment and uprightness on the earth.

16 And in the eleventh jubilee Jared took to himself a wife, and her name was Bâraka, the daughter of Rûsûjâl, a daughter of his father's brother, in the fourth week of this jubilee, and she bare him a son in the fifth week, in the fourth year of the jubilee, and he called his name Enoch.

17 And he was the first among men that are born on earth who learnt writing and knowledge and wisdom and who wrote down the signs of heaven according to the order of their months in a book, that men might know the seasons of the years according to the order of their separate months.

18 And he was the first to write a testimony, and he testified to the sons of men among the generations of the earth, and recounted the weeks of the jubilees, and made known to them the days of the years, and set in order the months and recounted the Sabbaths of the years as we made (them) known to him.

19 And what was and what will be he saw in a vision of his sleep, as it will happen to the children of men throughout their generations until the day of judgment; he saw and understood everything, and wrote his testimony, and placed the testimony on earth for all the children of men and for their generations.

20 And in the twelfth jubilee, in the seventh week thereof, he took to himself a wife, and her name was

Ednî, the daughter of Dânêl, the daughter of his father's brother, and in the sixth year in this week she bare him a son and he called his name Methuselah.

21 And he was moreover with the angels of God these six jubilees of years, and they showed him everything which is on earth and in the heavens, the rule of the sun, and he wrote down everything.

22 And he testified to the Watchers, who had sinned with the daughters of men; for these had begun to unite themselves, so as to be defiled, with the daughters of men, and Enoch testified against (them) all.

23 And he was taken from amongst the children of men, and we conducted him into the Garden of Eden in majesty and honour, and behold there he writeth down the condemnation and judgment of the world, and all the wickedness of the children of men.

24 And on account of it (God) brought the waters of the flood upon all the land of Eden; for there he was set as a sign and that he should testify against all the children of men, that he should recount all the deeds of the generations until the day of condemnation.

25 And he burnt the incense of the sanctuary, (even) sweet spices, acceptable before the Lord on the Mount.

26 For the Lord hath four places on the earth, the Garden of Eden, and the Mount of the East, and this mountain on which thou art this day, Mount Sinai, and Mount Zion (which) will be sanctified in the new creation for a sanctification of the earth; through it will the earth be sanctified from all (its) guilt and its

uncleanness throughout the generations of the world.

27 And in the fourteenth jubilee Methuselah took unto himself a wife, Ednâ the daughter of 'Âzrîâl, the daughter of his father's brother, in the third week, in the first year of this week, and he begat a son and called his name Lamech.

28 And in the fifteenth jubilee in the third week Lamech took to himself a wife, and her name was Bêtênôs the daughter of Bârâkî'îl, the daughter of his father's brother, and in this week she bare him a son and he called his name Noah, saying, "This one will comfort me for my trouble and all my work, and for the ground which the Lord hath cursed."

29 And at the close of the nineteenth jubilee, in the seventh week in the sixth year thereof, Adam died, and all his sons buried him in the land of his creation, and he was the first to be buried in the earth.

30 And he lacked seventy years of one thousand years; for one thousand years are as one day in the testimony of the heavens and therefore was it written concerning the tree of knowledge: "On the day that ye eat thereof ye will die." For this reason he did not complete the years of this day; for he died during it.

31 At the close of this jubilee Cain was killed after him in the same year; for his house fell upon him and he died in the midst of his house, and he was killed by its stones; for with a stone he had killed Abel, and by a stone was he killed in righteous judgment.

32 For this reason it was ordained on the heav-

enly tables: "With the instrument with which a man killeth his neighbour with the same shall he be killed; after the manner that he wounded him, in like manner shall they deal with him."

33 And in the twenty-fifth jubilee Noah took to himself a wife, and her name was 'Ĕmzârâ, the daughter of Râkê'êl, the daughter of his father's brother, in the first year in the fifth week: and in the third year thereof she bare him Shem, in the fifth year thereof she bare him Ham, and in the first year in the sixth week she bare him Japheth.

The Fall of the Angels and Their Punishment; the Deluge Foretold

V

1 And it came to pass when the children of men began to multiply on the face of the earth and daughters were born unto them, that the angels of God saw them on a certain year of this jubilee, that they were beautiful to look upon; and they took themselves wives of all whom they chose, and they bare unto them sons and they were giants.

2 And lawlessness increased on the earth and all flesh corrupted its way, alike men and cattle and beasts and birds and everything that walketh on the earth— all of them corrupted their ways and their orders, and they began to devour each other, and lawlessness increased on the earth and every imagination of the thoughts of all men (was) thus evil continually.

3 And God looked upon the earth, and behold it was corrupt, and all flesh had corrupted its orders, and all that were upon the earth had wrought all manner of evil before His eyes.

4 And He said: "I shall destroy man and all flesh upon the face of the earth which I have created."

5 But Noah found grace before the eyes of the Lord.

6 And against the angels whom He had sent upon the earth, He was exceedingly wroth, and He gave commandment to root them out of all their dominion, and He bade us to bind them in the depths of the earth, and behold they are bound in the midst of them, and are (kept) separate.

7 And against their sons went forth a command from before His face that they should be smitten with the sword, and be removed from under heaven.

8 And He said "My spirit will not always abide on man; for they also are flesh and their days shall be one hundred and twenty years."

9 And He sent His sword into their midst that each should slay his neighbour, and they began to slay each other till they all fell by the sword and were destroyed from the earth.

10 And their fathers were witnesses (of their destruction), and after this they were bound in the depths of the earth for ever, until the day of the great condemnation, when judgment is executed on all those who have corrupted their ways and their works before the Lord.

11 And He [shall destroy] all from their places, and there [shall not be] left one of them whom He [shall not have] judged according to all their wickedness.

12 And He [shall make] for all His works a new and righteous nature, so that they should not sin in their whole nature for ever, but should be all righteous each in his kind alway.

13 And the judgment of all is ordained and written on the heavenly tables in righteousness—even (the judgment of) all who depart from the path which is ordained for them to walk in; and if they walk not therein, judgment is written down for every creature and for every kind.

14 And there is nothing in heaven or on earth, or in light or in darkness, or in Sheol or in the depth, or in the place of darkness (which is not judged); and all their judgments are ordained and written and engraved.

15 In regard to all He will judge, the great according to his greatness, and the small according to his smallness, and each according to his way.

16 And He is not one who will regard the person (of any), nor is He one who will receive gifts, if He saith that He will execute judgment on each: if one gave everything that is on the earth, He will not regard the gifts or the person (of any), nor accept anything at his hands, for He is a righteous judge.

17 And of the children of Israel it hath been written and ordained: If they turn to Him in righteousness,

He will forgive all their transgressions and pardon all their sins.

18 It is written and ordained that He will show mercy to all who turn from all their guilt once each year.[2]

19 And as for all those who corrupted their ways and their thoughts before the flood, no man's person was accepted save that of Noah alone; for his person was accepted in behalf of his sons, whom (God) saved from the waters of the flood on his account; for his heart was righteous in all his ways, according as it was commanded regarding him, and he had not departed from aught that was ordained for him.

20 And the Lord said that He would destroy everything which was upon the earth, both men and cattle, and beasts, and fowls of the air, and that which moveth on the earth. [In the remainder of chapter V, Noah builds an ark and survives the Great Flood.]

Noah Offers Sacrifice; the Cursing of Canaan:
    Noah's Sons and Grandsons and Their Cities.
    Noah's Admonitions.

VII

1 And in the seventh week in the first year thereof, in this jubilee, Noah planted vines on the mountain on which the ark had rested, named Lûbâr, one of the Ararat Mountains, and they produced fruit in the fourth year, and he guarded their fruit, and gathered it in this year in the seventh month.

---

2. See Lev. 16; Heb. 9:7.

2 And he made wine therefrom and put it into a vessel, and kept it until the fifth year, until the first day, on the new moon of the first month.

3 And he celebrated with joy the day of this feast, and he made a burnt sacrifice unto the Lord, one young ox and one ram, and seven sheep, each a year old, and a kid of the goats, that he might make atonement thereby for himself and his sons.

4 And he prepared the kid first, and placed some of its blood on the flesh that was on the altar which he had made, and all the fat he laid on the altar where he made the burnt sacrifice, and the ox and the ram and the sheep, and he laid all their flesh upon the altar.

5 And he placed all their offerings mingled with oil upon it, and afterwards he sprinkled wine on the fire which he had previously made on the altar, and he placed incense on the altar and caused a sweet savour to ascend acceptable before the Lord his God.

6 And he rejoiced and drank of this wine, he and his children with joy.

7 And it was evening, and he went into his tent, and being drunken he lay down and slept, and was uncovered in his tent as he slept.

8 And Ham saw Noah his father naked, and went forth and told his two brethren without.

9 And Shem took his garment and arose, he and Japheth, and they placed the garment on their shoulders and went backward and covered the shame of their father, and their faces were backward.

10 And Noah awoke from his sleep and knew all that his younger son had done unto him, and he cursed his son and said: "Cursed be Canaan; an enslaved servant shall he be unto his brethren."

11 And he blessed Shem, and said: "Blessed be the Lord God of Shem, and Canaan shall be his servant.

12 God shall enlarge Japheth, and God shall dwell in the dwelling of Shem, and Canaan shall be his servant."

13 And Ham knew that his father had cursed his younger son, and he was displeased that he had cursed his son, and he parted from his father, he and his sons with him, Cush and Mizraim and Put and Canaan.

14 And he built for himself a city and called its name after the name of his wife Nê'êlâtamâ'ûk.

15 And Japheth saw it, and became envious of his brother, and he too built for himself a city, and he called its name after the name of his wife 'Adâtanêsês.

16 And Shem dwelt with his father Noah, and he built a city close to his father on the mountain, and he too called its name after the name of his wife Sêdêqêtêlĕbâb.

17 And behold these three cities are near Mount Lûbâr; Sêdêqêtêlĕbâb fronting the mountain on its east; and Na'êlâtamâ'ûk on the south; 'Adatanêsês towards the west.

18 And these are the sons of Shem: Elam, and Asshur, and Arpachshad—this (son) was born two years after the flood—and Lud, and Aram.

19 The sons of Japheth: Gomer and Magog and Madai and Javan, Tubal and Meshech and Tiras: these are the sons of Noah.

20 And in the twenty-eighth jubilee Noah began to enjoin upon his sons' sons the ordinances and commandments, and all the judgments that he knew, and he exhorted his sons to observe righteousness, and to cover the shame of their flesh, and to bless their Creator, and honour father and mother, and love their neighbour, and guard their souls from fornication and uncleanness and all iniquity.

21 For owing to these three things came the flood upon the earth, namely, owing to the fornication wherein the Watchers against the law of their ordinances went a whoring after the daughters of men, and took themselves wives of all which they chose: and they made the beginning of uncleanness.

22 And they begat sons the Nâphîdîm,[3] and they were all unlike,[4] and they devoured one another: and the Giants slew the Nâphîl, and the Nâphîl slew the Eljô, and the Eljô mankind, and one man another.

23 And every one sold himself to work iniquity and to shed much blood, and the earth was filled with iniquity.

24 And after this they sinned against the beasts and birds, and all that moveth and walketh on the earth: and much blood was shed on the earth, and every

3. i.e., the Nephilim.
4. The text is probably corrupt.

imagination and desire of men imagined vanity and evil continually.

25 And the Lord destroyed everything from off the face of the earth; because of the wickedness of their deeds, and because of the blood which they had shed in the midst of the earth He destroyed everything.

26 And we were left, I[5] and you, my sons, and everything that entered with us into the ark, and behold I see your works before me that ye do not walk in righteousness; for in the path of destruction ye have begun to walk, and ye are parting one from another, and are envious one of another, and (so it cometh) that ye are not in harmony, my sons, each with his brother.

27 For I see, and behold the demons have begun (their) seductions against you and against your children, and now I fear on your behalf, that after my death ye will shed the blood of men upon the earth, and that ye, too, will be destroyed from the face of the earth.

28 For whoso sheddeth man's blood, and whoso eateth the blood of any flesh, will all be destroyed from the earth.

29 And there will not be left any man that eateth blood.

> Or that sheddeth the blood of man on the earth,
> Nor will there be left to him any seed or descendants living under heaven;

---

5. From this verse to the end of the chapter, Noah speaks in the first person. This section may be a fragment of the lost Book of Noah.

For into Sheol will they go,

And into the place of condemnation will they descend.

And into the darkness of the deep will they all be removed by a violent death.

30 There shall be no blood seen upon you of all the blood there shall be all the days in which ye have killed any beasts or cattle or whatever flieth upon the earth, and work ye a good work to your souls by covering that which hath been shed on the face of the earth.

31 And ye shall not be like him who eateth with blood, but guard yourselves that none may eat blood before you: cover the blood, for thus have I been commanded to testify to you and your children, together with all flesh.

32 And suffer not the soul to be eaten with the flesh, that your blood, which is your life, may not be required at the hand of any flesh that sheddeth (it) on the earth.

33 For the earth will not be clean from the blood which hath been shed upon it; for (only) through the blood of him that shed it will the earth be purified throughout all its generations.

34 And now, my children, hearken: work judgment and righteousness that ye may be planted in righteousness over the face of the whole earth, and your glory lifted up before my God, who saved me from the waters of the flood.

35 And behold, ye will go and build for yourselves cities, and plant in them all the plants that are upon the

earth, and moreover all fruit-bearing trees.

36 For three years the fruit of everything that is eaten will not be gathered: and in the fourth year its fruit will be accounted holy and they will offer the first-fruits, acceptable before the Most High God, who created heaven and earth and all things. Let them offer in abundance the first of the wine and oil (as) first-fruits on the altar of the Lord, who receiveth it, and what is left let the servants of the house of the Lord eat before the altar which receiveth (it).

37 And in the fifth year [break in text]

. . . . . .

make ye the release so that ye release it in righteousness and uprightness, and ye shall be righteous, and all that you plant will prosper.

38 For thus did Enoch, the father of your father command Methuselah, his son, and Methuselah his son Lamech, and Lamech commanded me all the things which his fathers commanded him.

39 And I also will give you commandment, my sons, as Enoch commanded his son in the first jubilees: whilst still living, the seventh in his generation, he commanded and testified to his son and to his sons' sons until the day of his death....

Noah's Sons Led Astray by Evil Spirits;
  Noah's Prayer; Mastêmâ; Death of Noah.

X

1 And in the third week of this jubilee the unclean demons began to lead astray the children of the sons of Noah, and to make to err and destroy them.

2 And the sons of Noah came to Noah their father, and they told him concerning the demons which were leading astray and blinding and slaying his sons' sons.

3 And he prayed before the Lord his God, and said:

> "God of the spirits of all flesh, who hast
>   shown mercy unto me,
> And hast saved me and my sons from the
>   waters of the flood,
> And hast not caused me to perish as Thou
>   didst the sons of perdition;
>
> For Thy grace hath been great towards me,
> And great hath been Thy mercy to my soul;
>
> Let Thy grace be lift up upon my sons,
> And let not wicked spirits rule over them
> Lest they should destroy them from the
>   earth.

4 But do Thou bless me and my sons, that we may increase and multiply and replenish the earth.

5 And Thou knowest how Thy Watchers, the

fathers of these spirits, acted in my day: and as for these spirits which are living, imprison them and hold them fast in the place of condemnation, and let them not bring destruction on the sons of thy servant, my God; for these are malignant, and created in order to destroy.

6 And let them not rule over the spirits of the living; for Thou alone canst exercise dominion over them. And let them not have power over the sons of the righteous from henceforth and for evermore."

7 And the Lord our God bade us to bind all.

8 And the chief of the spirits, Mastêmâ,[6] came and said: "Lord, Creator, let some of them remain before me, and let them hearken to my voice, and do all that I shall say unto them; for if some of them are not left to me, I shall not be able to execute the power of my will on the sons of men; for these are for corruption and leading astray before my judgment, for great is the wickedness of the sons of men."

9 And He said: "Let the tenth part of them remain before him, and let nine parts descend into the place of condemnation."

10 And one of us[7] He commanded that we should

---

6. The word apparently = *mastim*, "to be adverse," "inimical"; the Heb. noun *mastēmâ* = "animosity," in Hos. 9:7–8. Thus the word = Satan ("adversary"). As a proper name it is practically confined to the Jubilees literature. The evil spirits under the guidance of Mastêmâ tempt, accuse and destroy men.

7. The angel Raphael is referred to here, as indicated in the Hebrew Book of Noah.

teach Noah all their medicines; for He knew that they would not walk in uprightness, nor strive in righteousness.

11 And we did according to all His words: all the malignant evil ones we bound in the place of condemnation, and a tenth part of them we left that they might be subject before Satan on the earth.

12 And we explained to Noah all the medicines of their diseases, together with their seductions, how he might heal them with herbs of the earth.

13 And Noah wrote down all things in a book as we instructed him concerning every kind of medicine. Thus the evil spirits were precluded from (hurting) the sons of Noah.

14 And he gave all that he had written to Shem, his eldest son; for he loved him exceedingly above all his sons.

15 And Noah slept with his fathers, and was buried on Mount Lûbâr in the land of Ararat.

16 Nine hundred and fifty years he completed in his life, nineteen jubilees and two weeks and five years.

17 And in his life on earth he excelled the children of men save Enoch because of the righteousness, wherein he was perfect. For Enoch's office was ordained for a testimony to the generations of the world, so that he should recount all the deeds of generation unto generation, till the day of judgment.

THE TESTAMENTS OF THE TWELVE PATRIARCHS
(EXCERPTS)

TESTAMENT OF REUBEN
The First-Born Son of Jacob and Leah.

CHAPTER 2

Reuben continues with his experiences and his good advice.

1 Pay no heed, therefore, my children, to the beauty of women, nor set your mind on their affairs; but walk in singleness of heart in the fear of the Lord, and expend labour on good works, and on study and on your flocks, until the Lord give you a wife, whom He will, that ye suffer not as I did.

2 For until my father's death I had not boldness to look in his face, or to speak to any of my brethren, because of the reproach.

3 Even until now my conscience causeth me anguish on account of my impiety.

4 And yet my father comforted me much, and prayed for me unto the Lord, that the anger of the Lord

might pass from me, even as the Lord showed.

5 And thenceforth until now I have been on my guard and sinned not.

6 Therefore, my children, I say unto you, observe all things whatsoever I command you, and ye shall not sin. ....

17 Flee, therefore, fornication, my children, and command your wives and your daughters, that they adorn not their heads and faces to deceive the mind: because every woman who useth these wiles hath been reserved for eternal punishment.

18 For thus they allured the Watchers who were before the flood; for as these continually beheld them, they lusted after them, and they conceived the act in their mind; for they changed themselves into the shape of men, and appeared to them when they were with their husbands.

19 And the women lusting in their minds after their forms, gave birth to giants, for the Watchers appeared to them as reaching even unto heaven.

TESTAMENT OF SIMEON
The Second Son of Jacob and Leah.

CHAPTER 2

11 And now, my children, make your hearts good before the Lord, and your ways straight before men, and ye shall find grace before the Lord and men.

12 Beware, therefore, of fornication, for fornica-

tion is mother of all evils, separating from God, and bringing near to Beliar.

13 For I have seen it inscribed in the writing of Enoch that your sons shall be corrupted in fornication, and shall do harm to the sons of Levi with the sword.

14 But they shall not be able to withstand Levi; for he shall wage the war of the Lord, and shall conquer all your hosts.

15 And they shall be few in number, divided in Levi and Judah, and there shall be none of you for sovereignty, even as also our father prophesied in his blessings.

TESTAMENT OF LEVI
The Third Son of Jacob and Leah.

CHAPTER 3

43 Now, therefore, observe whatsoever I command you, children; for whatsoever things I have heard from my fathers I have declared unto you.

44 And behold I am clear from your ungodliness and transgression, which ye shall commit in the end of the ages against the Saviour of the world, Christ, acting godlessly, deceiving Israel, and stirring up against it great evils from the Lord.

45 And ye shall deal lawlessly together with Israel, so He shall not bear with Jerusalem because of your wickedness; but the veil of the temple shall be rent, so as not to cover your shame.

46 And ye shall be scattered as captives among the

Gentiles, and shall be for a reproach and for a curse there.

47 For the house which the Lord shall choose shall be called Jerusalem, as is contained in the book of Enoch the righteous.

THE TESTAMENT OF DAN
The Seventh Son of Jacob and Bilhah.

CHAPTER 2

A prophecy of the sins, captivity, plagues, and ultimate restitution of the nation.

1 Observe, therefore, my children, the commandments of the Lord, and keep His law; depart from wrath, and hate lying, that the Lord may dwell among you, and Beliar may flee from you.

2 Speak truth each one with his neighbour. So shall ye not fall into wrath and confusion; but ye shall be in peace, having the God of peace, so shall no war prevail over you.

3 Love the Lord through all your life, and one another with a true heart.

4 I know that in the last days ye shall depart from the Lord, and ye shall provoke Levi unto anger, and fight against Judah; but ye shall not prevail against them, for an angel of the Lord shall guide them both; for by them shall Israel stand.

5 And whensoever ye depart from the Lord, ye shall walk in all evil and work the abominations of the

Gentiles, going a-whoring after women of the lawless ones, while with all wickedness the spirits of wickedness work in you.

6 For I have read in the book of Enoch, the righteous, that your prince is Satan, and that all the spirits of wickedness and pride will conspire to attend constantly on the sons of Levi, to cause them to sin before the Lord.

7 And my sons will draw near to Levi, and sin with them in all things; and the sons of Judah will be covetous, plundering other men's goods like lions.

8 Therefore shall ye be led away with them into captivity, and there shall ye receive all the plagues of Egypt, and all the evils of the Gentiles.

9 And so when ye return to the Lord ye shall obtain mercy, and He shall bring you into His sanctuary, and He shall give you peace.

10 And there shall arise unto you from the tribe of Judah and of Levi the salvation of the Lord; and he shall make war against Beliar.

11 And execute an everlasting vengeance on our enemies; and the captivity shall he take from Beliar the souls of the saints, and turn disobedient hearts unto the Lord, and give to them that call upon him eternal peace.

12 And the saints shall rest in Eden, and in the New Jerusalem shall the righteous rejoice, and it shall be unto the glory of God for ever.

13 And no longer shall Jerusalem endure desolation, nor Israel be led captive; for the Lord shall be in

the midst of it [living amongst men], and the Holy One of Israel shall reign over it in humility and in poverty; and he who believeth on Him shall reign amongst men in truth.

THE TESTAMENT OF NAPHTALI
The Eighth Son of Jacob and Bilhah.

CHAPTER 1

21 So then, my children, let all your works be done in order with good intent in the fear of God, and do nothing disorderly in scorn or out of its due season.

22 For if thou bid the eye to hear, it cannot; so neither while ye are in darkness can ye do the works of light.

23 Be ye, therefore, not eager to corrupt your doings through covetousness or with vain words to beguile your souls; because if ye keep silence in purity of heart, ye shall understand how to hold fast the will of God, and to cast away the will of Beliar.

24 Sun and moon and stars change not their order; so do ye also change not the law of God in the disorderliness of your doings.

25 The Gentiles went astray, and forsook the Lord, and changed their order, and obeyed stocks and stones, spirits of deceit.

26 But ye shall not be so, my children, recognizing in the firmament, in the earth, and in the sea, and in all created things, the Lord who made all things, that

ye become not as Sodom, which changed the order of nature.

27 In like manner the Watchers also changed the order of their nature, whom the Lord cursed at the flood, on whose account He made the earth without inhabitants and fruitless.

28 These things I say unto you, my children, for I have read in the writing of Enoch that ye yourselves also shall depart from the Lord, walking according to all the lawlessness of the Gentiles, and ye shall do according to all the wickedness of Sodom.

29 And the Lord shall bring captivity upon you, and there shall ye serve your enemies, and ye shall be bowed down with every affliction and tribulation, until the Lord have consumed you all.

30 And after ye have become diminished and made few, ye return and acknowledge the Lord your God; and He shall bring you back into your land, according to His abundant mercy.

31 And it shall be, that after that they come into the land of their fathers, they shall again forget the Lord and become ungodly.

32 And the Lord shall scatter them upon the face of all the earth, until the compassion of the Lord shall come, a man working righteousness and working mercy unto all them that are afar off, and to them that are near.

THE TESTAMENT OF BENJAMIN
The Twelfth Son of Jacob and Rachel.

CHAPTER 2

4 And I believe that there will be also evil-doings among you, from the words of Enoch the righteous: that ye shall commit fornication with the fornication of Sodom, and shall perish, all save a few, and shall renew wanton deeds with women; and the kingdom of the Lord shall not be among you, for straightway He shall take it away.

5 Nevertheless the temple of God shall be in your portion, and the last temple shall be more glorious than the first.

6 And the twelve tribes shall be gathered together there, and all the Gentiles, until the Most High shall send forth His salvation in the visitation of an only-begotten prophet.

7 And He shall enter into the first temple, and there shall the Lord be treated with outrage, and He shall be lifted up upon a tree.

8 And the veil of the temple shall be rent, and the Spirit of God shall pass on to the Gentiles as fire poured forth.

9 And He shall ascend from Hades and shall pass from earth into heaven.

10 And I know how lowly He shall be upon earth, and how glorious in heaven.

Concerning the Good Tidings of Seth, to Which We Must Give Ear

And the Lord grew compassionate toward Adam, and sent his angel unto him, saying, "Know thy wife that thou mayest have a son instead of Abel."

Adam said, "I cannot know my wife, for I knew her twice, and that was a greater punishment than my expulsion from the Garden. For as long as I see Abel covered with blood, my heart is grieved and vexes me; and when I turn and see Cain's punishment, my tears run down. And if I know my wife again, that might be the cause of another grief and affliction."

The angel said, "Fear not, Adam; for God shall give thee a son and thou shalt call his name Seth, which being interpreted is, 'consolation'. He shall be the blessed seed, and the head of patriarchs, and shall be a comfort unto thee; forasmuch as Cain's wickedness has caused thee sorrow, so much comfort shall Seth afford thee. And thy seed and the seed of Seth shall multiply, and the world shall be filled with it. But let not the seed of Seth, or the seed of others of thy children, be mixed with that of Cain's generation; for if they mix themselves with that generation, thy good children shall become wicked, and then all shall be punished together."

Now when the angel gave unto Adam the good tidings regarding Seth, he had no other child of the seed of Cain. When Seth was born, there were three hundred and ninety women, and twenty-four men. Cain, thirty years after he was married, murdered Abel, who would have been married in the same year; but this did not take place, and so he became a virgin martyr. When Seth and others of his brothers were born, his parents were comforted on account of him, according to the tidings of the angel. So the seed of Seth and of his brethren multiplied; but they chased away the seed of Cain and did not mix with them, and they lived virtuously.

And the son of Seth, Enoch, the good Fruit, asked his father, saying, "Why is Adam, our grandfather, grieved?"

Seth said, "He is afflicted for having tasted of the fruit, for which he was expelled from the Garden."

And Enoch said unto his father, "The debt of the father must be paid by the son."

Wherefore Enoch did not marry. He planted a vineyard. It was a large vineyard, filled with all good things, and he worked in it sixty-four years. Every man tasted of its fruits, but he, Enoch, did not taste at all. He wore on his head an iron helmet, that he should not look up into the fruits of the trees; and for sixty-four years he was a vine-dresser, but he did not eat of the vineyard. And God commanded His angels, and they took him up in his body, and placed him in Paradise, where he is until this day.

And when the other children of Seth and Adam saw that Enoch, on account of his purity and fasting, was taken up into Paradise, many of them departed and retired to mountains, and devoted themselves to purity and mortification.

APPENDIX 1

THE LAW AND THE PROPHETS
QUOTED BY JESUS CHRIST

THE LAW AND THE PROPHETS
QUOTED BY JESUS CHRIST

GOSPELS	OLD TESTAMENT
Matt. 4:4	Deut. 8:3
4:7	Deut. 6:16
4:10	Deut. 6:13; 10:20
5:21	Exod. 20:13; Deut. 5:17
5:27	Exod. 20:14; Deut. 5:18
5:31	Deut. 24:1, 3
5:33	Lev. 19:12; Num. 30:12; Deut. 23:21
5:38	Exod. 21:24
5:43	Lev. 19:16–18
9:13; 12:7	Hos. 6:6
10:35	Mic. 7:6
11:10	Isa. 40:3; Mal. 3:1
12:3–5	I Sam. 21:1–6
12:40–41	Jon. 1:17; 1:2; 3:5
13:14	Isa. 6:9–10
15:4	Exod. 20:12; Deut. 5:16; Exod. 21:17; Lev. 20:9
15:7–9	Isa. 29:13
19:4–5	Gen. 1:27; 5:2; 2:24

GOSPELS	OLD TESTAMENT
19:8	Deut. 24:1–4
19:18–19	Exod. 20:13–16; Deut. 5:17–20; Exod. 20:12; Lev. 19:18
21:13	Isa. 56:7; Jer. 7:11
21:16	Ps. 8:2
21:42	Ps. 118:22–23
22:32	Exod. 3:6
22:37	Deut. 6:5
22:39	Lev. 19:18
24:29	Isa. 13:9–10; Joel 2:31; 3:15
24:37–39	Gen. 6:5; 7:6–23
27:46	Ps. 22:1
Mark 2:25–26	I Sam. 21:1–6
2:27	Exod. 23:12; Deut. 5:14
7:6–8	Isa. 29:13
7:10	Exod. 20:12; Deut. 5:16; Exod. 21:17
8:18	Ezek. 12:2
9:12–13	Isa. 53; Mal. 4:5–6
9:44, 46, 48	Isa. 66:24
10:6, 7	Gen. 1:27; 5:2; 2:24
10:19	Exod. 20:12–16; Deut. 5:16–20
11:17	Isa. 56:7; Jer. 7:11
12:10–11	Ps. 118:22–23
12:26	Exod. 3:6
12:29–31	Deut. 6:4–5; Lev. 19:18
12:36	Ps. 110:1

GOSPELS	OLD TESTAMENT
13:14	Dan. 9:27; 11:31; 12:11
13:24–25	Isa. 13:10; 34:4
14:62	Ps. 110:1
15:34	Ps. 22:1
Luke 4:4	Deut. 8:3
4:8	Deut. 6:13; 10:20
4:12	Deut. 6:16
4:18–19	Isa. 61:1–2
4:25–26	I Kings 17:8–24
4:27	II Kings 5:1–14
6:3	I Sam. 21:1–6
7:22	Isa. 61:1
12:53	Mic. 7:6
17:26–27	Gen. 6
17:28	Gen. 19
18:20	Exod. 20:12–16; Deut. 5:16–20
20:17	Ps. 118:22
20:37	Exod. 3:6
20:42–43	Ps. 110:1
22:37	Isa. 53:12
23:30	Hos. 10:8
John 3:14	Num. 21:5–9
4:37	Job 31:8
6:45	Isa. 54:13
7:22	Gen. 17:10; 21:4
8:17	Deut. 19:15; 17:6
10:34	Ps. 82:6
13:18	Ps. 41:9
15:25	Pss. 35:19; 69:4

APPENDIX 11

CONFRONTATIONS: THE WATCHERS VS.
JOHN THE BAPTIST AND JESUS CHRIST

CONFRONTATIONS: THE WATCHERS VS. JOHN THE BAPTIST AND JESUS CHRIST

1. John rebukes Pharisees and Sadducees who come to his baptism (Matt. 3:1–12; Luke 3:1–18).
2. John bears witness of only begotten Son before priests and Levites from Jerusalem (John 1:19–34).
3. Jesus casts moneychangers out of temple (John 2:13–25).
4. Jesus preaches in synagogue, reading from Esaias (Luke 4:16–30).
5. Jesus challenges scribes and Pharisees who say within themselves, "This man blasphemeth" (Matt. 9:2–8; Mark 2:1–12; Luke 5:17–26).
6. Jesus admonishes scribes and Pharisees who question his eating with publicans and sinners (Matt. 9:10–17; Mark 2:15–22; Luke 5:29–39).
7. Jesus answers Jews who persecute him for healing impotent man at Bethesda on sabbath (John 5:1–47).
8. Disciples pluck ears of grain on sabbath and Jesus reproves Pharisees who therefore question him (Matt. 12:1–14; Mark 2:23–3:6; Luke 6:1–11).
9. Jesus rebukes scribes and Pharisees who accuse him of casting out devils by Beelzebub (Matt. 12:22–37; Mark 3:22–30; Luke 11:14–26).
10. Jesus counters "an evil generation" seeking a sign (Matt. 12:38–45; Luke 11:16, 29–36).

11. In synagogue at Capernaum, Jesus reproves Jews and many disciples who murmur in disbelief because he said, "...Whoso eateth my flesh, and drinketh my blood, hath eternal life..." (John 6:22–7:1).

12. God's commandments vs. man's tradition: Jesus rebukes scribes and Pharisees of Jerusalem and calls the multitude to understand (Matt. 15:1–20; Mark 7:1–23).

13. Jesus rebukes Pharisees and Sadducees who tempt him, seeking a sign (Matt. 15:39–16:4; Mark 8:9–12).

14. Jesus teaches in temple at Jerusalem, speaking boldly and prophesying of the Spirit; Pharisees and chief priests send officers to take him (John 7).

15. Jesus challenges scribes and Pharisees who accuse woman taken in adultery (John 8:1–11).

16. Central conflict between Jesus and Pharisees: origin of Christ (John 8:12–59).

17. Jesus heals blind man on sabbath and affirms divine Sonship before Pharisees; the Good Shepherd (John 9; 10:1–21).

18. Jesus answers testing of a lawyer; the good Samaritan (Luke 10:25–37).

19. Woes upon scribes and Pharisees for hypocrisy and upon lawyers for taking away key of knowledge (Luke 11:37–54).

20. Jesus looses woman from infirmity on sabbath, confronting ruler of synagogue (Luke 13:10–17).

21. Jesus sends Pharisees to testify before "that fox," Herod (Luke 13:31–35).

22. Jesus answers Pharisees who test him concerning divorce (Matt. 19:3–12; Mark 10:2–12).

23. Jesus testifies of his oneness with the Father to Jews "not of my sheep" who gather round to stone him (John 10:22–42).

24. Jesus rebukes covetous Pharisees (Luke 16:14–18).

25. Jesus demanded of Pharisees when kingdom of God should come (Luke 17:20, 21).

26. Triumphal entry into Jerusalem: Jesus answers Pharisees who say, "Master, rebuke thy disciples." (Luke 19:29–44).

27. Jesus again casts moneychangers out of temple and answers chief priests and scribes who question the children's "Hosanna to the Son of David!" (Matt. 21:12–17; Mark 11:15–19; Luke 19:45–48).

28. Jesus confounds chief priests and elders who challenge his authority (Matt. 21:23–46; 22:1–14; Mark 11:27–33; 12:1–12; Luke 20:1–19).

29. Jesus confutes Pharisees who question tribute unto Caesar (Matt. 22:15–22; Mark 12:13–17; Luke 20:20–26).

30. Jesus silences Sadducees who say there is no resurrection (Matt. 22:23–33; Mark 12:18–27; Luke 20:27–40).

31. Jesus answers lawyer who tests him regarding the great commandment (Matt. 22:34–40; Mark 12:28–34).

32. Jesus silences Pharisees by asking them, "What think ye of Christ? Whose son is he?" (Matt. 22:41–46; Mark 12:35–37; Luke 20:41–44).

33. Jesus announces seven woes upon scribes and Pharisees (Matt. 23:13–39).

34. Jesus reproves chief priests and elders of the people who come to arrest him (Matt. 26:47–56; Mark 14:43–52; Luke 22:47–53; John 18:2–12).

35. Jesus before Caiaphas, the high priest (John 18:13–24; Matt. 26:59–68; Mark 14:55–65; Luke 22:66–71).

36. Jesus before Pontius Pilate, the governor (Matt. 27:2, 11–31; Mark 15:1–20; Luke 23:1–5, 13–25; John 18:28–19:16).

37. Jesus before Herod—answering nothing (Luke 23:6–12).

And the fifth angel sounded, and I saw a star fall from heaven unto the earth: and to him was given the key of the bottomless pit.

And he opened the bottomless pit; and there arose a smoke out of the pit, as the smoke of a great furnace; and the sun and the air were darkened by reason of the smoke of the pit.

And there came out of the smoke locusts upon the earth: and unto them was given power, as the scorpions of the earth have power.

And it was commanded them that they should not hurt the grass of the earth, neither any green thing, neither any tree; but only those men which have not the seal of God in their foreheads.

And to them it was given that they should not kill them, but that they should be tormented five months: and their torment was as the torment of a scorpion, when he striketh a man.

And in those days shall men seek death, and shall not find it; and shall desire to die, and death shall flee from them.

And the shapes of the locusts were like unto horses prepared unto battle; and on their heads were as it were crowns like gold, and their faces were as the faces of men.

And they had hair as the hair of women, and their teeth were as the teeth of lions.

And they had breastplates, as it were breastplates of iron; and the sound of their wings was as the sound of chariots of many horses running to battle.

And they had tails like unto scorpions, and there were stings in their tails: and their power was to hurt men five months.

And they had a king over them, which is the angel of the bottomless pit, whose name in the Hebrew tongue is Abaddon, but in the Greek tongue hath his name Apollyon.

Revelation 9:1–11

ANGEL WITH THE KEY OF THE ABYSS

CREDITS

Grateful acknowledgment is made for permission to reproduce the following material:

Excerpts from *The Screwtape Letters,* by C. S. Lewis, copyright © C.S. Lewis Pte. Ltd. 1942. Reprinted by permission.

Archangel Gabriel, Messenger of God (frontispiece) and *Archangel Michael* (page 349), stained-glass windows by Tiffany Studios, installed at St. Peter's Chapel, Mare Island, Vallejo, Calif. Used with permission of the Mare Island Historic Park Foundation.

POCKET GUIDES
TO PRACTICAL SPIRITUALITY:

Karma and Reincarnation

Alchemy of the Heart

Your Seven Energy Centers

Soul Mates and Twin Flames

Violet Flame to Heal Body, Mind and Soul

The Art of Practical Spirituality

How to Work with Angels

Creative Abundance

Access the Power of Your Higher Self

The Creative Power of Sound

———————————

FOR MORE INFORMATION

Summit University Press books are available at fine bookstores worldwide and at your favorite on-line bookseller. For a free catalog of our books and products or to learn more about the spiritual techniques featured in this book, please contact:

Summit University Press
PO Box 5000
Corwin Springs, MT 59030-5000 USA
Telephone: 1-800-245-5445 or 406-848-9500
Fax: 1-800-221-8307 or 406-848-9555
E-mail: info@summituniversitypress.com
www.summituniversitypress.com

Elizabeth Clare Prophet is a world-renowned author. Among her best-sellers are *Soul Mates and Twin Flames*, her Pocket Guides to Practical Spirituality series, *The Lost Years of Jesus: Documentary Evidence of Jesus' 17-Year Journey to the East*, *Kabbalah: Key to Your Inner Power*, *Reincarnation: The Missing Link in Christianity* and *Fallen Angels and the Origins of Evil*.

She has pioneered techniques in practical spirituality, including the creative power of sound for personal growth and world transformation. Since the 1960s, Elizabeth Clare Prophet has conducted seminars and workshops around the world on spirituality, personal growth and the mystical paths of the world's religions. She has been featured on NBC's *Ancient Prophecies* and A&E's *The Unexplained* and has talked about her work on *Donahue, Larry King Live, Nightline, Sonya Live* and *CNN & Company.*